Contingent Kinship

Contingent Kinship

THE FLOWS AND FUTURES OF ADOPTION IN THE UNITED STATES

Kathryn A. Mariner

UNIVERSITY OF CALIFORNIA PRESS

University of California Press, one of the most distinguished university presses in the United States, enriches lives around the world by advancing scholarship in the humanities, social sciences, and natural sciences. Its activities are supported by the UC Press Foundation and by philanthropic contributions from individuals and institutions. For more information, visit www.ucpress.edu.

University of California Press
Oakland, California

An earlier version of Chapter 4 was previously published: Kathryn A. Ludwig, "Unfulfilled Futures: The 'Fall-Through' Phenomenon in Domestic Private Adoption," *Advocates' Forum* (2012): 13–27. Chapters 1 and 2 are derived in part from an article published in *Ethnos* 2018, copyright Taylor & Francis, available online at www.tandfonline.com/10.1080/00141844.2017.1377744.

Cataloguing-in-Publication Data is on file at the Library of Congress.

ISBN 9780520299559 (cloth : alk. paper)
ISBN 9780520299566 (pbk. : alk. paper)
ISBN 9780520971240 (ebook)

Manufactured in the United States of America

28 27 26 25 24 23 22 21 20 19
10 9 8 7 6 5 4 3 2 1

*to my real parents
and
for Devonte
and all his kin*

CONTENTS

ILLUSTRATIONS

ACKNOWLEDGMENTS

This book is made of kinship and contingency, imagined and incubated in the best of company.

My first thank you goes to Judith Farquhar, serving as Director of Graduate Studies in the Department of Anthropology at the University of Chicago when I matriculated in 2008. When I went to her in the winter of my first year in the PhD program, twenty-two years old and awash in anxiety, and shared that I planned to change my research focus from indigenous languages of Central America to transracial adoption in the United States, she encouraged me and showed continued kindness and support for the next seven years as I pursued my degree and a new set of interests. I am very appreciative of her facilitation of my circuitous path. I am supremely grateful for the guidance and support of my dissertation committee: Joe Masco (for his constructive critique and numerous thorough readings), John Comaroff (for his responsiveness, critical interventions, and much-needed pep talks, often from halfway around the globe), Summerson Carr (for providing a social work perspective and offering crucial feedback on seminar papers, workshop papers, and resulting chapter drafts), and Julie Chu (for encouraging me to write the ethnography that I would want to read, and for reminding me that invisibility itself is a worthy object of analysis). Their encouragement and inspiration sustained me intellectually throughout the project and beyond.

During my doctoral program, I had the benefit of receiving less formalized (but no less important) feedback from my colleagues in a range of contexts. Jennifer Cole and the participants in her Winter 2013 and Winter 2015 Ethnographic Writing seminars helped greatly in the development of the project as a whole. I would also especially like to thank the participants and coordinators of the U. S. Locations Workshop, the Reproduction of Race and Racial Ideologies Workshop, and the Clinical Ethnography Workshop at the University of Chicago, as well as the Susan B. Anthony Institute Work-in-Progress Seminar at the University of Rochester. Special thanks is also due to the coordinators, discussants, participants, and attendees at panels where I presented my work at conferences hosted by the American Anthropological Association, the National Women's Studies Association, the Alliance for the Study of Adoption and Culture, the Adoption Initiative, and the University of Colorado–Boulder Department of Anthropology. Several of my fellow graduate students also played an important role in the development of this project outside of classroom, conference, and workshop contexts, particularly my 2014 writing group (Duff Morton, Adam Sargent, and Gabriel Tusinski) and other valued interlocutors (Ella Butler, Christine El Ouardani, Karma Frierson, Jonathan Rosa, Aaron Seaman, Lisa Simeone, Matilda Stubbs, and Talia Weiner). Toward the end of dissertation writing, the support and cama-raderie of Shirley Yeung, Madeleine McLeester, Mary Adekoya, and Haley Stinnett was invaluable.

Special recognition is owed to my friends and colleagues at the University of Chicago School of Social Service Administration. Particularly valuable were courses taught and guidance offered by Summerson Carr, Gina Samuels, Joan Palmer, and William Borden. The editorial team at *Advocate's Forum* offered critical peer review that helped shape and refine an earlier version of chapter 4. I am indebted to my Mellon Mays Undergraduate Fellowship family at Stanford, University of Chicago, and beyond, for their friendship, fellowship, and continued faith in my ability to succeed, particularly partici-pants at the 2011 Proposal Writing and Dissertation Development Seminar and the 2014 Preparing for the Professoriate Seminar. Since I am at heart a social animal, I am hugely appreciative of various writing groups, "boot-camps," and retreats: I am grateful for UChicagoGRAD, the Mellon Mays Graduate Initiatives Program, the University of Rochester Susan B. Anthony Institute Writing Group, and my incredibly consistent and intrepid account-ability partner, Molly Ball.

My research was supported by generous funding from the National Science Foundation Graduate Research Fellowship Program, the Illinois Board of Higher Education's Diversifying Faculty in Illinois Fellowship, the University of Chicago Division of Social Sciences Graduate Aid Initiative and Orrin Williams Travel Grant, the University of Chicago Office of Multicultural Student Affairs Research Initiative Grant, and grants from the

Mellon Mays Graduate Initiatives Program (supported by the Social Science Research Council and Woodrow Wilson Foundation). The final year of dissertation writing was made possible by the generous support of a Mellon / American Council of Learned Societies Dissertation Completion Fellowship. Many thanks are due to Anne Chien at the University of Chicago Department of Anthropology for her administrative work "behind the scenes," which made so many aspects of both my training and this project possible; I certainly could not have done this without her. Additionally, I would still be in my office transcribing interviews and staff meetings if it were not for my careful (and miraculously speedy) transcriptionist, Rebecca Hannah Fraimow.

The University of Rochester provided a supportive environment in which to develop my dissertation into this full-fledged book. I am grateful to the Frederick Douglass Institute for African and African-American Studies (under the leadership of Cilas Kemedjio and the administrative support of Ghislaine Radegonde-Eison), which provided funding and both the physical and mental space to let the project breathe. I am also grateful to the Department of Anthropology (under the leadership of Daniel Reichman and the administrative support of Donna Mero), which has proven a warm and collegial institutional home. I am especially grateful to the Humanities Center (under the direction of Joan Rubin with the administrative support of Jennie Gilardoni), which provided a generous internal fellowship in the fall of 2018, and also hosted a full-day manuscript workshop in April 2017 in which Laurence Ralph, Linda Seligmann, and Eleana Kim provided generous and thoughtful critiques of the text. I am indebted to these scholars for their insights, which have greatly shaped the present manuscript, alongside conversations with numerous others including Stevie Larson, and also Katherine McKittrick, who in particular helped me hold the weight of wrecked cars and hearts. Sometimes one conversation can change everything.

I am fortunate to have landed amid an invaluable clutch of incredible colleagues at the University of Rochester, who have provided feedback, support, advice, mentorship, tea, cheese, and chocolate: Samira Abdur-Rahman, Molly Ball, Stefanie Bautista, Joel Burges, Kristin Doughty, Joshua Dubler, Signithia Fordham, Robert Foster, Tom Gibson, Margarita Guillory, Rachel Haidu, Jennifer Kyker, John Osburg, Rachel Remmel, Llerena Searle, Elana Shever, Indrani Singh, Dena Swanson, and all of my Space Invaders. Special thanks are due to Anna Rosensweig for friendship and support beyond measure or articulation. To extra-university colleagues, friends, family, and loves as well: Judy Asuzu, Miguel Cardona, William Cleeton-Gandino, Jordi

Handcox, Lea Kearns, Phillip Mariner, Danielle Rinallo, Jennifer Tan, and all my therapists. I am especially grateful for Mackenzie Price, without whose weekly check-in calls I would never have finished my dissertation. And to Molly Cunningham and Kaya Williams, for helping me dream big freedom dreams and always inspiring me to be a better and braver anthropologist.

At University of California Press, Kate Marshall and Reed Malcolm were instrumental in guiding this book into the world. Thanks is also due to the Editorial Committee for their time and attention. Additional support—from administrative assistance to editing, proofing, indexing, design, and marketing—was provided by Victoria Baker, Bradley Depew, Jessica Moll, Enrique Ochoa-Kaup, Sabrina Robleh, Tom Sullivan, and Paul Tyler. Further thanks to any others who touched the book after it was out of my writerly hands. I want to especially thank Kevin O'Neill for his availability, encouragement (this is an understatement, but I am at a loss for a better word), and willingness to read literally "anything." The book is stronger and more engaging because of his key interventions. Thank you to my cohort of fellow Atelier authors: Jatin Dua, Anthony Fontes, and Jacob Doherty. Thank you to Dean Gloria Culver at the University of Rochester for providing access to funding for cover art and indexing, and generally supporting my work and well-being. My research assistants, Amelia Kelly, Ethan Okoshi, and Julia Tulke, were a joy to work with during the final phases of manuscript revision.

I thank the woman who pushed me screaming into this crazy beautiful world, tipping the first domino in a chain reaction that has delivered me exactly where I need to be, and I thank my parents for their unwavering support, and for demonstrating the truth that kinship is so much more than biological relatedness. Finally, I thank the individuals in whose hopes, dreams, lives, loves, and losses this ethnography is rooted. Although I cannot name them here, they made this project possible by allowing me to observe and participate in the everyday contours of their intimate and professional lives. Over a decade, an incredible and beautiful storm of interactions, inspirations, and influences paved the way for the delivery of this book. Any errors are my own, and to anyone I may have forgotten, please know that you too are appreciated, and that your omission is due to the limits of my memory rather than that of your contribution.

Prologue

IT WAS A BITTERLY COLD and bright day in the middle of 2014's Polar Vortex. Stella and I piled into her little car and headed off to a far north suburb of Chicago to visit Dawn, a new expectant mother. Stella hunched over the steering wheel, squinting. A thick blanket of fresh snow reflected the midday sun, and despite it being December, I regretted not grabbing a pair of sunglasses on my way out of the house. The drive up was a little over an hour, and Dawn texted Stella—the "birth mother worker" at First Steps—several times along the way. We followed the turn-by-turn directions issuing forth from Stella's smartphone, and finally turned down Dawn's street, pulling up to a beige two-story, a large unassuming house that had been converted into smaller apartments.

Stella texted Dawn that we had arrived, to which Dawn responded, also via text message, that she was "using the washroom" and would be "out in one second." Shortly thereafter, a smiling and visibly pregnant brown-skinned woman emerged, and Stella—accustomed to chronic difficulties in locating expectant mothers—was noticeably relieved to see her. In her mid-twenties, Dawn wore a puffy black coat, black pants, and navy Nike sneakers, her hair pinned up into a crown of black and gold twists. She approached us with a swaying gait typical of the third trimester, crunching a trail of small footprints into the snow, an ephemeral tether between her swollen frame and the front door of the house.

Like so many pregnant women approaching First Steps—the small private adoption agency where I conducted fieldwork—for adoption services, Dawn struggled economically. Stella and I had arrived to take her grocery shopping and deliver money for rent and laundry. Dawn had two children who were not currently living with her, and she told Stella that she could not afford to care for another child. The couple she had chosen to adopt her baby was helping with everyday expenses. The prospective adoptive mother had armed Stella and me with a cooler of premade meals, to help ensure Dawn and the infant she carried were receiving adequate sustenance.

Stella introduced me, and Dawn and I exchanged smiles and hellos before I scrambled clumsily into the backseat of the two-door hatchback, wriggling into an uncomfortable yet familiar folding of my nearly six-foot frame. When Stella drove expectant mothers somewhere (usually to the doctor, to the store, and so on) I always sat in the backseat—a mix of politeness and respect, and a feeble attempt to minimize my own power. On this particular day I reflected on buses and black folks and the simultaneous strangeness and normalcy of young women of color being chauffeured around by an older white female social worker. I sat in the back silently, listening as Stella made small talk with Dawn. Stella mentioned that I was a student, opening up a space for me to briefly describe my research project and collect verbal consent from Dawn for the observation. I gazed out over Dawn's shoulder at the frosty path unfolding before us, and thought about my own birth mother.

"The personal is theoretical," writes Sara Ahmed (2017: 10). It is also methodological. I did not simply choose this project; I was born into it, in a sense. And Dawn was gestating it. Our relative positions within the adoption triad meant that we shared intimate kinship connections with people who aligned with important aspects of each of our own subjectivities. Dawn was on the verge of making the same decision that the woman who once carried me had made, a decision that a minuscule fraction of American women make every year. A decision that drastically alters individual trajectories. In my fieldwork, I struggled to understand the implications of these decisions without influencing them. The classic anthropological conundrum of how much to observe, how much to participate.

As we rumbled along, Stella, trying to be helpful, suddenly asked me to tell Dawn about my schooling.[1] Caught off-guard, I felt constrained, somewhat reluctantly desiring to establish my institutional authority as a researcher but more urgently wanting to minimize it. How could I humanize our interaction? I wasn't sure. We were there for support, yes. (Even lumping Stella and me together into an institutional "we" is a move that reflects a complex positionality.) But we were really there for the baby. In her ethnography of life among addicted, pregnant, poor women in San Francisco's daily rent hotels, Kelly Ray Knight (2015) has described the vulture-like tendencies of anthropologists.[2] I was a buzzard in the backseat. Though well intentioned, at times the social workers appeared predatory as well.

But these dynamics were more complicated. In Dawn's presence, I suddenly felt like a child, awkward and afraid, and my brain buzzed trying to figure out how to articulate my overprivileged, overachieving, degree-laden trajectory from Stanford to the University of Chicago. What was I even doing there? *But I attended an underfunded rural public high school before all that,* I thought to myself, self-consciously grasping for something— anything—that might help to level our experiences. The gap between us felt simultaneously vast and nonexistent. Our subjectivities aligned in a few socially important ways (young women of color, members of the adoption triad) while diverging sharply in others (capital of all kinds). There were probably only fifteen seconds of silence, but it felt like three hours. Suddenly, Stella interrupted her own question to ask Dawn about directions to the grocery store. They started chatting about something else. There was a levity that felt out of sync with the gravity of our visit's purpose. And I felt a sense of relief, as though I had been forgotten in the backseat. Neither in their line of sight nor on their minds. Something akin to "ethnographic countertransference" had crashed through the little car like a wrecking ball.[3] Our closeness in age was suddenly irrelevant; in the same way that I had often become a promising image of an expectant mother's own future-relinquished child, Dawn became my own birth mother, and the notion of alienating her or offering myself up for her potential rejection was debilitating. And it didn't matter that she had already agreed cheerfully to be observed for my project. There she was in the front, and there I was in the back, and despite the power imbalance between us, all I could feel was a discouraging sense of unease, an acute case of what John Jackson (2005) has termed ethnographobia.[4]

I noticed that later, when we were in the grocery store, I struggled to meet Dawn's gaze, and my awareness of this horrified me. *I can't see you because when I see your pain—your resourcelessness, your powerlessness—I am in pain.* This is not an uncommon refrain within the context of social work practice, in which practitioners often experience trauma vicariously through their clients and develop coping mechanisms to ease their own suffering.[5] But I wasn't even a social worker in that moment; I needed something from Dawn and I had nothing to offer in return. I didn't know what to say. We had just met, so personal questions about her experience as a prospective birth mother and the circumstances that prompted her adoption plan felt grossly inappropriate. Stella, as the "proper" social worker, seemed in a better position to ask them. I felt chilled, like the wintered world outside. Dawn quietly added items to the cart as the three of us moved slowly down the frozen food aisle, its walls lined with chrome-trimmed and fluorescent-lit glass boxes of cold.

After dropping Dawn off at her house, as we drove down the alley toward the GPS's highlighted route home, Stella asked, as she always did after an expectant mother visit, "What do you think? Think she'll place?" Even after decades of experience, she was always uncertain. As was I. In an effort to assess whether Dawn would follow through with the adoption plan, Stella reemphasized the nature of expectant mothers' situations, which, she reasoned, often led to the necessary development of circumspect tactics, a sort of "hidden transcript" (Scott 1990): "She's just used to asking people for help and getting help and needing help. Her house looked empty enough. I just feel like there's a whole lot she's not saying." *Perhaps,* I thought to myself, *because she is participating in a process in which she is structurally silenced.* The food in her belly was literally contingent upon her continued interactions with Stella.

The sun sat low on the horizon as Stella and I made our way back to the freeway, the northern suburbs fading into the rearview mirror. We did not really know Dawn any better on the drive back than we did on the drive up. My own troubling inability to see Dawn suddenly rendered visible other ways in which she was being erased. Neither Stella nor I—nor the prospective adoptive couple—heard from or saw Dawn again after that day. The adoption fell through.

·   ·   ·

end, n. A piece broken, cut off, or left; a fragment, remnant.[6]

·   ·   ·

Introduction

TO SPECULATE INTIMATELY

> Had a baby girl on the 10th. 8lbs 7oz beautiful. named her
> CLEO. can you please tell robert and william I send them my
> deepest apology? one look at her and And I just culdnt bring
> myself to giving her away.
>
> —*Text message from Selene to Stella, September 2010*

THIS IS A BOOK ABOUT the contingency of kinship. The above text
message from a new mother to her adoption social worker illustrates a phenomenon known among adoption professionals as a "fall-through." In the
summer of 2010, social workers at First Steps—a small private nonprofit
adoption agency just outside of Chicago—were growing increasingly exasperated by a sharp uptick in fall-throughs, which sometimes occurred when
a pregnant woman initiated an adoption plan with the agency, often early in
her third trimester, and progressed to the stage at which social workers
"matched" her with a waiting prospective adoptive family. This match was
nonbinding, and an adoption was considered a fall-through if, at any point
beyond this match, the expectant mother decided to parent—rather than
place—her baby, effectively terminating the adoption plan and foreclosing
the possibility of adoptive kinship. The language is not neutral; to refer to
this scenario as a fall-through gestured toward a particular desired end, an
outcome aligned with a specific set of interests.

Fall-throughs were emotionally distressing to social workers and prospective adoptive parents for a variety of reasons. But at the start of my fieldwork,

these emotional losses were increasingly complicated by financial losses in the form of "legally allowable birth parent expenses," which were paid to the expectant mother by the prospective adoptive family. This investment—which included money for food, clothing, shelter, and any necessary legal fees—was irrecoverable in the case of a fall-through. In the years following the financial crisis of 2008, prospective adoptive parents were sometimes experiencing multiple fall-throughs and losing hundreds and thousands of dollars. Social workers openly wondered if the increase in fall-throughs was due in part to the economic downturn, which had hit low-income communities of color—where the majority of expectant mothers resided—the hardest. Suspicions arose that economically desperate mothers-to-be were "gaming the system" with no intention of placing their babies. One thing was clear: investments of multiple kinds were being made, and lost, in these unborn children. A multivalent adoption economy determined the futures of children, parents, and social workers alike. Money changed hands, but this adoption economy could not be reduced to market forces or some preexisting and overarching economic "logic."[1] For adoption also encompasses a range of other economies: moral, affective, visual, and temporal. That is to say, adoption is a site of messy circulations and investments in which valuable entities as disparate as dollars, kin ties, hours and years, gazes, and imagined children are produced and exchanged by parents and social workers. Adoption at First Steps constituted an elaborate traffic in imagined futures. Depending on a number of factors, this traffic at various times resulted in the creation, dissolution, and preservation of both adoptive and biological kinship, connections that were, as a result, highly contingent.

For decades—perhaps more than a century—American adoption has been haunted by anxieties about origins, background, and history. The fight for access to birth records, efforts toward search and reunion, and concerns with confidentiality, secrecy, and illegitimacy all reveal an anxiety about roots. Questions of racial / ethnic identity, heritage, belonging, and culture-keeping point backwards. Where do adoptees come from? How are their divergent biological and cultural histories incorporated into new adoptive family formations? Departing from this trend, *Contingent Kinship* takes up the *process* of private agency adoption, revealing an equally profound emphasis on the future, produced through complex modes of circulation, investment, and affective engagement.[2] Examining the adoption process entails a shift in focus from the adoptee or the adoptive family as its seemingly logical outcome. Rather than focusing on a singular result, this ethnography traces adoption to various possible ends, attending to the practices and processes that produce those ends. These processes coalesce into what I term *intimate speculation:* a set of practices mobilized by adoption professionals (social workers, clinicians, educators, attorneys), prospective adoptive parents, and expectant mothers that involves differential investment in an imagined future child.

This ethnography identifies and explores three different speculative modes within adoption, based on the following tripartite definition of the term speculation:[3]

> The conjectural anticipation of something.
> The exercise of the faculty of sight; the action, or an act, of seeing, viewing, or looking on or at; examination or observation.
> Engagement in any business enterprise or transaction of a venturesome or risky nature, but offering the chance of great or unusual gain.[4]

Within the context of adoption in the United States, and perhaps much more broadly, intimate speculation is a theoretical concept that knits together modes of anticipation, observation, and risky investment. Adoption is a particularly potent site in which to interrogate how the production and dissolution of kinship in America fluctuate alongside larger economic and affective shifts, and within pervasive and enduring structures of uncertainty and inequality.

Intimate speculation in turn produces a form of contingent kinship.[5] Contingency is an uncertainty about what the future holds, with risk a close cousin.[6] Indeed, risk might be said to arise from contingency, with uncertainty through risk stemming from an outcome's dependence upon the decisions of others.[7] Through this lens, infant adoption represents the epitome of risk, the entire process hinging on the decision of an expectant mother (at times considered "at risk" herself), and involving the circulation of personal knowledge and information.[8] However, this risk was not the calculable sort.[9] For many prospective adoptive parents, the possibility of a fallen-through adoption—which often resulted from a potential birth mother's decision to parent—constituted one of the most anxiety-provoking future outcomes, as it foreclosed the possibility of adoptive kinship and necessitated a starting over. Throughout the adoption process, actors attempted to engineer a particular sort of happening; when I describe adoptive kinship as contingent, I am pointing to the ways that it hangs in the balance of a complex web of risks, decisions, events, and pressures. Contingency, by its very nature, complicates the predictability of ends, often disrupting imagined futures.

Thus, the practice of adoption offers a powerful lens through which to consider the question of who can have a future in the United States, and who cannot, wherein child and future become synonymous in particular ways. This question reverberates broadly beyond the issue of adoption, with implications for how we think about the figure of the child and the family, as well as the intersection of race, class, intimacy, and violence at the neoliberal, post-welfare dawning of the twenty-first century. The story of adoption in the United States is a story of blood and biology, choice and abandonment, family and intimacy. It is a story about power, but also, relative powerlessness. As much as it is a story about family formation, it is also—and necessarily—a story about familial dissolution.[10]

THE STRUCTURE OF AN AGENCY

An adoption agency is a particularly good vantage point from which to witness the simultaneous production of contingency and kinship.[11] This ethnography investigates the adoption process from within a small nonprofit private adoption agency—First Steps—located on the periphery of Chicago between an affluent and progressive suburb and one of the city's low-income and predominantly African American neighborhoods. Bordered on the east by Lake Michigan and to the north, south, and west by sprawling suburbs, Chicago is a complex space of race and class inequalities. According to the U.S. Census and the American Community Survey, during my fieldwork, 18.6% of families and 22.6% of individuals in Chicago experienced everyday life below the poverty line.[12] In addition, across the United States, 48.5% of black children were living in poverty, more than three times the number of white children.[13] In 2010, one-third of Chicago's total population was African American, and those inhabitants were overwhelmingly represented in the city's poorest neighborhoods, effectively segregated from the more affluent white population.[14] Chicago, in fact, ranked fifth on a list of most segregated U.S. cities with respect to African Americans and whites.[15] Perhaps predictably then, Chicago is also home to some of the most racially segregated public schools in the country, with white students comprising only 9% of the city's total public school population in 2015.[16] Moreover, in 2013–14, 85% of students enrolled in Chicago public schools were designated low-income, and low-income students consistently score lower on average on reading assessments than their higher-income counterparts.[17]

The physical location of First Steps illustrated the inadequacy of a stark distinction between city and suburb, and reflected the spatial dynamics of domestic adoption in a highly segregated metropolitan area. The village of River Glen is technically a suburb.[18] The adoption agency, however, was located on River Glen's edge, just a few blocks' walking distance from the Chicago city limits, and was served by one of Chicago's elevated CTA rail lines, as well as several city buses. First Steps' physical position in a borderland—an anomalous space between city and suburb—was mirrored by its conceptual location as a space of mediation between prospective adoptive parents and expectant parents, the former often residing in the suburbs and the latter usually residing in the city. The agency thus functioned as a boundary place: "a privileged material and spatial setting in which worlds that are incompatible in other settings become temporarily—and at least partially—compatible" (Koster 2014: 128). This spatial arrangement relocated the center of the adoption exchange to the physical periphery of Chicago.[19] It also reified the role of social workers as the mediators and brokers of adoption transactions. This mediator role is reflected in the ways that communication between expectant mothers and prospective adopters was routed and filtered through social workers at the agency, illustrated sharply by Selene's text message to Stella.

Specializing in the adoption of African American and biracial children, First Steps was founded in 1992 by a white adoptive mother and social worker, Dotty, and had a completely white staff of mostly women. The agency was born in the midst of a sea of shifting priorities among adoption professionals concerning the best interests of black children. In the United States, transracial adoptions increased following the Civil Rights Movement, before declining sharply after a fierce condemnation of the practice by the National Association of Black Social Workers (NABSW) in 1972, essentially equating the adoption of black children by white parents with cultural genocide.[20] This condemnation prompted many social workers to turn to race-matching. In the early 1990s, adopting across racial lines was still somewhat taboo. In 1994, in response to concerns that race-matching practices were delaying the placement of certain children, the Multiethnic Placement Act was passed and later amended and strengthened by the Interethnic Placement Act in 1996, prohibiting the use of race in placement decisions by federally funded agencies (Fogg-Davis 2002: 10). When First Steps was founded, many agencies either avoided transracial adoption or literally devalued black children by charging higher adoption fees for white babies than black babies. A point of pride for Dotty, up until the closing of the agency, was that First Steps never altered its fee structure based on the race or health conditions of the child.[21]

From its inception until its closing more than two decades later, First Steps facilitated the movement of children from predominantly low-income, African American neighborhoods on the South and West Sides of Chicago to mostly white middle- and upper-middle-class families residing in whiter neighborhoods within the city, as well as the suburbs and out of state. The vast majority of First Steps' domestic placements were newborns.[22] During my time at the agency, First Steps also participated in a number of fleeting international programs—often in an attempt to "save" the struggling nonprofit in the face of dwindling domestic numbers.[23]

This book is based on ethnographic fieldwork conducted at First Steps between 2009 and 2016, including approximately a year and a half of sustained participant-observation, and many more months of peripheral or intermittent involvement during seven years spent living and studying in Chicago. In addition to my involvement at First Steps, I also carried out research at a number of auxiliary sites, including several large national adoption conferences, prospective adoptive parent training sessions, an adoption clinic, and a suburban "culture camp" for children adopted transracially and internationally. The latter proved a fruitful source of three dozen narratives from adoptive parents with some distance from the adoption process, as those in the midst of the process were sometimes more difficult to access. Although the project is quite local and grounded in the particular, it is situated within the context of a broader adoption landscape.

There is no view from nowhere. My perspective—and thus this book—springs from an embodied and subjective experience of my time in the field: of being a woman of "child-bearing age," of being brown and somewhat ambiguously raced, of having white parents, of being adopted, of being classed in particular ways, of being trained as a clinical social worker as well as a cultural anthropologist, of being a transplant from the Pacific Northwest rather than a Chicago native, of being literally haunted by my object of study.[24] Indeed there are reflexive issues inherent in the very mode of research, which required me to serve as an observer, and in which my own visibility was highly conditioned by gender, race, and visible markers of social and economic capital. As somewhat of a native *and* nonnative anthropologist, throughout my fieldwork I certainly felt parts of myself—to use Kirin Narayan's (1993: 673) language—both "tugged into the open" and "stuffed out of sight" (often through no effort of my own), and herein I have strived, consciously, to attend to instances in which these tuggings and stuffings have become ethnographically generative while actively resisting the temptation to "delete" myself from the text.[25]

During my time at the agency, particularly in the early years, I filled the native role of social work intern. Later into my fieldwork, that positioning became a more natural—though not wholly comfortable—fit, as I completed professional graduate training in social work in 2013.[26] I answered phones, organized placement files, and helped plan agency functions. I spent hundreds of hours in the agency office, accompanied social workers on home visits and other various errands, attended staff meetings and agency fundraisers, sat in on trainings and conference presentations, observed home study interviews, and participated in outreach efforts. I took detailed field notes and audio-recorded as many events and interactions as possible. I also gained insights from critical analysis of online content, official and unofficial adoption documentation, adoptive family profiles, promotional materials, and various state and government documents, including bureaucratic forms and policies, legislation, and reports. In addition, I spoke with adoption professionals (including social workers, agency board members, medical personnel, and the two attorneys who worked with the agency), prospective and adoptive parents, and a few expectant mothers.

Much of my time at First Steps was spent in the agency office, which was located in an old building a short walk from River Glen's downtown. Once buzzed in on the ground floor, staff and applicants ascended a narrow flight of carpeted stairs to a suite of offices on the second floor. The space was shared with a realty office, and was downsized twice during my fieldwork: the first time in 2009 when a wall was constructed in the middle of the large existing office space, and again a couple of years later when the whole operation moved down the hall into a small cluster of rooms including a small office for Stella—then the director—a multipurpose room (the only room with a window), a copy room, and a long, narrow office for the other staff. The staff office occupied approximately two hundred square feet, and housed four desks (one for Jenny, the business manager; one for Holly, the director of international adoptions; and two more for rotating staff and interns), and an imposing band of no less than seventeen filing cabinets. The lights were fluorescent, the walls an innocuous shade of beige. The ceiling sloped along the length of both long walls, increasing the space's cramped quality. A large framed print of a series of African masks adorned a far wall.

When I was not in the office, I was often in the car or out in the city with Stella, who had been the director of domestic adoptions when I began my fieldwork and was promoted to agency director a couple of years before the agency closed. Dotty, the agency's founder and director before Stella, retired during my fieldwork. The full-time staff consisted of Stella and Dotty (until her retirement). Jenny and Holly, in the above-mentioned roles, worked part-time, and the small staff was supplemented by a handful of contract social workers and social work interns from nearby graduate schools.

In the United States, adoption policy is determined at the state level, but the process of private agency adoption—to be distinguished from foster care and private non-agency-assisted adoption—is fairly similar across state contexts.[27] When I arrived at First Steps in 2009, a domestic adoption took about one-and-a-half to two years from start to finish, with the wait time increasing to two-and-a-half years by 2015. First Steps was not religiously affiliated, and prided itself on radical inclusiveness; social workers worked with any individual who could demonstrate parental fitness. Historically, within the context of American adoption, the parameters (both explicit and implicit) for parental fitness have been fairly narrow: white, middle- or upper-class, heterosexual, two-parent households. First Steps, however, had a long track record of placing children with single parents, considered itself minority- and LGBT-"friendly," and even worked with terminally ill parents. First Steps was equally inclusive of parents wishing to relinquish, and would "never turn away a birth mother."

Dotty, the agency's founder, often told prospective parents, with a mix of pride and sadness, that First Steps was sometimes considered the "agency of last resort" by social workers at other agencies. Early on, she would receive calls from these social workers referring expectant mothers with severe mental illness, or children they found "hard to place," such as African American children or children with medical or developmental special needs. When speaking with new prospective parents, Dotty often recounted a story about the placement of a baby with no arms and no legs: it had apparently only taken her one phone call to find willing adopters. In more than two decades of operation, First Steps boasted the successful placement of over 800 children, including more than 70 who were HIV+. However, these placements were not evenly distributed across the life of the agency.

In the spring of 2015, First Steps closed permanently. An amalgam of factors led to this outcome: a decrease in domestic adoption numbers at the agency, and likely more broadly; precarious and unstable international programs (such as one in Liberia that buckled in the midst of the 2014 Ebola outbreak); and, further back in the agency's history, a difficult shift from for-profit to nonprofit status following a 2005 Illinois adoption reform law that required an expensive buyout of the original business and crippled the agency with debt. These factors converged to produce a devastating lack of funds and the assessment by staff that it would be irresponsible to continue to accept new applicants when the future was so uncertain. The private agency always operated as a fee-for-service organization and subsisted on fees from adoptive parents and donations rather than public or private grants. In its final years, there was constant anxiety about whether or not the monthly income would exceed the accrued debt and payroll expenses. The margin simply grew smaller and smaller, until the only choice was to shutter, rendering First Steps a casualty of economic pressures produced by the Recession and changing trends in adoption more broadly. In a way, this closure was the institutional version of a fall-through.

The agency was small, and this contributed both to its perpetual financial precarity and the personal level of attention its employees were able to offer clients. As one board member opined after the closing, "What people really appreciated about First Steps was personal contact, consistency of personnel, an intimate kind of relationship." Holly insisted, "You had to have gone with us because you didn't like the big, the companies and the this and the that, like, you liked that you knew me by name and knew my kids and my cell number, you know what I mean? That's why people went with us." She explicitly positioned First Steps in opposition to "companies," an index for larger neoliberal forces seen to be encroaching on the intimate territory of family-building. Regardless of First Steps' status as small and nonprofit, however, its adoption process was neither immune to nor protected from the forces of economic exchange. In fact, particular economic logics were *generated* by the very structure of the adoption process, and vice versa. My ethnographic positioning within the agency helped to elucidate these structures and processes.

The accounts herein are based on the experiences of a group of staff and agency clients, which dwindled before being cut off abruptly at the end of my formal fieldwork when First Steps closed. When I began my research in 2009, I reached out to several agencies, large and small, in the Chicago area. Dotty was the only agency director to respond, perhaps because her pride in the agency's work made her eager to share it with others. Later in my fieldwork, I reached out again in the hopes of being able to offer a comparative perspective, and was generally met with silence. One agency responded that although my dissertation sounded "both very interesting as well as an important piece of research," due to a rebranding and some upcoming projects, the agency "would not be a good match for you as an agency able to take on a researcher" and "would not be able to provide the attention to adequately support you." Similarly, in 2016, when I reached out to the agency that took the bulk of First Steps' in-process cases after the closure, I did not receive a response. Despite my multifaceted insider status, access was a recurring challenge in this project.

As a result, this book tells the story of what adoption looks like from inside a single agency, but my time in the adoption community leads me to believe that little about the overall adoption process was unique to First Steps. Because of the nature of my fieldwork, my position at the agency, and my overarching concern with charting the process of adoption, the loudest voices in this ethnography are those of adoption professionals. While I always operated under the approval of a human subjects review board that set the minimum ethical standards for my work, certain of my own—and others'—sensitivities and concerns around access, privacy, confidentiality, and the emotional intensity of the adoption process limited my gathering of certain types of data (narratives from expectant mothers in the midst of the adoption process, for example, or discussions with prospective adopters in the wake of a fall-through). All names of individuals and private institutions have been replaced by pseudonyms to protect confidentiality.[28] Adoption work and work on adoption are both sensitive undertakings, and the ethnography to follow is greatly shaped by concerns about privacy, exposure, inequality, morality, and emotionally charged decision-making. The result is a story about the futures that hung in the balance. In advancing a theory of the imagined child as a highly contingent future, the story of First Steps is linked intimately to larger American discourses of the child as a future in—and of—the United States.

CLIENT AS CHILD, CHILD AS FUTURE

One evening in the fall of 2013, Barbara—First Steps' most senior contract social worker—interviewed a prospective adoptive mother, as was customary in the beginning phase of the adoption process. Early in the three-hour interview, Barbara veered away from questions about the hopeful adoptive mother-to-be's motivations to adopt and desires for a child, and instead offered a digression on the problem of the client in adoption social work—namely the question: "Who is the social worker's client in an adoption?" This is an important and fraught question, since the two parties engaged in the exchange—the prospective adoptive parent(s) and the expectant / birth parent(s)—often have deeply divergent interests and needs. However, this sort of "parent vs. parent" thinking, according to Barbara, is flawed. "My client is the child," she said matter-of-factly. So while Barbara completed a home study with a prospective adoptive parent (often months or even years in advance of a match with an expectant mother, and thus months or years before the child—her client—was even conceived), she was working on behalf of a client that did not even exist yet. In the case of domestic private agency adoption, the pre-adoption process is one of ensuring and protecting the future of an unborn—often pre-conceived—child. The client then—the child-to-be itself—becomes a future worth investing in, a potential waiting to be fulfilled. These logics of futurity rooted in the child are reflected more broadly in America's landscape of race, class, and social inequality.

Two visual mobilizations of black youth as futures appeared prominently in Chicago during my fieldwork. The first, a public service campaign from an antiviolence nonprofit called CeaseFire Illinois, produced a near-ubiquitous sticker on car bumpers throughout the city. The sticker contained a close-up photograph of a very young black child, overlaid with prominent white text, reading "DON'T SHOOT, I want to grow up." The second representation came from a fundraising campaign conducted by the United Negro College Fund, billboards for which portrayed an older black boy, perhaps a teen, smiling and wearing a collared shirt, next to text reading "What if the future of kids was a stock you could invest in?" Both public service announcements featured an image of a young African American—a toddler and a potentially college-bound student, respectively—and both implored the reader to imagine these children as futures, holders of positive potential. They both depicted futures at risk—the first, at risk of being cut short as a result of gun violence, the second, at risk of educational and intellectual atrophy as a result of a lack of investment in higher education—and suggested concrete ways that the viewer / reader could invest in, and thus protect, these futures.

These ads were set against a stark reality: severe racial inequality reflected in national rates of gun violence and academic achievement. Four hundred and fourteen people were killed in Chicago in 2013, and over 80 percent of those deaths were attributed to gun violence. Seventy-five percent of Chicago's gun violence victims in 2012 were African American or Latinx. In addition, between 2008 and 2012, almost half of Chicago's homicide victims were under the age of 25.[29] The CeaseFire PSA was a plea to stop this violence, which so profoundly affects the lives (and potential) of so many of Chicago's low-income children of color. The UNCF billboard responded to another disturbing trend: educational disparity. A stubborn racial and class-based academic achievement gap persists between groups of students in the United States, illustrating an important link between race and class.[30] The UNCF Better Futures program is a nonprofit fundraising campaign framed in the register of stock market investing. In the language of cost-benefit analysis, a calculator on the UNCF website allows users to "see how your investment creates Better Futures™." By investing in Better Futures (fictional stock exchange symbol: BTFR) through making a tax-deductible donation to UNCF, investors can create "social return." In electric orange text alongside a portrait of an African American student shown in profile, the donation page of the website declares, "A mind is a terrible thing to waste, but a wonderful thing to invest in." "Please invest below," it implores, "to ensure that deserving students can go to college with help from UNCF. It's an investment in a better future for us all."[31]

American culture is filled with similar messages of children as potent symbols of individual, national, and international futures in need of protection and investment. The tragedy implied by both representations is one in which a child's future is left unprotected, a future wasted through an absence of investment. Both of these representations prompt us to imagine other, better futures. In this message the child and the future are one—when one dies (or is wasted), so does (and is) the other. The Illinois Safe Haven program, which targets women wishing to anonymously relinquish their newborn infants, draws upon this very discourse.[32] The statewide symbol for Safe Havens—firehouses, police stations, and hospitals where mothers can leave newborn infants, "no questions asked"—is a large hand gingerly cradling a baby's head. Echoing the CeaseFire advertisement, the inside of the Safe Haven brochure entreats the mother, "If you are unable to keep your child, please give him or her a chance to grow up." Infants surrendered under Safe Haven laws in Illinois are referred out to private adoption agencies, such as First Steps.[33]

The Save Abandoned Babies Foundation, a nonprofit organization that raises awareness about Illinois's Safe Haven laws, includes on its website links to printable posters showing signs left on dumpsters ("It smells. It's dirty. And unfortunately it's where some women leave their babies.") and in public restrooms ("Even more upsetting than how many babies are born here is how many die here."). The posters—in addition to shaming mothers as a strategy for protecting infant life—call on viewers to raise awareness, and to imagine a different outcome: "Tell a friend. Talk about it. You might save a life." The website features a sixty-two-second video, intended for use as an educational tool in schools. The video opens with the question, "How has Apple changed your life?" After a series of images of popular Apple products, it is revealed that Steve Jobs, founder and former CEO of the tech giant, was adopted. White text flashes across a black and white photo of Jobs: "Your life changed thanks to Steve Jobs … who was ADOPTED. But what if he had been thrown in the trash?" The word "trash" flares red, superimposed on an image of a dumpster, spray painted with the words "NO BABIES." A montage of racially diverse crying infants follows. The screen reads, "Give them a chance. Every life is precious." The film concludes with a full-screen Safe Haven logo, Twitter hashtag, and Facebook group link. Two vastly different, diametrically opposed futures are laid out for children relinquished by their mothers (either to a garbage can or the loving arms of a Safe Haven representative, a firefighter perhaps, or a cop): the first marked by death and abandonment, the second by monumental achievement, economic success, and influence as the founder and CEO of one of the world's most recognizable multinational corporations. This striking binary does a great deal of ideological work. It forecloses the possibility of keeping one's child by presenting only two options: death in a dumpster or public restroom, or a meteoric rise to wealth and fame. Adoption here is portrayed as a positive investment in everyone's future, in a national future, not just the future of the child. Indeed, the future of anyone who owns or uses an iPod, iPhone, or Mac.[34] In short, adoption is framed as the condition of possibility for the Steve Jobses of the world.

The case of Devonte Hart represents another compelling example of this linking of adoption to the construction of particular American futures. In the fall of 2014, nationwide protests followed on the heels of two grand jury decisions not to indict white police officers in the deaths of unarmed African Americans: Michael Brown in Ferguson, Missouri, and Eric Garner in New York City. In November of that year, an African American child—12-year-old Tamir Rice—was shot and killed on a playground by police for brandishing a toy airsoft gun. The 2012 shooting death of 17-year-old Trayvon Martin—which touched off the Black Lives Matter movement—was fresh in the memories of those who saw these acts of violence as symptoms of larger entrenched structures of racism and inequality.

Later in 2015, two more incidents sparked national attention: a white police officer trained his weapon on an unarmed group of black teens at a pool party in Texas, pinning one bathing-suit-clad teenage girl to the ground,

FIGURE 1. Twelve-year-old Devonte Hart and Sgt. Bret Barnum share a hug at a Ferguson rally in Portland, Oregon, in November 2014. Photographer: Johnny Nguyen.

and a white officer stationed in a South Carolina school dragged a black female student out of her desk and violently threw her to the floor. Amid the protests that followed these wide-ranging acts of violence against black bodies, black male youth—Tamir, Trayvon, Michael Brown (18 at the time of his death, often pictured in his high school graduation cap and gown by mainstream media coverage), and Devonte Hart (pictured in figure 1)—became at once symbols of death and rebirth, of despair and hope for a better future.[35]

The photograph in figure 1 was taken by freelance photographer Johnny Nguyen at a rally in Portland, Oregon, after the Ferguson grand jury decision. In it, Devonte Hart—a 12-year-old African American boy—engages in a tearful hug with a white police officer, Sgt. Bret Barnum. It is a powerful image of "interracial intimacy" (Kennedy 2004) in a time of egregious interracial violence and tension—a comforting embrace between a white adult and a vulnerable and distraught child of color. Even amid rumors that the photograph was staged and that Barnum was an alleged supporter of Darren Wilson, the officer who fatally shot Michael Brown, the photo quickly went viral, becoming "one of the most shared images of the Ferguson protests" (Saul 2014). It became known not only as "the hug that moved a nation"

(Homer 2014), but also "the hug felt 'round the world" that "melted millions of hearts" (Jonsson 2014). It is ironic that journalists would choose a metaphor stemming from a violent—gun violence, no less—act of war (whether referring to the first shot of the American Revolutionary War or the assassin's bullet often cited as ground zero for the First World War) to describe this image and the intimacy it depicted. Indeed, this hug felt 'round the world was only made possible by the six gunshots that struck Michael Brown, contemporary shots heard 'round the world.[36] However, those shots were not its only condition of possibility.[37]

The image of Devonte is instructive because he was adopted, across both race and class lines. This image and its reception are exceptionally illustrative of how children—particularly African American children—can become contested symbols of a hopeful national future, even in a world where they are often victims of extreme physical and structural violence. This stark duality is reflected further in U.S. domestic adoption—a practice rendered possible through complex histories of racial disparity and economic abandonment—which painfully severs existing kinship ties at the same time that it joyfully builds new ones. The photograph—more commonly recognized as protest imagery—is part of a larger visual canon of adoptive interracial intimacy circulated by the mainstream media.

Actress Mariska Hargitay nuzzles her African American infant daughter Amaya in numerous tabloid photos. The cover of *People Magazine* portrays Sandra Bullock lifting her newly adopted African American three-month-old Louis above her head in jubilation.[38] Brangelina's modern-day Bakeresque "rainbow tribe" is gazed upon with awe. Even former Massachusetts governor and Republican presidential hopeful Mitt Romney bounces baby Kieran, his adopted African American grandson, on his knee in a family portrait. There is a sense that these children's trajectories have been altered dramatically, but how are these new families formed? What is the process, the labor, of creating the condition of possibility for these images of transracial intimacy, of American pluralism and post-raciality, of a "land of equals," in a nation riddled by systemic inequity? How is it that these children become symbols of utopian, rather than dystopian, futures?

A couple of weeks before the Portland rally where Devonte was iconically photographed—in some strange feat of journalistic prescience—New Zealand news site *Paper Trail* published a story about him, which was later picked up by *Huffington Post*. According to writer Chloe Johnson (2014), who spoke with Devonte's white adoptive mothers—who at that time, it should be noted, lived with Devonte and his siblings in West Linn, Oregon, the state's fifth-most affluent community—Devonte was born "into a life of drugs, extreme poverty, danger and destined for a bleak future." "By the time he was 4 years old," writes Johnson, "he had smoked, consumed alcohol, handled guns, been shot at, and suffered severe abuse and neglect." Her details confirm what readers think they know about America's black and broken inner cities, and the conditions that produce thugs, super-predators, and a generation of lost- cause crack babies. "It was life with little hope and a future that seemed over before it began," the journalist concludes; "That is, until Jen Hart and her wife Sarah entered Devonte's life and adopted him and his two siblings seven years ago."

The white savior narrative is not subtle, and Johnson tells a story of adoption as a practice of drastically altering futures: "With their unconditional love, nurturing natures, patience and acceptance, Devonte defied all odds and has grown into a young charismatic man with a heart of gold." The implication here is that were it not for adoption, Devonte's heart might have been made of something less shiny and precious. According to one of his adoptive mothers, quoted in the article, "His future is most definitely not bleak, he is a shining star in this world." She continues, "Yes indeed he is living proof that our past does not dictate our future." Devonte's story seems quintessential in the moment of Black Lives Matter: transracial adoption as a mechanism that can produce a little black boy who loves white cops.[39] This story of adoption is one of profound social transformation made possible by egregious social inequality, underscoring adoption's (dys)function as an individual solution to a set of deep structural problems.

I first wrote about Devonte in 2015. As I was finishing the final revisions of this manuscript in late March 2018, Jennifer Hart drove her SUV off a cliff in Mendocino County, California, with her partner Sarah and at least five of their six adopted black children inside. The bodies of the adoptive mothers and four children were recovered at the scene, and the remains of a fifth child were later identified. As this book goes to press, Devonte remains missing, presumed dead. Authorities investigated the incident as intentional, a murder-suicide. This is a devastating example of how even the most "happily ever after" endings of adoption may, in exceptional cases, be shot through with violence. And how the conditions of transracial adoption remain intimately entwined with the conditions of black life in the United States. Much of the apparatus of the adoption process is built around trying desperately to prevent this type of outcome: a future careening off a cliff. This un / expected ending reminds us to question the assumption that an adoptive future is always a better future. To understand adoption and its outcomes, however, it is necessary to explore further its conditions of possibility.

PROCESS AND PROCESSING

What is the work of imagining futures? *Contingent Kinship* is an ethnography of both process and processing, the social glue that links structures of inequality to individual and familial trajectories. As a nonnormative version of family-making in the United States—one with an abundance of fictionalized portrayals and distortions—adoption as a process is often rather opaque to those without direct personal experience. Its inner workings are complex and fragile, and they amplify the forms of uncertainty and stress that accompany biological reproduction.[40] The best way to illustrate the doing and undoing of adoption at First Steps is through a diagram that Stella created to teach potential clients about the adoption process. As an unconventional sort of hybrid kinship-diagram-timeline-map, her "Adoption at a Glance" visualizes the ways in which subjects both process and are processed into and out of certain kinds of subjectivities.

The work of the day (visiting expectant mothers, making phone calls, filing papers) was done, and I was sitting with Stella in the adoption agency conference room. I employ the term "conference room" loosely. A well-worn dining table—which, on a good day, could seat maybe four—was pushed against the wall, taking up far too much space in a small room that also contained a rocking chair, an overstuffed love-seat, and a changing table often piled high with diapers and onesies. When the agency had occupied a slightly larger space on the same floor, there had also been a rocking horse. The chair in which I was seated was backed up against a tall bookshelf crammed with adoption-related titles like *Childhood: A Multicultural View, Adoption: A Handful of Hope, Raising Black Children,* and *Be My Baby: Parents and Children Talk about Adoption.* On the wall were two bulletin boards displaying an impressive collection of family and baby photos. Most of the adults in the photos were white, most of the children were black.

I sat in this room often, observing meetings between social workers and prospective adopters, and it was where Stella and I regularly caught up over

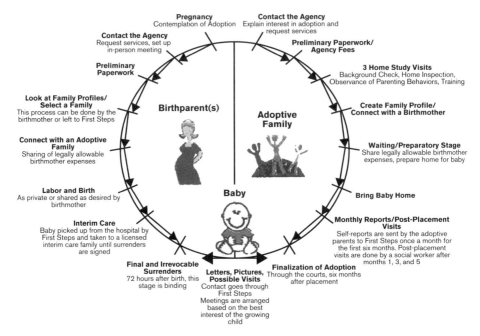

Pregnancy
Contemplation of Adoption

Contact the Agency
Explain interest in adoption and request services

Contact the Agency
Request services, set up in-person meeting

Preliminary Paperwork/
Agency Fees

Preliminary Paperwork

3 Home Study Visits
Background Check, Home Inspection, Observance of Parenting Behaviors, Training

Look at Family Profiles/
Select a Family
This process can be done by the birthmother or left to First Steps

Birthparent(s)

Adoptive Family

Create Family Profile/
Connect with a Birthmother

Connect with an Adoptive Family
Sharing of legally allowable birthmother expenses

Waiting/Preparatory Stage
Share legally allowable birthmother expenses, prepare home for baby

Labor and Birth
As private or shared as desired by birthmother

Baby

Bring Baby Home

Interim Care
Baby picked up from the hospital by First Steps and taken to a licensed interim care family until surrenders are signed

Monthly Reports/Post-Placement Visits
Self-reports are sent by the adoptive parents to First Steps once a month for the first six months. Post-placement visits are done by a social worker after months 1, 3, and 5

Final and Irrevocable Surrenders
72 hours after birth, this stage is binding

Letters, Pictures, Possible Visits
Contact goes through First Steps Meetings are arranged based on the best interest of the growing child

Finalization of Adoption
Through the courts, six months after placement

FIGURE 2. "Adoption at a Glance" diagram used by agency staff to explain the adoption process to clients.

lunch. It was late afternoon, and shafts of sunlight spilled through the open blinds of the room's only window, warming the broad wooden table between us, where an array of papers was spread out. I asked Stella to tell me about a diagram I had seen her draw numerous times as an explanatory aid while meeting with expectant parents. She began,

> I really like it as a tool, and the way it came about was the intern came with me [to visit expectant mothers] and saw what I was doing and I would draw it out—on paper, always. And that's what I was doing. When I was a therapist I would often draw their lives, and draw a map, and draw possible decisions. It's something I've often done.

Stella reproduced this diagram by hand with expectant mothers every time I accompanied her to a preliminary paperwork meeting—indeed it served as one of the most important artifacts of this initial meeting, as well as a crucial pedagogical tool. In my time at the agency, the document was transformed from a hand-drawn image created in the moment of interaction to a reproducible digital graphic immortalized by the aforementioned social work intern, and then a standard part of the preliminary paperwork packet for expectant parents. It was also often shown to prospective adoptive parents in their initial meeting with either Stella or their home study worker (see figure 2).

Stella's diagram depicts and simplifies the entire adoption process on paper—a process that takes months, even years, in real time is explicated and diagrammed in a matter of moments within the initial encounter of social worker and expectant / prospective parent. The diagram's most prominent feature is its circularity. Visually, the diagram resembles a clock (with many more hour marks than a normal twelve-hour clock, emphasizing the extension of what we might call adoption time)—or rather two half clocks, dual temporalities unfolding, drawing the eye, like a second hand sweeping downward, toward the future, the infant.[41]

One half of the circle lays out the adoption process for the "birthparent(s)," while the other depicts the process for the prospective adoptive parents / family—this division mirrors a conceptual and lived distinction between First Steps' two client populations. The same social worker very rarely worked with both sets of parents-to-be in a given adoption. Aside from fielding occasional initial visits and phone calls from prospective adoptive parents, Stella had traditionally been the "birth mother worker," while an array of different social workers handled the home study process for prospective adoptive parents.[42] The logic of this division of labor was that it prevented one worker from representing the often-conflicting interests of both sides. It was not unlike the representational logic of a divorce—it is generally not thought to be ideal for the same counsel to represent both parties.[43]

As Barbara told one prospective adoptive mother, "Oddly enough, I have met rarely any birth moms. That, I just, I'm not part of that, and there was a time when people did a little of both, and I find it's better that I'm not." The applicant nodded, and Barbara continued, "Just because there's a little bit of conflict of interest in that, you know? And I feel like I'm here for you. I can't be there for the mom too." Barbara's admission reveals a belief that the interests of expectant parents and prospective adoptive parents are at least "a little bit" divergent. The diagram, with its cascade of forking and then reconnecting arrows, confirms this. In Sara Dorow's 2006 ethnography of transnational adoption from China in which she explores "how adoption as a social process speaks to a range of broader questions" (8), she observes: "The (impossible) trick was to keep the child at the center of professional social work practice even as the [prospective adoptive] parent, the 'secondary client,' was the one directly paying for services" (85).[44] In domestic adoption, it can be difficult to separate imagined children from the expectant mothers carrying them, even when this appears to be the overarching goal of the process.

Returning to Stella's diagram, each step depicted was contingent upon the steps that came before it, giving the process a sense of linearity in addition to its circularity. In a typical first meeting with an expectant mother or prospective adoptive couple, Stella would begin at the top of the diagram and narrate the process as it would unfold simultaneously for each set of parents, while moving down either side of the circle, retracing the image with a pen, making hash-marks at important stages or milestones. The twin—perhaps fraternal rather than identical—processes meet at the bottom center of the circle, where Stella would normally write, in large capital letters, "BABY": the finish line, a shared, but also split, future encapsulated in an imagined child. The arrows on the left side of the diagram—the consanguineal side of this odd kinship chart—appear to point backwards at first, hinting at an undoing.

Aside from the mention of the possible exchange of letters and pictures via open adoption, the potential for radical family formations is foreclosed—*this* kinship relationship will be dissolved and *this other one* will replace it. Somehow, the "baby's" arrows do not really point toward anyone or anything. This end is left completely open—where do the arrows go?—a moment of contingency, an end that depends on the neat stacking of one arrow / step / decision on top of another. The diagram elides the fact that broken, missing, and lengthened arrows often created gaps and clogs, splintered shafts and shredded fletching gumming up the works like proverbial wrenches.[45]

Like all diagrams of social processes, for all its detail, Stella's map is of course an oversimplification of the adoption process. The simplicity and directionality of the diagram artfully obscure the fits, starts, and circling back necessitated by disruption, delay, and failure. Cost is another important aspect of the process that is not reflected in the diagram. When I began my fieldwork, the total fee for a domestic adoption was approximately $13,000, paid in installments at different stages of the process. By the time the agency closed, that fee had been doubled to approximately $27,000. In the face of these omissions, the clipart speaks volumes. Notably, the expectant mother is singular and faceless—if anything, she might be interpreted as in pain or discomfort, her hand placed on her lower back. Her partner is absent, reflecting wider assumptions about birth fathers, which are tied very closely to American stereotypes of absent black fathers or "deadbeat dads" (Cassiman 2008). In practice, the vast majority of "birth parent work" at First Steps occurred between social worker and expectant mother only. In contrast, the adoptive family is multiple, multicolored, and joyful.

The social worker constitutes another striking absence from Stella's diagram. The collection of icons at the center of the circle conveys a version of the "adoption triad," a term commonly used among those in the adoption community denoting the grouping of birth parent(s), adoptive family, and child, usually represented by an equilateral triangle.[46] The relation examined in this book, which—like Stella's diagram—shifts the temporal frame of analysis to the months leading up to the birth of the child, includes the central and mediating role of the social worker and collapses the child into the expectant mother. Indeed, for much of the adoption process, the child does not yet exist as such. This reformulation creates a model of the adoption *process*, leaving open the possibility for various outcomes. In it, the child remains a potentiality, a not-yet. The problem of adoption is shifted from unknown origins and a troubling past to contingent and unknown futures. In this way the practice of American adoption might be imagined as an emergent phenomenon, and an exercise in intense contingency.[47]

To understand adoptive kinship, it is necessary to comprehend how it comes to be, and a reformulated triad—expectant mother, prospective adopter(s), social worker—is the best model to illustrate the relational dynamics that I watched unfold during my time at First Steps. Dorow (2006: 24) calls for a shift in analytical focus from the "post" of adoption to "the powerful heterogeneity of the 'pre' of adoption." I would argue that the language of pre- and post-, while organizationally useful from a temporal perspective, is limiting because the adoption itself is never a given. In order for the adoption to happen—and not fall through—each arm of the triad needed to be fixed. If one arm could not be fixed, the whole thing would collapse. At First Steps, this triad often became an inverted pyramid teetering precariously on the expectant mother's decision. At other times, the social worker perched at the apex as an instrument of surveillance, shining a figurative cone of light onto her clients below. The prospective adopters, though often voicing feelings of disempowerment or lack of control, provided the capital that kept the whole fee-for-service enterprise running. Anticipation. Observation. Investment. The chapters to follow examine these relationships and dynamics in a great deal more detail. Rather than telling stories of the adoptive family as the outcome of adoption, this book explores the tangle of steps and decisions that make such outcomes (im)possible.

Reimagining the triadic relationship in this way foregrounds the role of the social worker as the facilitator, mediator, and ultimately, the broker of these complex relationships.[48] Put most simply, a broker is an actor who "bridges" two other actors who would not otherwise share a connection (Spiro, Acton, and Butts 2013). In adoption, in many ways, she is a kinship gatekeeper. The tasks of the adoption social worker as broker include various forms of affective, intimate, emotional, and reproductive labor.[49] Affective labor reveals "how relations of intimacy are constructed through processes of labor" (Mankekar and Gupta 2016: 17). In examining how adoption professionals market adoption to potential adopters, Elizabeth Raleigh (2017: 67) has referred to this labor as "emotion work." As the following chapters will show, the social worker labors to produce connection, kinship (a "happy family"), hope, certainty, and particular imaginaries of future children and families. At various times, her work also results in separation, commodification, and erasure. She is to varying degrees a mother, a detective, a state agent, a bureaucrat, a matchmaker, a counselor, a coach, a liaison, an educator, a giver, and a taker. Brokerage itself has the potential to produce inequality, and brokers derive power from the fact that the individuals or entities that they connect cannot do so without them.[50] Indeed, the brokerage function was the reason for the adoption agency's existence. In order to understand the contingency of the adoption process, we must attend to what Martijn Koster (2012: 48) has identified as "the complexity and ambiguity of brokerage . . . its conflict-prone and fragile nature." As brokers, adoption social workers regulate complex and unstable flows of infants, money, time, power, and knowledge.

CONVOLUTED FLOWS

Social scientists often use the concept of "flow" to describe and interrogate circulations of power, capital, people, and objects over space and time.[51] Adoption at First Steps was clearly a form of circulation. Babies were literally moving—across racial, class-based, and geographical borders. Money was changing hands. Power and knowledge were in constant flux. Social workers and parents were trading in futures at risk. But upon closer inspection, the adoption process is revealed to be one characterized much less by smooth and circular flows than by choppy swells and troughs. The concept of flow remains conceptually attractive, however, not just for the sake of alliteration, but because it resonates with adoption in a native sense, one of "going with the flow" as a strategy of flexibility to weather the uncertainties of life, the bumps in the road.

In 2013, sitting in the office of First Steps, Stella told me how she had to adjust her ways of working to accommodate a new group of expectant mothers approaching the agency from out-of-state. "Very doable," she said, appraising the feasibility of working across such long distances. "And plus, nowadays you gotta do it if you want to keep your head up. Because you know they're all [expectant mothers and prospective adoptive parents] on that internet." At this point, the World Wide Web was already supplanting the brokerage function of the agency, and the notion of increased competition was implicit in Stella's account. I nodded, and she continued, "And that means national, and so we gotta go with the flow." This was a kind of flexible accumulation within the intimate industry of adoption. Just as this social worker saw the need to attune her practice to the changing landscape of American adoption, this sense of flux, change, and disruption also characterized each individual adoption, unfolding at a much smaller scale. The following chapters chart these ebbs and flows of futures-in-the-making, revealing how modes of intimate speculation function to create futures for some, while dissolving them for others. By examining adoption practice through the final seven years of First Steps' institutional life, *Contingent Kinship* reveals the challenges and intricacies of making kin and futures in the twenty-first-century United States.

. . .

Before continuing this journey, however, a note on terminology is necessary, as the temporality of the adoption process is encoded in the very language used to describe its participants. Below is a brief vocabulary for adoption as a form of intimate speculation.

expectant mother   The question of what to call the woman who may relinquish a child reveals the temporal dimensions of adoption as a process of future-building grounded in larger systems of oppression. Social workers and adoptive parents have dispensed with terms like "real mother" and "natural mother" in favor of "positive" or "preferred" adoption language that does not reflect an assumption that adoptive ties are "fake" or "unnatural," although both terms ("real" and "natural") are embraced by those in the birth / first parent community, begging the question, "positive" for whom?[52] The more clinical "biological mother" was rarely uttered in my field site, although I did hear the shorthand "biomom" once or twice. Social workers and adoptive parents, as well as those outside the adoption community, commonly refer to the woman who may relinquish her child as a "birth mother." For example, at First Steps, social workers regularly referred to "birth mother paperwork," "birth mother visits," and "legally allowable birth mother expenses."[53] To aid in the selection process, it was not uncommon for prospective adopters to craft "dear birth mother" letters to include in the profiles—essentially auto-biographical photo albums—that would be shown to expectant mothers. There has been a growing trend, spurred by women whose babies were taken during the "Baby Scoop Era" of the 1960s, to use the term "first mother."[54] Although "first mother" was never used in my field site (likely because it implies that adoptive motherhood is "second"), the term starkly reflects the temporality of adoption through the sequential ordering and ranking of kin-ship ties and claims to motherhood.

Using "birth mother" within the context of the adoption process reduces a woman's connection to her child to the moment of birth. It fast-forwards her existence to a future state in which she has given birth and relinquished. For she is only a "birth mother" after she has given birth and surrendered her parental rights. Before that moment, in fact, she is an expectant mother, like any other pregnant woman. Calling her a "birth mother" overdetermines her. When she is referred to as a "birth mother," she has always already made her decision to place the child for adoption. This means she has always already decided *not* to parent the child herself. When she is called a "birth mother," she is prefigured as an unfit parent—or at least a second-best option, despite her impending status as "first mother." She is effectively recruited to the role of the woman who has already surrendered her parental rights. As a result, it feels like a betrayal to social workers and prospective parents when she "changes her mind," or decides to parent. In this way, the very words used to describe her have profound implications for the fall-through.[55]

In light of these complexities, I use the terms "expectant" and "potential" when referring to those considering relinquishment prior to birth. Indeed, the expectant mother is imbued with expectations. After birth but before surrenders have been signed, I refer to those considering relinquishment in an unmarked and unmodified way, simply as "mother / father / parent." I use the term "birth mother" when designating women who have already placed their children, when referring to reported speech by others, and when discussing the figure of the birth mother constructed by the adoption process.

prospective adopter(s)   In this book, "adoptive parents" will only appear without the qualifier "prospective" when I am discussing individuals or couples who have *already* adopted. Prospective adoptive parents are those hoping to adopt, but whose adoptions are not yet finalized. This distinction is crucial. Throughout the vast majority of the process, these are speculative parents of the child-to-be-adopted. Like "expectant" in the case of expectant mothers, "prospective" is a speculative adjective that more accurately reflects the temporal realities of the adoption process and avoids perpetrating the ontological violence of premature categorization.

imagined child   I refer to the imagined / future child, the child-to-be, or the unborn child, emphasizing the child's ability or potential to be adopted in the future. Although technically the object of investment is a fetus, or the mere idea of one, the word "fetus" was rarely, if ever, uttered in my field site, further underscoring the social import of the child as anticipatory subject. By referring only to the "child," "baby," or "adoptee" (not "child-to-be" or "fetus") when discussing the contents of a pregnant woman's uterus, social workers and prospective adoptive parents discursively create a speculative future. They are hailing a child—and a future—that does not yet exist. This book is not so much about actual children as it is about imagined children, and often, a very particular imaginary of the black child.

ONE

Suspect and Spectral (M)others

I see you are not there.

—AVERY GORDON (2008: 16)

ADOPTION RATES EBBED AND FLOWED with the seasons at First Steps, and 2010 had seen a very slow summer. Staff usually did not arrive at the office until 10:00 a.m. and rarely stayed past 3:00 or 4:00 in the afternoon, and an extended lunch break in the middle of the day was not unusual. After a couple of meetings in the city, Stella and I met up with Dotty—First Steps' founder and director—and her sister-in-law at a small café around the corner from the agency. After polite chitchat, the conversation shifted to the general goings-on at the agency, and inevitably to the serial fall-throughs that staff and prospective parents had been experiencing. In referring to expectant mothers as a group, and particularly the ones who seemed prone to "changing their minds" about the adoption plans they had made, Dotty, nonchalantly and in between bites of her salad, called them "slippery little eels," a metaphor at once direct and loaded with a range of implications. The conversation continued without missing a beat.

Several structural issues informed Dotty's conception of First Steps' expectant mothers as "slippery little eels," a crude metaphor that can be understood as a resurrection of the figure of the "welfare queen" of the 1970s, 1980s, and 1990s. First Steps was a very small nonprofit agency that struggled each year to stay afloat financially. In 2010, Dotty and Stella were the only full-time employees, and the only social workers, aside from seasonal interns, who interacted with expectant mothers. A handful of contracted social workers carried out home studies with prospective adoptive families. Due to the logics of supply and demand, social workers were stressed by an imbalance in caseload in which prospective adoptive parents greatly outnumbered expectant mothers. Every year the situation seemed bleaker, the list of waiting adoptive parents—final installments of fees from whom could not be collected until after the successful placement of a child—grew longer, and the "link list" of expectant mothers seemed to grow shorter.

Intimate speculation entails a set of practices for making subjects visible in the service of gaining predictive knowledge. This whole book is very much about birth mothers, but there are very few birth mothers in these pages. Indeed, that is, and was, precisely the problem—both for the agency and for my research. In order to understand the nature of fallen-through adoptions, it is necessary to begin at the source, which is a space and subject position of intense marginality, highly constrained choice, and often, disappearance and invisibility. This story of adoption, therefore, is best begun with absence. Indeed, a disappearing mother can lead us to important methodological, historical, and ethnographic insights. In my field site, the absence of expectant mothers—at first a methodological conundrum—proved an important, and critically revealing, ethnographic fact. Everyone was always looking for "birth mothers": social workers, adoptive parents, adoptees, and ethnographers. The particular modes by which they were located (or not) and visually conjured provide insight into the roles of surveillance, power, and knowledge in the adoption process. Through examining the structural modes by which expectant / birth mothers are rendered (and are perceived to render themselves) absent, invisible, spectral, and ultimately unknowable, this chapter demonstrates how power dynamics in the adoption process are highly conditioned by questions of who can see and be seen, who looks and is looked at, when, how, and to what effect.

REACHING OUT

There were two primary reasons for the growing list of prospective adopters and the dire financial situation in which First Steps found itself. The first was that there were simply fewer expectant mothers working with the agency. Social workers were not sure why. Perhaps they were flocking to some other agency, or placing their babies informally with relatives, a practice common in black communities (Roberts 1997: 54; Stack 1974). Indeed, my first summer at First Steps had been spent delivering flyers to the city's hospitals, women's clinics, and shelters as a mode of "outreach" in an effort to reverse this trend.

A couple of times each week, the social work intern, Christine—a bubbly white woman in her early twenties—and I would set out in her small, well-worn car to visit area hospitals and medical clinics. It was 2009. We were armed with stacks of flyers describing the agency's services to potential birth mothers. The hospitals and clinics we visited were primarily in low-income neighborhoods with which both Christine, a suburbanite, and I, having only arrived in Chicago a year prior, were unfamiliar. It comforted Stella to know that we traveled in a pair, particularly in the heat of the summer, which was known as the most violent time of year in Chicago. On our first day, we went as far south as 111th Street and visited a total of fifteen establishments, mostly women's health and family planning clinics, a YWCA, one shelter, and one hospital. Most, but not all, of the people with whom we spoke were African American. The second day, we distributed flyers on Chicago's West Side, where we visited twelve clinics, only to find that six of them did not exist (Christine had compiled a list of likely targets using Google and other data-bases and we had mapped them out before leaving the agency). It was a lot of driving, but not much else. It was oppressively hot and muggy, and the air freshener dangling from Christine's rearview mirror made me nauseous. The two of us, pounding the proverbial pavement during those early July days, constituted the closest thing First Steps had to a marketing department.

The flyers were printed in color. The lines of the text and agency logo were smooth and crisp. The single glossy image—of a light-brown-skinned woman, man, and baby—occupied a third of the page. The baby looks directly into the eyes of the viewer. Her (she is wearing a pink jumper) ostensible parents' eyes are closed or downcast. Mom's lips are pursed into a kiss planted on Baby's right temple. Dad rests his cheek on the other side of Baby's head. It is left up to the person viewing the flyer to decide whether these adults are this baby's birth parents or her adoptive parents. This ambiguity widened the image's potential appeal. All of the cultural clues are there to let us know that they love her very much, regardless of the qualifier we apply to "parent." At the top of the flyer, two questions are posed, the former loudly, the latter more of a whisper: "UNPLANNED PREGNANCY? Looking for adoption services?" An unexpected pregnancy produces an expectant mother. The flyer then answers its own questions, using the second person along with future and conditional verb tenses to great effect: "First Steps will provide you with an adoptive family who will give your child everything you would . . . if only you could!" The reader is somehow benevolently cast as an unfit parent. The monologue is interrupted by the image of parental love, before the entreaty continues below with a list: "Many qualified families waiting . . . Open or closed adoptions . . . Special needs accepted . . . Culturally sensitive staff . . .

Confidential." The reader is then encouraged to "Call Toll Free." This form of marketing / outreach—along with connections at area hospitals for "born babies"—was one of the primary ways First Steps sought to locate new expectant mothers.

At the 2013 staff holiday party, Dotty and Stella reminisced about a time earlier in the life of the agency when placing over seventy infants annually was the norm. Dotty told me about one year when there were eighteen babies in August alone. She had four newborns in the office at one time, lined up in their car seats, she said chuckling, with adoptive parents waiting to fill out paperwork. She recalled worrying she might mix up the infants, literally switching them at birth. By the time of my fieldwork, placements had steeply declined. In both 2013 and 2014, only thirteen babies were placed per year, scarcely more than one each month on average. Fewer expectant mothers at First Steps meant fewer babies and fewer adoptions, which in turn meant less revenue for the agency.

Let us return to the "slippery little eels" comment. In addition to the dearth of expectant mothers, the second phenomenon informing Dotty's eel metaphor was the recent spike in fall-throughs. Most of the time these fall-throughs occurred after social workers had spent a considerable amount of time on the case, and after prospective adoptive families had also become involved and invested, emotionally as well as financially, in the form of "legally allowable birth mother expenses." In the summer of 2010, the agency seemed to be experiencing fall-through after fall-through, and social workers lamented not only the loss of "business" but also the emotional fallout experienced by adoptive families. From my vantage point, it seemed as though expectant mothers were frustratingly slipping through Stella's grasp, despite her numerous efforts to retain them. This is not to say that Stella and Dotty did not believe wholeheartedly that expectant mothers had a legal right to parent, and they did their best to support mothers in making that decision, but their existence as brokers—and adoptive parents themselves—depended on relinquishment. Regardless of individual intention or motivation, the system itself was oppressive. Indeed, the social workers at First Steps operated within a structure that was—and remains—a great deal more violent than they ever were as individuals. Their moral stance, however, did little to stem the frustration they felt when it seemed like every single adoption plan was failing midstream. It also did little to prevent them from carrying out everyday practices of erasure and marginalization, even if they intended otherwise. Even progressive adoptive professionals committed to the mission of social work were not immune from ideas circulating about poor black women.

A conversation I had with Stella one day while out running errands illustrates simultaneously her awareness of the marginalized position of expectant mothers and her frustration with what she perceived as inherent expectant mother unknowability. In discussing an expectant mother who had recently approached the agency, she said, "I think there's a lot about this girl that I don't know. Is she a scammer? I don't know." Her repetition of "I don't know" illustrates the central place of uncertainty in the adoption process rooted in the figure of the expectant mother and the need for social workers to manage it (and her).[1] Stella talked about the structural inequities affecting the lives of many expectant mothers as producing social norms of guarded secrecy and mistrust: "It would seem more normal not to disclose. You learn very quickly that you don't tell everybody everything. Then you add in shame, guilt." Guilt factored not only in terms of remorse, but also in social workers' framing of expectant mothers as potential "scammers." The expectant mother's structural position rendered her always already *suspect,* a word whose etymology suggests a distrustful look (Ayto 2006). Visual, temporal, and moral logics were intimately bound up in social workers' encounters with expectant mothers.

Stella spoke briefly about another expectant mother she had been working with out-of-state, who had suffered from postpartum depression and bipolar disorder and had not initially disclosed that while pregnant she had overdosed on sleeping pills in an attempted suicide: "People in her position have learned not to share a whole lot of information about themselves." Here Stella alludes to the social and economic constraints that put certain groups of people into positions in which control over presence, visibility, and self-disclosure is one of the few powers they possess. The expectant mother's lies of omission link her to the welfare queen, who was defined by guilt and dishonesty. A perceived dynamic in which expectant mothers "choose" whether or not to disclose certain information (and whether or not to render themselves visible in particular ways), places social workers in a position with little control over certain forms of predictive knowledge about expectant mothers, and this dynamic contributes to the construction of the expectant mother as a shadowy and unpredictable figure, an object of suspicion.

As I believe it was intended to, Dotty's comparison of expectant mothers to "slippery little eels" engendered feelings of aversion and disgust in me—toward the metaphoric eels, and by extension the expectant mothers, but also toward Dotty for the way she so boldly and insensitively described this subset of Chicago's low-income women confronted by unexpected pregnancies. At the same time, I empathized with her. I can imagine how one might find this sentiment of an adoption social worker toward her most vulnerable clients horrifying—a product of the perhaps unrealistic idea that social workers can hold *only* unconditional positive regard toward their clients—and dismiss it as callousness or insensitivity at best (racism, classism, and sexism at worst). But much can be gleaned from a more careful consideration of Dotty's chosen analogy, for it reflects a sense of frustration produced by the perceived difficulty of her work, and begins to reveal the structures and practices through which the "birth mother" is constructed as a spectral figure—the ways in which the adoption process produces and enables certain types of erasure and invisibility.

From Dotty's perspective, slippery little eels, and by extension expectant mothers, were adept at disappearing. They slid through her frantic grasp; in some cases, when she did succeed in catching them, she got a nasty shock. Her analogy also gives a sense that expectant mothers were mischievous, conniving, or bad in some way, mirroring a cultural association with snakes. Indeed "slippery little *fish*" would not have produced the same response as "slippery little eels." "Slippery" conveys slickness or smoothness, but also sneakiness, untrustworthiness, difficulty, and stealth. In the cultural context in which Dotty was speaking, there is a general aversion to eels, which is reflected in popular media, and informs both the use and reception of Dotty's metaphor.[2] Expectant mothers, as imagined within the metaphor, often slithered away into the depths, difficult to track. First Steps was located in the suburbs, and expectant mothers often disappeared into what Dotty may have construed as the dark—really, black—dangerous, and murky depths of the South and West Sides of Chicago. In the case of a fall-through, social workers would grasp for contact, and they were often met with silence, darkness. The loss was usually ambiguous, and the social workers were left to make the official call of failure. The expectant mother had simply "disappeared."

Throughout the adoption process, even in cases that did not end in fall-through, First Steps' expectant mothers were generally difficult to locate. They often vanished from social workers' field of vision, and therefore constituted a problematically unknown entity—at once opaque and transparent. Cheryl Mattingly (2010) mobilizes the notion of the "familiar stranger" in her analysis of racially and socioeconomically fraught interactions between low-income African American patients and upper-class white clinicians in a pediatric hospital: "a troublesome familiar stranger is the sort of character whose actions are predictable but unreasonable, unaccountable, deeply flawed, possibly immoral" (107). For social workers, the expectant mother who "scammed" or "fell through" was a sort of familiar stranger, one who often acted in expected but unfortunate (for social workers and prospective adoptive families) ways. As perceived by social workers, expectant mothers as a group were predictably unpredictable—they often missed scheduled appointments, and they were difficult to track. Their motivations and intentions were impossible to discern. After every meeting with a new expectant mother, Stella would invariably ask me if I thought she would complete the adoption. The outcome was always uncertain. Did she intend to place? Would she change her mind? Or was she simply "flipping the script"?[3]

For prospective adoptive families, the expectant mother becomes a *familial* stranger, unpredictable, no longer (or not) familiar, but rather a stranger subject who must be somehow integrated into the imagined kinship formation—at least until the surrenders are signed, but possibly long after—for the adoption to occur. Following from one trainer's characterization of adoption as a form of "high-risk pregnancy," for social workers, and by extension prospective adoptive parents, this is a form of stranger pregnancy.[4] And encoded in the stranger is a sense of threat: "stranger danger"—that memorable artifact of a national discourse of child protection—has a new sort of purchase here. Ahmed (2014a) notes, "strangers become objects not only of feeling but also of governance; strangers are bodies that are managed. Or perhaps we should say: the governing of bodies creates strangers as bodies that require being governed." During the pre-adoption process, prospective adoptive parents do not know the "birth mother." Most of the time, they can't even find her. They can't know her—not as a birth mother, at least, because she does not exist as one yet. The language of "slippery little eels" fits neatly into a larger discursive apparatus of referring to "birth mothers" in advance of their arrival, a technique of fixing a stranger subject. This temporal condition had important implications for my access to expectant mothers.

In March of 2014, I gave a paper at an academic conference on adoption in Tallahassee, Florida. After the talk, a middle-aged African American woman approached me with a look of concern on her face. "I have a question," she said. I nodded, and she continued, eyes narrowed, "Aren't you worried that talking to birth mothers during the adoption process might influence their decisions about whether or not they will place?" The question echoed an anonymous grant proposal reviewer for a major anthropology funding agency, who had responded to an early sketch of my research design in 2013 with the statement: "Although the applicant is aware that there are some ethical concerns, and that she will be working with parents, birth mothers and social workers, I see serious ethical concerns . . . Adoption in this case is a sensitive issue." The reviewer went on,

> The applicant will trace the adoption process from the time the expectant mother contacts the agency. She is proposing to participate in all stages of the adoption process, to accompany social workers, prospective parents, and birth mothers. Her constant presence may have implications in terms of the possible research bias.

Funds were not awarded. While I cannot recall exactly how I responded to the woman at the conference—it was certainly in the affirmative: yes, absolutely, I worry about this all the time—I remember with an intense and visceral clarity the way that her question articulated foundational concerns and anxieties I had been experiencing throughout my fieldwork as I tried and failed repeatedly to produce what I felt were ethnographically "useful" encounters with expectant mothers.

Although she never voiced it explicitly, I suspect Stella shared my anxieties. Given the institutional pressures to produce successful placements and the resultantly immense implications of my potential "meddling," how could she not? Every time there was a new expectant mother, and I expressed interest in an interview or private conversation, much talk ensued about whether she would be a "good" candidate and whether it was the "right" time. Stella— my key interlocutor and ethnographic gatekeeper—often implied that some kind of "closer" relationship would be the ideal environment for conversations with expectant mothers, but the cultivation of such a relationship proved impossible for me within a handful, or less, of encounters in which Stella was always—literally and figuratively—in the driver's seat. Although it may sound crass, I have no doubt that the increased numbers of failed adoptions made her especially wary of a researcher "spooking" the potential suppliers.

As my failed funding application revealed, I began my fieldwork under the impression that I could offer a balanced, tripartite account of the experiences of adoption professionals, prospective adoptive parents, and expectant mothers. After running into a number of methodological obstacles, I quickly realized that my position within the adoption agency—in addition to a number of structural features of the adoption process itself—skewed my ethnographic account toward the experiences and narratives of social workers. However, what this unexpected stumbling block to my proposed research plan allowed me to *see* were the myriad ways the adoption process rendered the expectant mother invisible, while producing a figure of the "birth mother" that is inherently unknowable and contradictory. At First Steps, "birth mothers" often went missing, in more ways than one, and these absences were central to the production of contingent kinship and the assumptions that structured it.

During my time in the field, I can recall countless instances of missed connections between expectant mothers and social workers. I would arrive with Stella or another social worker for a scheduled meeting, only to find that the expectant mother was nowhere to be found. Casper and Moore (2009: 14) ask: "How do we as scholars come to understand the missing if their lives and indeed their very corporeal essence are systematically ignored, erased, unseen, or missing in action? How do we 'measure' the absent subject? And how do we 'operationalize' invisibility?" I contend that one way of measuring the absence, the invisibility, the vanishing of the "birth mother," is by attending to the failed attempts of those perpetually in search of her, and the ghostly manifestations of her that haunt the imagination of those who look at, for, and through her.

HYPERVISIBLE BODIES, ILLEGITIMATE SUBJECTS

Expectant mother invisibility must be located within the context of the simultaneous hypervisibility of poor black mothering in the United States.[5] To speak of "poor black mothering" within this context is to invoke a tangled and intersectional history of race, class, and gender. Many histories of American adoption describe trends in terms of markets and demographics, attending only to the experiences of those who gain children, thereby effacing the stories of those who lose them, in particular, poor women of color (Briggs 2012; Roberts 2002). But the invisibility of expectant and birth mothers is tied intimately to a particular kind of hypervisibility, both of black motherhood and the black pregnant body. Raced and classed notions of il/legitimate mothering have fluctuated throughout American adoption's fraught history.

In the early days of formal adoption, which was first legally codified by the Massachusetts Adoption Act of 1851, birth mothers were primarily white and poor (Herman 2008).[6] During the Progressive Era, adoption was deeply intertwined with notions of the "deserving" versus "undeserving" poor. Following World War II, adoption practice developed and remained a solution for poor families who did not have the resources to raise a child. In the postwar decades, a new group of women were surrendering their infants: young, unmarried, middle-class women faced with the shame of illegitimacy (Fessler 2006). These women were predominantly white, as black infants were not considered "adoptable" until the mid-1960s during the Civil Rights Movement.[7] During the 1950s and 1960s, foster care greatly expanded and many "illegitimate" black children were removed from "unsuitable homes"; black single motherhood and illegitimacy were identified as the pathological roots of poverty in the infamous Moynihan Report (1965), formally titled *The Negro Family: The Case for National Action,* and endorsed by a number of prominent civil rights activists (Briggs 2012). From the 1970s onward, adoption trends have shifted with the increasing social acceptance of single motherhood and transracial—and more recently "special needs"—adoption. According to historian and gender studies scholar Laura Briggs (2012: 7), the most important precursor to the declining adoption rate in the 1970s was the "ability and willingness of single mothers to raise their children." But only a certain subset of single mothers.

The post-Recession pregnancies ending with relinquishment at First Steps were not so much unwanted (or the product of an unwillingness) as they were economically untenable. With improved sex education and the wider availability of birth control for middle- and upper-class women, there has been a shift back to a pattern of poverty as the primary precursor to relinquishment. By the 1980s, relinquishment among the middle class had sharply declined, and adoption again became an issue that primarily affected poor women. As Solinger (2001: 113) notes, "Politicians and others in this era [the '80s] routinely urged adoption of illegitimate children as the stone to kill several nasty birds at once: unwed motherhood, poverty, childlessness, and the dearth of adoptable white infants." Ronald Reagan explicitly touted adoption as a solution to America's "abortion problem."[8] His economic and "pro-family" policies during the 1980s were disastrous for poor women and their children, and reflected the nation's lack of relative economic mobility (Maril 2013; Solinger 2001; Zimmerman 1989).

The 1980s and 1990s solidified the social and public construction of the welfare queen—a highly raced and gendered figure defined in terms of her perceived hyper-fertility and laziness (Hancock 2004). Expectant mothers considering adoption were already defined by the former of these two qualities; by definition, they had more children than they could care for. Patricia Hill Collins (1991: 69) traces a genealogy from the mammy to the matriarch to the welfare mother, as controlling images of black womanhood, "part of a generalized ideology of domination." A conversation I had with one of First Steps' social workers over dinner following the closure of the agency highlights the connection between notions of the welfare queen and the socioeconomic logics of adoption. Of the several social workers I encountered at First Steps, Barbara had been there the longest. She recounted some of her journey to me in June of 2016. She had worked at a homeless shelter on Chicago's North Side in the 1980s, before earning her graduate degree in social work. She recalled, "I mean, we had so many birth moms that were basically—or, I should just say, single moms with several kids that were just having more kids because that meant their check was going up, and there was no push for them to have to work and do a job outside of raising their kids, so there was a big incentive, you know." Here, Barbara points to the problematic notion of reproduction as an economic tactic, a standard element of welfare queen rhetoric. She continued, "And if you have more kids, you get a bigger apartment in CHA [Chicago Housing Authority]. What a different mentality." She was telling me this story as a way to explain a perceived decrease in domestic adoptions. "So working with women at that end to now, I mean, I think black girls in poorer neighborhoods now realize that there's other alternatives besides having babies. You know, they can get an education and get a decent job, and—so I believe that's part of it," she finished. While it was uncommon for social workers at First Steps to speak about expectant mothers in ways that aligned so explicitly with welfare queen rhetoric, this was an important part of the history that informed adoption ideology and practice during my fieldwork. As Collins (1991: 69) notes, these "controlling images" are "remarkably tenacious."

Perceived similarities between low-income expectant / birth mothers and welfare queens placed women considering or engaging in relinquishment squarely within the category of the undeserving poor. During the 1980s, the social stigma of illegitimacy was relaxed (much to the chagrin of those in favor of "pro-family" policies), but only toward women perceived as being able to afford children. During this time, poverty was highly feminized and racialized (Gilens 2003). Solinger—who has described motherhood in the United States as a class privilege—explains (2001: 130) that there is "a two-tiered public perception of single mothers that has remained vibrant through the end of the century: middle-class, never-married mothers are legitimate mothers (of their own and other people's children), but poor never-married mothers are not." Poor mothers were affected by notions of illegitimacy on two fronts; not only were their children deemed illegitimate, but so too were their very identities as mothering subjects. When expectant mothers were identified and labeled as "birth mothers" through their participation in the adoption process, they became fixed as illegitimate and "unfit" mothering subjects. There was no way for a pregnant woman to occupy a role within the framework of adoption that did not fit into the stereotypes of the unfit mother: either she relinquished her child because she was unfit and self-aware, or she fell through, either by scamming the agency to keep the child—dishonesty evincing her unfitness—or keeping the child out of weakness and a "change of heart." In approaching the agency, only certain ends were possible. The pregnant body became the site at which these complex histories and projections intersected.

See(k)ing "birth mothers" at First Steps and within the context of adoption more broadly required visual examination of the pregnant body. In the case of First Steps, the woman in possession of this body—in addition to being pregnant—was also likely African American and poor. If, as according to Yancy (2008: 49), seeing the black body—"the phantasmic object of the white imaginary"—is an act of constructing the black body, then the figure of the "birth mother" was constructed through social workers' attempts to surveil expectant mothers. As Simone Browne (2015: 9) has argued, "blackness is a key site through which surveillance is practiced, narrated, and enacted." Cross-racial surveillance of blackness is informed by long and complex histories of marking the black body as Other (Fanon 2008; Spillers 1987; Yancy 2008: 3). In describing "the new surveillance," Gary T. Marx identifies "categorical suspicion" as a process by which "the presumption of guilt is assigned to some based on their membership within a particular category or grouping" (quoted in Browne 2015: 15). Therefore, suspicion and surveillance are intimately connected. Informed by a long history of racial attitudes and dominant beliefs about poor black women and reproduction in America, the figure of the "birth mother" becomes a suspect specter.

The racialized body of the expectant mother is further marked by her poverty and the embodied reality of pregnancy. John Gilliom (2001: xii–xiii) describes how the welfare state surveils poor women: "In their pursuit of food, health care, and shelter for their families, they are watched, analyzed, assessed, monitored, checked, and reevaluated in an ongoing process involving supercomputers, caseworkers, fraud control agents, grocers, and neighbors. They *know* surveillance." Expectant mothers at First Steps became subjects of a racialized and classed gaze by virtue of their subject positions as black and poor, and pregnancy added yet another layer of social and medical surveillance:

> Traditionally, the pregnant female body has been the object of medical scrutiny and surveillance, as well as a mystical (if unrepresentable) reverence and awe in Western culture. The pregnant body—even clothed—is a source of abjection and disgust in popular culture: the woman is represented as awkward, uncomfortable, and grotesquely excessive. In a culture that places such a premium on thinness, the pregnant body is anathema. Not only is it perhaps the most visible and physical mark of sexual difference, it is also the sign for deeply embedded fears and anxieties about femininity and the female reproductive system. With the advent of visual technologies, the contents of the uterus have become demystified and entirely representable, but the pregnant body itself remains concealed. (Stabile 1998: 183)

In the case of poor African American expectant mothers considering adoption, the "pregnant body's ability to shock and horrify the spectator" (183) also conjures notions of poor African American women as inherently hypersexual and oversexed: "pregnancy literally signifies the consequences of unprotected, heterosexual sex," Stabile adds (185).

The nature of the raced and classed pregnant body as a site of surveillance is additionally informed by the power dynamics produced in the act of seeing. Casper and Moore (2009: 9) contend, "Because society is stratified along lines of gender, race, class, sexuality, age, disability status, citizenship, geography, and other cleavages, some bodies are public and visually dissected while others are vulnerable to erasure and marginalization." Through adoption, expectant mothers were both "visually dissected" by technologies such as the ultrasound, *and* "vulnerable to erasure and marginalization" by virtue of their simultaneously central and liminal status within the adoption exchange, which was only made possible by their resourcelessness. Expectant mothers at First Steps embodied intersecting subjectivities, which have traditionally foreclosed the possibility of being "entitled to look" (Brighenti 2010: 2).[9] The adoption process is therefore—for expectant mothers—an elaborate structure of invisibility, which, in its attempts to render visible certain types of bodies, actually contributes to their erasure. Surveillance strategies are often anticipatory, aiming to "reduce risk and uncertainty" (Marx 1989: 218). Throughout the adoption process, social workers attempted to surveil expectant mothers' bodies—inside and out—in order to arrive at a desired outcome: placement. They were met with mixed success, and more absences than presences. Let us now consider a series of these absences: a missing mother, a "fake" fetus, an invisible ethnographer, and a putative father.

MISSING MOTHER

Stella and I drove to Englewood on a July afternoon for a second meeting with an expectant mother named Sheena. These meetings were generally conducted in the home, and on our first visit Stella had given Sheena some preliminary paperwork to fill out and a few prospective adoptive family profiles to peruse, and Sheena had selected a single mother, Janice. Stella and I arrived with a money order for Sheena's rent, and plans to conduct a conference call with Janice, but we could not connect. Sheena had been borrowing a friend's cell phone because she did not have her own, so all communication between her and Stella was routed through a third party. When we arrived at Sheena's house, the friend texted Stella to tell her that Sheena had "walked her baby to school." Stella was somewhat perplexed because she had arranged a predetermined time to meet, but she was not surprised by the missed connection; they happened all the time. They were inconvenient, but expected.

Still hoping to catch Sheena, Stella and I went through the front gate, and into a stuffy vestibule and buzzed to see if she had returned. Stella pressed the button and soon we heard the clang of keys as someone walked down the stairs, but the noise receded as they disappeared through a door on the other side and never came to the vestibule. Before giving up, I tried the front door and to our surprise, it swung open. We climbed two flights of stairs in a concrete stairwell, the temperature increasing with our ascent. At the top of the stairs were two doors, one that led into Sheena's top-floor apartment. We knocked, but no one came to the door. We returned to the car to escape the concentrated heat, and waited for about fifteen minutes before driving slowly along the road to a convenience store Sheena frequented, hoping to find her walking along the way. She was not there. About the time we made our way back to the expressway leading back to the agency, some distance from Sheena's house, her friend called saying she had returned. But it was too late; we had missed her. Stella told her we would need to reschedule, and sped us back to the agency. A week later, we successfully met up with Sheena, and completed the conference call with the prospective adoptive mother. However, that was the last time that either Stella or I saw Sheena. She became unreachable, and each time I asked Stella if she had heard anything, her response was, "She's disappeared" or "She's gone." One day, she even said, "Sheena's dead," and I stopped asking.

·   ·   ·

end, n. (a) Termination of existence; destruction, abolition. (b) The death (of a person); a mode or manner of death.[10]

·   ·   ·

Sheena had not actually died, at least as far as Stella knew, but her language points to a form of social death that other scholars have observed in the case of adoption.[11] Stella's use of the death analogy signaled her official surrender. Like a doctor in the emergency room, Stella had "called" the time of death, and Sheena became the ghost of a fall-through. The fall-through foreclosed future interactions between Stella and Sheena, and severed Sheena's tie to the agency. From Stella's perspective, there was nothing more to be done. It was frustrating. As a broker, Stella had failed to bridge her two clients. Suddenly I understood with more gravity why Barbara—in a spectacular display of biologically determinist kinship ideology—often compared fall-throughs to miscarriages for the prospective adoptive family. From Stella's perspective, and that of the prospective adoptive parents, the child-to-be was simply gone. The descriptor "gone" is often used euphemistically to indicate that a person has died. This is also reflected in Stella's interchanging of the terms when discussing Sheena. Stella would often refer to "slow" periods in which there was a dearth of expectant mothers as "dead times." "What is Christmas like around here," I asked her one day as I made travel arrangements for the upcoming winter break. "Kind of dead," she said. "People don't start things; it's kind of a dead time," she added. Furthering this connection between absence and death, Gordon (2008: 17) contends, "to write stories concerning exclusions and invisibilities is to write ghost stories." Indeed, the primary indicator of a fall-through was Stella getting "ghosted" by the expectant mother.[12] The logics of surveillance and visibility run deeper than simple absence and presence, however, and are also rooted in the physicality and visuality of the pregnant body. Social workers' surveillance tactics included the biometric (Browne 2015).

I can recall vividly two instances in which expectant mothers, at the end of a meeting with Stella, uncovered their bellies, as if to reassure her of the presence of a fetus. In one instance, Fiona—a warm and cheerful black woman in her thirties, who repeatedly referred to Stella as "my best friend"— lifted up her shirt multiple times, explicitly exposing her bare and swollen stomach, to "show" the baby to Stella. In the second example, the exposure was subtler. At the end of the visit I described in the Prologue, Stella gave Dawn a hug—which the pregnant woman heartily returned with a smile— and asked if she needed anything. In response, Dawn unzipped her puffy coat, exposing a visibly pregnant belly covered by a thin yellow camisole, as if to remind Stella of the terms of the exchange, and asked for help with laundry, which Stella promised to address in a couple of days. "I don't have any clean brassieres," Dawn said quietly, gently cupping her own breast. Stella gave Dawn forty dollars in cash out of her wallet and we left. Belly and breast, as organs of reproduction, functioned as sites of embodied evidence, both of pregnancy and need. Both of these women insisted on being visible within adoption's structures of erasure.

A conversation Stella and I had about Sheena earlier in the summer exemplifies the primacy of visible physicality in the search for expectant mothers. Stella was worried about the status of the pregnancy because Sheena's appearance was ambiguous—it was difficult to tell by looking at her that she was pregnant. There were limits to Stella's willingness to give expectant mothers the benefit of the doubt.[13] An ultrasound, reasoned Stella, would serve as a useful form of confirmation. As part of an assemblage of authoritative and lay knowledge practices legitimating a woman's status as "birth mother," the ultrasound played an important role in transforming her kinship tie to her child. Her legitimacy as "birth mother" often derived from the visual representation of the unborn child in her womb—one of few accepted forms of what social workers called "proof of pregnancy."

The most reliable form of "proof" for social workers was a form signed and dated by a medical professional attesting to a particular woman's pregnancy status. However, as Stella told me, "It varied mom to mom what we actually had in hand . . . each scenario has its own twists and turns to be maneuvered to protect everyone, and cooperation cannot always be mandated or ensured." Here she gestures toward the simple fact that, unlike with prospective adopters—who were abundant and beholden to a particular desired outcome (becoming parents)—it was difficult to incentivize compliance with exact preferred agency protocol among expectant mothers, who were scarce and prone to attrition. The expectant mothers approaching First Steps for services often did not have regular access to standard prenatal care. Furthermore, the agency was located far from where most potential birth mothers resided, which meant that face-to-face meetings were irregularly scheduled, and it was often difficult for social workers to procure these documents; sometimes they would wait weeks or months for "proof." As Stella offered, "So much depended on timing of birth mother call, what type of setting she accessed healthcare: comm[unity] clinic, hosp[ital] clinic, ER, and then her own willingness to follow up." Due to this irregular access to resources, in many cases the only form of "proof" was an ultrasound.

When social workers could not obtain other forms of proof, such as a signed clinic document, they viewed the sonogram as evidence of fetal presence. The image itself proved the expectant mother's status as such.[14] As feminist scholars have argued extensively, although an ultrasound is technically a picture of the mother, the target of the gaze is the fetus, and the aim of the ultrasound is literally to see *through* the expectant mother.[15] She is no longer the subject of the image, but merely its backdrop or frame, displaced by the fetus (Berlant 1997: 123). If, as Donna Haraway (1997: 177) has argued, "the sonogram is literally a pedagogy for learning to see who exists in the world," then by rendering the mother transparent and visually privileging the fetus she carried, the ultrasound simultaneously functioned to erase her from existence. When an ultrasound served as "proof of pregnancy" for social workers, seeing the contents of a woman's uterus—and therefore rendering the woman transparent—became an essential part of verifying her legitimacy as a birth mother, despite the fact that she had not yet given birth. An empty womb did not a birth mother make. The ultrasound served no other function at this stage.[16]

When I asked about "proof of pregnancy" in regards to Sheena, Stella said that she had not received an ultrasound yet, "but she's been talking about the doctor. Throughout our experiences, telling me, the clinic. All of this has been consistent. I don't think she's lying, but I don't have that documentation yet." From Sheena's forthrightness about medical information and the consistency of her accounts, Stella reasoned that she was not "scamming." But she reported that she would like to get the ultrasound "ASAP." I nodded. She went on, "But you know, so many people have passed me the document and then changed their mind. It's—the family deserves that ['proof'], and I will tell them I don't have it at this point in time. It wasn't that she didn't—" she continued, "at first when I saw her, but I saw the belly. So I kind of assessed that she did look pregnant at the end, by the end of the interview, but at the point I first saw her in that dress, I expected her to be bulging out." I remember watching Sheena walk toward us on that oppressively hot day. Her dark brown skin glowed with a thin slick of sweat, and her belly swelled almost imperceptibly under her floral-print maxi dress. Sheena's refrigerator was broken, and Stella was worried that she was not getting enough to eat: "Yeah. So, that's another thing, maybe, why she's not showing. I don't know. I think she's eaten well. She understands nutrition, but I don't know if she's eaten a lot." Knowing is inherently linked to "showing"—a colloquial term for being visibly pregnant. Unable to render Sheena transparent in order to visually access her interior, Stella assessed the exterior of Sheena's body to determine the possible outcome of the adoption plan. Obtaining visual access to the fetus within, however, produced a new set of invisibilities.

FAKING BABY

Stella and Holly had attended a Saturday brunch with a new expectant mother, Denise, and the prospective adoptive parents that Denise had chosen to adopt her baby. On Monday, Stella appeared in the office holding an ultrasound image she had just received from Denise. "I think I've got a problem," she said, frowning. She handed the image to Holly, another social worker, asking, "Is that too old for that? It looked like a foot," questioning the timeline of Denise's pregnancy, based on the date printed on the image and the visible development of the fetus. Jenny, the agency's business manager, leaned over and, referring to the date on the ultrasound, said, "Yeah, that would be like eight months ago." As quickly as she had appeared, Stella rushed out. "I've gotta go stop that money," she said curtly over her shoulder, referring to the hundreds of dollars she had just wired to Denise's landlord for her monthly rent, part of Denise's "legally allowable birth parent expenses" furnished by the prospective adoptive parents.

After Stella left, Holly asserted, "But she was visibly pregnant at the thing on Saturday." As she spoke, she swept both hands in an arc in front of her midsection, miming an ample third-trimester belly. Jenny replied, rather skeptically, "But if you're already overweight, couldn't you just stick something [like a pillow or padding, for example] in there?" This exchange between Jenny and Holly illustrates the futility of exterior scrutiny—the proof needed to come from interior access. Otherwise, who could tell a fetus from a pillow? It was not enough to be "guessing at the inside" (Foucault [1963] 2003: 167). Stella returned about thirty minutes later. "Can't stop payment," she said breathlessly. "The only option we have now is the police I guess. It's no good, guys." Stella trudged down the hall to her office, and I asked Jenny when the last scam had occurred. Despite the fact that the term "scam" was commonly used by agency staff to describe similar phenomena, Jenny replied, " 'Scam' is a harsh word . . . you can't tell." And that was precisely the problem. This instance illustrated a catastrophic failure of the visual technology that social workers often relied upon to determine the legitimacy of a pregnancy, wherein legitimacy referred not only to the viability of the fetus, but also to its future adoptability.

While the agency office boasted two large bulletin boards overflowing with glossy color photos and holiday cards featuring beaming adoptive families, expectant mothers and birth mothers were primarily represented by ultrasound images, which were usually tucked away into files and desk drawers, never put on display. The ultrasound is a tool of seeing and knowing—a simultaneously literal and figurative speculum (Haraway 1997)—and plays a significant role in the production of authoritative knowledge for both doctors and pregnant women (Georges 1996). The notion that an ultrasound provides "proof" of anything, however, is specious. As Barbara Duden (1993a: 9) remarks on the peculiar temporality and contingency of the unborn:

> And yet, among the invisible, the unborn, which is invisible in the body of a woman, is an important historical subject. Two things distinguish it from others of its kind. It is never there with certainty. In spite of many signs and intimations of its presence, one can never be sure about it. Unlike the dead, one's guardian angel, or God, it cannot be grasped by faith; it remains a hope. And second, before a child comes to light it is a *nondum,* a "not-yet." It has a peculiar temporal dimension. It is the only one of the invisible beings that knocks at the door of existence and emerges an infant.

At First Steps, an ultrasound was an imperfect attempt to inject some certainty into the pregnant womb. It was believed that to see a fetus was to know that it was there, yet contingency remained, inevitably.[17]

At brunch that day, Denise had given Stella an ultrasound image from an earlier pregnancy, an image of a child recently born but unavailable for adoption—a child no longer residing within Denise's body. The image of her interior was temporally distorted. Although the ultrasound did document or "prove" a true pregnancy at an earlier point in time, by the time Stella encountered the image, its time frame rendered it a fake. The failure of the ultrasound was inherent to its structure and design as a technology of seeing through: by rendering Denise transparent, it also rendered her anonymous, unrecognizable, and therefore potentially interchangeable with any other sonogrammic mother—including her earlier self—at any other point in time. In Denise's case, the ultrasound actually became a tool of camouflage, disguising the temporal and corporeal truth of a birth that had already taken place.[18]

"Yeah, she looked very pregnant, and she waddled like she was pregnant, and who would wanna go meet two new people if you weren't pregnant?" Stella asked, puzzled and distraught. Her next statement—"She looked pregnant today; she wasn't hiding herself at all"—exemplified the primacy of visual scrutiny in the social work of adoption. One of the other women quickly chimed in, "Did you see that thing online, where you can make your own ultrasound?" Indeed, a quick internet search revealed the company FakeABaby.com, "Home of the $9.95 Fake Ultrasound." Ostensibly created to fill a need for gag gifts, the company celebrates "so many ways to fake a baby."[19] Although this particular technology was not used by Denise, it represented a major source of anxiety for social workers and a perceived threat to the integrity of the adoption process. FakeABaby transforms what was once imagined as a reliable mode of biomedical (in)sight into a fraudulent "gag." "Proof-of-pregnancy" does not prove anything anymore.

Stella shook her head, calling it quits and drawing attention to the performative aspect of Denise's tactics: "This, I just think it's over. She plays the part very well, I give it to her. I just feel terrible having to call the [prospective adoptive] family." Stella looked up at the ceiling as she recounted her interactions with Denise, backtracking to figure out where her detective strategies had failed. She reported that when Denise had given her the ultrasound, she had said, "See my name?" as if to offer visual proof of the authenticity of the document. Holly looked at the image again, and exclaimed, "You can see toes on there! That's a full baby foot. Oh, she had this baby a long time ago. Like that could be like, 'I'm due tomorrow' foot." Increasingly, the baby foot grew to have more and more in common with Big Foot. Blurry. Shadowy. Grayscale. Never there with certainty. The fantastical product of an overactive imagination. This instance illustrates the imperfection of social workers' systems of expectant mother inspection and surveillance—indeed an example of a mother co-opting a traditional form of surveillance for her own ends, which did not match up with the ends of the agency. Denise—and the wired money, and the baby—disappeared, despite Stella's attempts to surveil her.

Ultrasound technology seems a particularly appropriate mode of surveillance for adoption: it evolved from sonar, originally developed to first detect icebergs after the sinking of the *Titanic*, then the wartime threat of German U-boats during WWI (Casper 1998: 83; Stabile 1998: 192; Petchesky 1997: 139). Carole Stabile (1998: 192) has referred to this auspicious beginning as "the military origins of the sonogram." Through and through, as a quintessential technology of predictive knowledge, the ultrasound exists to detect future threat. It is at once a vital and useless tool of intimate speculation. Unfortunately, for all its power as a medically authorized instrument of visualization, the ultrasound is far from a foolproof mode of ensuring pregnancy and placement within the context of adoption.

Subversive acts to resist social scrutiny—such as Sheena's ghosting of Stella, and Denise's use of an asynchronous ultrasound—have been referred to by Gilliom (2001: 6–7) as "antisurveillance politics," acts which "create small and necessary spaces of personal control and autonomy" within larger state structures of surveillance. In the case of racialized surveillance, Browne (2015: 24) refers to these acts of resistance as "dark sousveillance," "a way to frame how the contemporary surveillance of the racial body might be contended with." The ultrasound has been taken apart extensively by feminist scholars to uncover its characteristics as a tool of (male) authoritative knowledge, which, through its rendering of a visible fetus, contributes to the invisibilization of the mother.[20] But it has yet to be examined as a tool that women might employ to take advantage of and / or subvert larger structures of gender / race / class inequality. It has unexpected potential as a "weapon of the weak" (Scott 1985), and an important element of what Scott (1990: 183) has termed infrapolitics: "an unobtrusive realm of the political struggle . . . beyond the visible end of the spectrum." Philosopher George Yancy (2008) offers, "Perhaps in the case of invisibility, though, one has a greater opportunity of not being seen while taking advantage of this invisibility" (76). Indeed, historically, feigning pregnancy and using pregnancy to avoid work were forms of slave resistance (126). Might feigning pregnancy serve a similar purpose among potential birth mothers? It is a way to survive within a larger racial and class system that systematically renders poor black mothers invisible, powerless, and resourceless. Knight (2015) observed similar dynamics in her work with poor addicted pregnant women in San Francisco: "The multiple times I witnessed and documented women hustling systems, it was obvious that their hustling was generated from an interpretation that they were already being hustled by the systems themselves" (188). As Knight notes, in these situations, lying becomes "a responsive strategy for meeting the demands of negotiating pregnancy and addiction within constrictive institutional settings" (189).

Deterrence is often a key form of social control exercised by the state over the poor (Gilliom 2001:40). However, at First Steps, deterrence was an ineffective strategy, as social workers' primary goal was to recruit and *retain* expectant mothers, rather than discourage them; as brokers, social workers were reliant on the presence of expectant mothers to stay in business. Retaining them required finding them, seeing them, knowing them, and removing as many barriers to the process as possible. This was one of the reasons that although a very high value was placed on prenatal care, social workers rarely required full compliance with the recommended regimen of doctor's visits and supplements as, ironically, it often functioned to deter an expectant mother from working with the agency, and social workers were cognizant of the material obstacles to participating in that clinical system (time, access, transportation, childcare, etc.).

This is one way in which the class- and race-based power dynamics one might expect to observe in these interactions between middle-class white social workers and poor African American women are troubled in the case of adoption—a case in which a very specific future-oriented form of power (i.e., control over the outcome of the adoption plan) resides with whomever has custody of the child. As brokers, social workers were beholden to two sets of clients—this defined their position in the triad. However, resourcelessness and structural violence eliminated poor women's ability to exercise choice in these matters in the same way that middle-class women exercise choice as an individual, rational, market-based concept (Solinger 2001). Denise's past ultrasound had stood in for an authentic current one just long enough for Stella to deliver a much-needed resource. Stella's frustration stemmed from her momentary misreading of the image. At First Steps, the ultrasound was a key strategy not only for visualizing an expectant mother, but for moving her closer to the category of "birth mother." In Denise's case, when mobilized as a tactic (De Certeau 1984), the co-optation of this visualization created a sort of mirage—an optical illusion caused by structural conditions—that actually provided precious resources needed to keep her kinship tie with the child in question *intact*. As pure-mother-sans-baby, Denise was the polar opposite of the rare yet much-desired "born" or "sky" baby—a term social workers used to describe babies for whom adoption plans were only made at the hospital, on the cusp of birth or shortly thereafter, thus eliminating the speculative position of the expectant mother—so named, according to Dotty, because they appear to simply "fall out of the sky." In 1986, I had been one such sky baby, appearing as if by magic in an emergency room, devoid of the messiness of a physically attached mother who had not already made her decision. Shortly after my birth, I left the hospital via a closed adoption, never to see my own birth mother again.

INVISIBLE ETHNOGRAPHER

Throughout my time at First Steps, I was conscripted into the adoption process in various ways, perhaps the most instructive of which involved my own refusal to be made visible in the service of attracting more potential birth mothers to the agency. In the spring of 2014, the First Steps website was undergoing its first major redesign in almost a decade. It was a major effort by Jenny and the board of directors to increase the agency's own visibility and transform the way its mission and services were being portrayed to an increasingly web-going clientele of prospective adoptive parents *and* expectant mothers. One of Jenny's major updates was the addition of video content to the website. Stella excitedly volunteered me to be the subject of a brief video for expectant mothers that would explain the adoption process. Jenny sent an email to agency staff with a list of proposed videos, and next to "Birth Mom 'Counselor,'" my name appeared in parentheses. The use of "birth mom" in this instance yet again illustrates the temporal slippage inherent to how agency staff imagined expectant mothers.

I immediately felt uncomfortable. Although I held a newly minted graduate degree in social work, I was *not* a birth mother counselor (as Jenny's own scare quotes seemed to indicate). But I *was* a woman of color, just shy of my twenty-eighth birthday, and it was clear that Stella believed that I would *look* approachable—"You're so pretty," she said—and that expectant mothers might see in me a bit of themselves reflected back, or perhaps even better, a bit of their future child. Although the agency's board of directors included people of color, the social workers were all white, and I was often closest in age to the expectant mothers First Steps sought. Straddling subjectivities that at certain times were instrumental, at other times contradictory, I inhabited a deeply liminal position—*in* the agency perhaps, but not *of* the agency. The specific layering of several aspects of my identity—age, race, gender, adoptee status, education / training—positioned me particularly well to be something of a poster child for the agency's efforts.[21] *Look! A(n) (ostensibly) well-educated, articulate, accomplished, attractive, approachable, well-adjusted, young, upwardly mobile, light-skinned, black, female adoptee. Adoption is surely the route to a better future for your child.*[22] I was fairly certain I had been complicit in similar recruitment strategies before. I could sense an assumption that my presence in the video might somehow make more expectant mothers appear—a phenomenon that might have actually increased my ethnographic access to them.

The request for my participation in the video series called forth a memory of sitting with an expectant mother during a home visit with Stella in the summer of 2009. When Stella introduced—"outed" may be a better term— me as an adoptee (something she did from time to time, according to no pattern I could readily identify), I could perceive a sort of transference happening in which the mother identified me with her future child. She began to ask me what it was like to be adopted, as though she was trying to figure out if she was making the right decision for her future child. For her, I was no longer an ethnographer or social work intern, I was a possible future embodiment of the child she carried in her womb. I myself became the very phenomenon I sought to study: a technology of forecasting, divining, of attempting to see an unknown future in the flesh. Throughout my fieldwork, I detected a trend of presenting older adoptees as a way to visualize and interact with future possibilities. It was very common in adoption trainings and at adoption conferences to assemble panels of adopted adults to share "the adoptee experience." At the end of one training for prospective adoptive parents, the trainer's transracially adopted adult son appeared to answer questions "from the adoptee's point of view." All in the service of preparing the uninitiated for some of the parenting challenges they were sure to confront in the future. Similarly, on the back of Stella's business cards—which she gave to each expectant mother—were photographs of her two teen sons, also black and adopted. Promising imagery of a possible future. Like these adopted sons, my very presence and subjectivity perhaps represented a possible future accessible to this mother through adoption. It was a wildly strange position to occupy.[23] Overlapping identities, adoptive and biological kinship ties, were being mobilized to produce particular outcomes, to alter particular futures.

At the time of Jenny's recruitment of me for the video, I was in the midst of leaving the agency because the doctoral phase of my anthropology fieldwork had come to an end, thus it was unlikely that any mothers "recruited" by my video would ever actually interact with me. Even if they did, it would not be in a counseling capacity. It felt like false advertising—to return to Dotty's eel metaphor, a kind of bait-and-switch—however well-intentioned. When I declined to be featured in the video, Jenny's email reply to my polite refusal was "What?!?!? Ok." For her—an adoptive mother—this was an unimaginable scenario. In this way, my own absence was linked individually and structurally to the perceived absences of expectant mothers.

PUTATIVE FATHER

The mechanisms of adoption that are set up both to protect an expectant mother's autonomy and to entice her to follow through with a placement decision create a space in which she is perceived by social workers and prospective adoptive parents alike as the bearer of immense power—a kind of "relative leverage" (Kim 2016: 6)—over her own in / visibility by virtue of the immeasurably valuable child she carries in her womb, one she retains custody of, and thus power over, until the moment that pen meets paper in the signing of her voluntary and irrevocable surrenders. The fact that her invisibility results in the imagining of her as a spectral and ultimately unknowable—and thus unpredictable—figure only adds to this attribution of power. This chapter has provided an elaborate genealogy for the question, "Where are the (birth) mothers?" But that question begs another: "Where are the (birth) fathers?"

In November of 2013, Stella told me about a new expectant mother with whom she had recently connected: "'Dad's nowhere to be seen,' she says. Mm, okay. Go see." "So what are you going to do about Dad's surrenders?" I asked. Stella replied, "She'll—there won't be any. And it'll be a legal risk, with her stating 'don't know.'" I nodded. "I think she thought there could possibly be two [fathers]," Stella continued. "And she hasn't seen either one of them since conception. One was living with her, he moved out abruptly. And wants nothing to do with fatherhood, which is believable." "Okay," I replied. "And common," she finished, "Lara has the same story."

The widespread feminization of parenting and care work is reflected in the general absence of fathers, both in this ethnography and in the field site on which it is based. The realities of embodiment further contribute to this absence: the child-to-be resides in its mother's womb; therefore she is the primary target for social workers' energies (and interventions) during the adoption process. The expectant mother, not the father, is inhabited by the precious resource desired by prospective adoptive parents. It seems strange to call the biological-father-of-a-child-that-has-not-yet-been-born-but-is-part-of-an-adoption-plan a "birth father," but social workers at First Steps did it often. As in the case of the "birth mother," the terminology seems premature, since the child has yet to be birthed, but it is stranger still because a father does not birth a child anyway.[24] It seems perhaps equally strange to refer to him as an expectant father, since in certain cases, he may not even be aware of the pregnancy, therefore, how can he be expecting? He is notably absent from the adoption process, conceptualized primarily by social workers as an embodiment of "legal risk." He often exists for adoption professionals and prospective adoptive parents as a negative future possibility. When a social worker refers to the father-to-be as legal risk, she refers to the difficulty in obtaining final and irrevocable surrenders from him, and the possibility that he could assert a claim for kinship in the future, resulting in either a fall-through or a disruption (the term for an adoption that fails *after* it is finalized).

When first meeting with a social worker from First Steps, an expectant mother had three options with respect to providing information about the father: (1) identify him by name; (2) decline identification; or (3) report that she does not know the identity of the father. If the father was identified by name, Stella would attempt to locate him in order to obtain surrenders. Illinois law allows the identified father to sign surrenders before the birth of the child, unlike the mother, who must wait until at least 72 hours have passed after the birth. If the expectant mother declined identification or was unable to identify the father, information about the pregnancy had to be entered into the Illinois Putative Father Registry, which is administered by the Illinois Department of Children and Family Services. The registry is structured by uncertainty: "A Putative Father is defined as a man who *may* be the child's biological father, but who is not married to the child's mother on or before the date of the child's birth and has not established his paternity through legal proceedings" (emphasis added).[25] The registry website continues:

Protect Your Rights as a Father

In Illinois, a father is supposed to be notified before his child can be adopted. But a father who isn't married to the child's mother may not be easy to find, or might not be legally recognized as the child's father. The Putative Father Registry is a way for such fathers to make sure that they can protect their rights.

Putative fathers have up to 30 days following the birth of the child to register, and must "begin legal proceedings to establish paternity within 30 days of registering." For prospective adoptive parents matched with an expectant mother who had either declined or been unable to identify the father, this meant that there was a risk of a father pursuing custody of the child for up to two months after the baby was born. The Putative Father Registry allowed social workers to ensure that a child of semi-unknown parentage was "legally free" for adoption.

Kimberly, one of two adoption attorneys who handled First Steps cases, characterized biological fathers as typically absent and unknowable: "In the typical scenario, the biological father is not there. He either isn't known or he's not being disclosed or he's not knowable. So we have no idea who he is, and we certainly don't have any background information about him." She went on to describe the fear that many prospective adoptive parents have that a father will appear unexpectedly to claim his parental rights: "The kind of litigation that is much more scary to people is a birth father who claims that he was denied due process, that he was not given notice, and that as a result the adoption is not valid because he was not given the rights to which he was entitled." She went on,

> Those kinds of cases are very scary for everybody involved. However, if there is an analysis before the match is made about the status of the birth father and all the efforts that have been made to locate him, and because of something called the Putative Father Registry in Illinois, there is a way to defend against those claims. In common parlance, however, people actually believe that somebody can come back ten years later and just take the child away.

These ghosts are scary. This potential return—of either mother or father—however unrealistic, was haunting. Legally, in Illinois, the voluntary surrender of parental rights was irrevocable. Kimberly went on,

> No, that is not going to happen, but it's still a common fear. So that kind of litigation revolves around proving that that person did in fact get due notice, which is what due process is really about. It's usually about notice, or if we know in advance that he's not going to agree but everyone believes that he is an unfit person.

This fear often led prospective adopters to turn abroad for children.[26] I asked one mother who had adopted from China if she had ever considered domestic adoption, and she responded:

We did not . . . Right around that time is when some adoptions—domestic adoptions—where the birth fathers came forward and got their kids back. I don't know if you remember Baby Richard or Baby Jessica. You know, we didn't want to deal with any birth parents showing up on our doorstep and saying, "I want my kid back," you know. So that was one reason.

Biological fathers—mothers too—were often imagined simultaneously as absent and problematically present. Haunting apparitions, everlastingly connected through kinship.

In May of 2014, Barbara discussed the role of fathers in an interview with a prospective adoptive couple. She had spent the past fifteen minutes or so discussing the couple's expectations and preparation for a child. "Mainly [I] want to know what you're open to, and again," she said, "it seems like you are, but I'm just going to go through this." She moved through a long list of possibilities including heroin exposure, mental illness, correctable and chronic medical issues, incest, and rape. "Legal risks. Okay. Well. Obviously the biggest one is if the birth dad hasn't been located and hasn't signed [surrenders]." The couple nodded in understanding. "And what percentage of our fam–, our birth moms don't know who the birth dad [is]? What do you think? It's high, isn't it?" Barbara asked, looking at me. I responded that I wasn't sure, to which she replied with a folk statistic: "I would say at least fifty percent don't know the whereabouts of the birth dad, so what do you wait for? You wait that ninety [sic] days. So it's a risk. He could surface, right?" "Do we, do we get the baby for that ninety days, or does it stay . . . ," the prospective mother started. Barbara cut her off:

> Mm-hmm. Mm-hm. Yep. So it's published [in the Putative Father Registry]. It's published almost immediately after we meet the birth mom, they'll go ahead and send it through. Usually if that birth dad hasn't surfaced before the birth, he'll surface, he'll either surface at the hospital or he won't. And so if he does surface at the hospital, sometimes, you know, it's been clear that there's no way he can parent and the birth mom is successful in talking him into signing. So it's happened where he's surfaced, and, you know, most of the time it gets turned around where he realizes he can't parent. But it's there.

This repeated language of "surfacing" calls to mind Dotty's likening of expectant mothers to eels. In 2013, a similar conversation unfolded during Annette's home study, when Barbara explained, "Legal risks. So what do we mean by legal risks? Well, you're going to have legal risks unless both parents sign off, right? And what are the options, what are the odds that we're going to have a birth dad sign off?" "Did you ever do any research on that?" Barbara asked me, turning away from Annette. "It's pretty low," she said, before I could respond. "Uh, yeah," I said. "I haven't done [quantitative] research on it, just, like, anecdotal evidence. I can only think of a couple. Like, usually the birth father's not there."

In my time at the agency, I had only observed one father present at a mother's signing of surrenders. Expectant mothers routinely met with Stella alone, or with their small children in tow. Although many easily identified the fathers and obtained surrenders from them, for some expectant mothers, identifying and locating the father was much more challenging. "Yep, yep," Barbara had agreed. "So because he's not [there], that is an automatic risk, right?" In practice, initial absence was actually nowhere near an "automatic risk," but this portrayal certainly contributed to fears and anxieties about the figure of the "birth father." Annette nodded, "Right." Barbara continued,

> I can't really think of any, if the birth dad comes back into the picture after the birth, it's usually while the mom's still at the hospital. That's what we've always typically seen. If he's been out of the picture for six months, didn't know she was pregnant, shows back up, you're probably going to know about it before mom signs surrenders, because she's then going to quick think, "Wait a second here. If he's not on board with me, and I sign, then he can take this child and I think he's a rotten guy."

"Exactly," Annette followed. Barbara finished, "'And I don't want him parenting.' So then she's going to take a step back and hopefully convince him that he can't parent, right?" Barbara was laboring intently to weave bits of experience and (non)knowledge into a picture of probability in order to enable Annette to assess future risk. She continued, "Now if he doesn't ever materialize and doesn't show up at the hospital, there's the ninety-day window, right? Where he can come back during that ninety days, even though she's signed. I can't think of a situation where he's come back."

Just as the perception of "birth mothers" as unpredictable and unknowable relies upon cultural understandings and material realities of poor black women, the notion that biological fathers are immaterial, ghostly, absent, and invisible is undergirded by stereotypes of poor black men as perpetually absent "deadbeat dads" (see Cassiman 2008). The construction of expectant fathers as problematic sources of legal risk—alongside the powerlessness that social workers and prospective parents feel in reducing that risk—illustrates a final form of erasure, and also contingency, for these marginalized parents-to-be.

CONCLUSION: ABSENCE MAKES
THE HEART GROW ANXIOUS

The politics of visibility are crucial to the temporal logics of intimate specula-tion. Etymologically, the Latin *spec* of speculation (from *specere,* which means to look at or to view) is the *spec* of visuality found in terms like spectator, spectacular, inspection, spectacle, specter, specimen, speculum, perspective, and introspection (and also specious, prospective, and expectant; the *e* becomes an *i* in suspicion and conspicuous).[27] A misperception abounds that "seeing the birth mother"—whether through ultrasound, personal encoun-ter, or bodily inspection—somehow affords privileged access to knowledge of her, knowledge about her, knowledge of the child she carries, and ulti-mately predictive knowledge of what she will do next with respect to that future child. Furthermore, within the context of adoption, expectant mother invisibility and knowability are in turn intimately linked to notions of risk. When social workers' efforts to see and know an expectant mother fail, the adoption attains a high level of risk. Aside from the risk to prospective par-ents that the baby may not in fact exist, if no prenatal care records are submit-ted, or no sociomedical history filed, prospective parents may worry more about substance exposure, trauma, or genetic issues. It is impossible to pre-pare for the unknown. And although the notion is stigmatizing, there is still a lingering sense within and outside the adoption community that when you adopt, "You don't know what you're gonna get." This well-known statement privileges biological forms of kinship formation, in which more information is often known about one or both parents, as well as a range of other rela-tives.[28] There is threat in the unknown; therefore there is threat in the unseen. If a social worker cannot know that a mother is truly pregnant (i.e., she refuses to submit an ultrasound, or as in Denise's case, the ultrasound is not accurate), this immediately raises doubt as to the veracity of her preg-nancy and her intentions to place. The construction of fathers as a problem-atic source of "legal risk" further undergirds this sense of uncertainty and discomfort among both social workers and prospective adopters.

The desire for adoption knowledge, particularly knowledge of a birth fam-ily, is reflected in the recent shift toward practices of open adoption, in which an ongoing relationship is cultivated between the birth family and the adop-tive family. In this sense, knowledge is viewed as curative, and access to it considered necessary for the "healthy" development of identities and rela-tionships. However, open adoption is an imperfect answer to the seemingly ultimate unknowability of the "birth mother." As one adoption trainer (and also adoptive mother) said, as a way of advocating for open adoption, "I definitely want to know her and know where she is. If I know where she is, then I know she's not going to just appear on my doorstep out of the blue!"

One prospective adopter spoke about a similar perspective she had encountered in a training: "It's just ironic to me, some of these—and part of it was their threat, these adoptive parents were so threatened. By the fact that that birth family could override anything that they said or did or would come into their lives unexpectedly, probably is the biggest fear." In this case, knowledge of the birth mother (and by extension, the ability to locate her, to see her coming) is yet another form of mitigating the unexpected, the unpredictable, the uncertain, and reducing the anxiety they engender. It is another way of constituting the birth mother as a source of threat. Although the appearance of the expectant mother *before* the birth of the child is a welcome surprise, prospective adoptive parents' imaginings of her unexpected appearance *after* the adoption is complete are often met with anxiety stemming from the concern that haunts many adoptive parents—that she may have come back for her child. Kinship gets renegotiated, but never entirely severed.

Rather than aiding social workers in their practices of surveillance and supervision, various mechanisms of the adoption process (discursive, medical, practical) actually function to erase expectant and birth parents from view. An ultrasound renders a mother-to-be merely a ghostly shadow of herself. A strategically exposed pregnant belly mitigates this erasure by rendering her solid, material, and worthy of support. A putative father—the "putative" label rendering always suspect his kinship tie to mother and child—may either "surface" or remain an invisible source of time-limited and disembodied legal risk. In their efforts to visualize the pregnant / parenting body, social workers attempt—often unsuccessfully—to eliminate elements of the unknown and the uncertain from the adoption process, thus reducing the risk of disappearance prior to the forging of legal kinship. Despite their considerable institutional authority, social workers are often left feeling powerless in their interactions with expectant mothers whose bodies and decisions they neither control nor trust. By contrast, the next chapter turns the ethnographic gaze to home study encounters between social workers and prospective adopters, examining the role of visual inspection in the production of predictive knowledge about future parental fitness, which hinges on particular performances of honesty and innocence in the present.

TWO

———

Protective Inspections

I MET JEANINE, A PROSPECTIVE adoptive parent and social worker, at a conference in the spring of 2013. She and her husband, Mark, were in the midst of a challenging transition from fertility treatment to adoption. White, middle income, and both approaching forty, the childless couple resided in one of Chicago's nearby northern suburbs. Their attractive two-story house was at the end of a street lined with similar homes and young deciduous trees. In December of 2013, shortly after her home study was finished, Jeanine invited me to dinner. It was snowing gently as I made my way up the front walk in the fading light, and Jeanine answered the door with a brilliant smile, pushing a warm mug of tea into my hands and ushering me inside.

Joined by Mark, we sat quietly at the dining room table, each with a steaming bowl of rice and vegetable soup. Jeanine had lit a few candles around the well-appointed living space, and the home glowed with warmth, the light absorbed and refracted by cozy wood tones, neutral colors, and soft textures. This was my first time meeting Mark, and I briefly described my research and asked how he found the home study process. Leaning over his stoneware bowl, mid-bite, he said quietly, "Humiliating." He swallowed. "The whole thing's humiliating," he repeated, matter-of-factly. "Someone else gets to judge whether or not you can have a baby." I nodded in understanding, having heard this lament from other adoptive parents. Indeed, someone else gets to judge whether or not you can have this future. "No, I mean, you know you're being judged. And . . ." he paused to chew his food, before telling me:

> I mean you have an understanding that they need, that, there's a reason for it. I mean, you wanna protect, ultimately, the children, but, they have this rigid process that they go through and they gotta get certain questions answered.

And, if you've ever seen one when it's written. Well I've only seen one, I saw ours. And to some extent it was like fill-in-the-blanks. But, I don't know, to some extent, like, it's just stuff that seems seemingly irrelevant, like you have to tell, like "This is their *exact* income," and it's not that like "They meet this income threshold, so they're fine." It's like "This is their exact income, and they spent this amount of money on that."

Pausing briefly to swallow, he resumed, "And then they start emailing that stuff. They completely violate any standards of—" "Privacy," Jeanine quietly finished Mark's sentence from across the table. "Privacy in financial protection," Mark continued.

You have to disclose health issues, so they're violating HIPAA—I don't even know that they're supposed to be compliant with HIPAA, but they know that this is private medical information that you're transmitting to people. And they're just sending it over the internet. And *these* are the people that are judging *us*. So the whole thing is just humiliating, and then they charge you a bunch of money, that's way in excess of the amount of time they spent.[1]

"So," Mark continued, "all that adds up to the humiliation." Mark touched on a constellation of affective, moral, and economic challenges presented by the home study—the complex vetting mechanism that applicants must "pass" in order to be approved to adopt. A deep sense of exposure underscores his testimony. In a way, Jeanine and Mark were being called to account through the home study, which entailed forms of audit and inspection.[2] This monitoring compelled a particular performance of good or "fit" parenting, in advance of the child's arrival. Indeed, the adoptive placement was contingent upon this performance.[3]

For both social workers and prospective adoptive parents, notions of public and private, prediction and protection, and the exercise of power and resulting experience of powerlessness are all deeply imbricated in the home study. It pries open intimate aspects of (often) white middle-class subjectivity in ways to which many prospective adoptive parents are not accustomed, so that social workers can make informed decisions about the granting of future kinship.[4] Therefore, these interactions between social workers and prospective parents—often centered on the visual or specular: monitoring, supervision, assessment, evaluation—have immense implications for the eventual formation of adoptive families. They can make or break imagined futures, imagined kinship.

Before a child or legal kin tie even exists, social workers mobilize an elaborate apparatus of monitoring and knowledge-gathering, which not only assesses parental fitness, but actually shapes adoption agency applicants into fit parental subjects.[5] In order to carry out their mission of preemptive child protection, social workers strive to generate predictive knowledge about future parenting ability. This chapter uses the home study as a window onto the speculative practices of adoption social workers and prospective adopters in their quest to create adoptive kinship. Social workers employ a penetrating gaze to predict and protect the future of a child-to-be, and in this way the home study is both specular and speculative. This mobilization of intermittent surveillance—which is really more like monitoring than the constant panoptic scrutiny described by Foucault, although it does reveal and produce power asymmetries—both overlaps with and diverges from that described in the previous chapter in complex and sometimes surprising ways.[6] Whereas the expectant mother is constructed as always already suspect / guilty, the home study is a mechanism by which the prospective adoptive parents can be verified as good / innocent, even in an environment characterized to some degree by mistrust.[7] This occurs at the same time that expectant / birth parents are perceived by those who attempt to watch them to exercise agency in their refusal to be surveilled. These intertwined forms of surveillance / monitoring reveal a power dynamic that is the reversal of what one would expect given the divergently classed and raced social locations of expectant parents and prospective adoptive parents.

PROTECTIVE LABOR

In the face of humiliation, Mark did concede, "You wanna protect, ultimately, the children." Much of social workers' focus in the adoption process is preemptive. The home study, like other forms of audit, is fundamentally about the management of risk.[8] A primary goal of the home study process in particular is the prevention of disruption or failure. It is one means to a happy end.

.   .   .

end, n. A final cause; the object for which a thing exists; the purpose for which it is designed and instituted.[9]

.   .   .

As Barbara evinced when emphatically stating that her client is the child, social workers' utmost stated goal is the protection of the children they place. First Steps was, first and foremost, a "licensed child welfare agency." This focus on child protection has its roots in the historical transformation of American adoption from a mode of redistributing both poverty and labor in the early nineteenth century to a form of intimate and sentimental kinship reconfiguration in the contemporary moment—what Herman (2008: 27) has referred to as "a momentous economic and cultural watershed in the history of childhood." Adoption of children has a relatively long history in the United States, stretching back into the 1700s, when it was used in informal arrangements to secure farm and household labor. These arrangements were known as "instrumental adoption" (Melosh 2002: 12). The birth of what adoption historians refer to as "modern" adoption, however, is usually traced to World War II, with formal adoption legislation dating back to the mid-nineteenth century as a response to urban and rural poverty (Carp 2002).

In the mid-nineteenth century, the social phenomenon of "placing out"—a term that came to encompass the placement of children with families other than those into which they were born—entailed the mass movement of America's poor from the densely populated central cities to the quickly developing West, often by train, the so-called "orphan trains" famously instituted by Charles Loring Brace, who founded the New York Children's Aid Society. According to Holt (1994: 3), these programs were a response to "the need to redistribute the nation's workforce." At its inception, placing out entailed the movement of both adults and children as a response to the "plight of the urban poor" (3), but as it progressed, those affected were increasingly children.[10] As Holt notes, "Families in the northeastern Illinois towns of Aurora, Geneva, Elgin, and 'other points along the railroads,' were urged to open their hearts to children arriving from New York and Boston" (29). In the early twenty-first century, families in these same suburbs open their hearts and homes to children arriving from the South and West Sides of Chicago, in addition to poverty-stricken regions all over the globe. The difference is that in the early years of placing out, a child's value was figured in labor (Jalongo 2010). Now, these children symbolize sentimental attachment and investment in a familial future to be protected.[11]

Key to these ongoing transformations was a historical process that Viviana Zelizer (1985, 2011) has referred to as "the sacralization of the child," through which the child became a sentimental subject perceived as existing outside the realm of monetary value. The residue of this process exists today in what we might call the discourse of protection that characterizes child welfare work, particularly adoption and foster care. The sacralization of the child took place between the 1870s and 1930s, following Brace's orphan train program, and coincided with the sweeping social reform of the Progressive Era. Zelizer notes a historical and cultural trend at the start of the twentieth century in which children ceased being economically valuable to their parents (in terms of providing labor) and began being viewed as *economically* worthless, yet quite expensive, and *emotionally* priceless. Placing out gradually transformed from a strategy to provide labor into a method of building families. It was the advent of what Nelson (1984) has called "protected childhood."[12] Zelizer (1985: 29) traces the social concern with "the conservation of child life" to the founding of the U. S. Children's Bureau in 1912. In discussing an ensuing concern with accidental child death, particularly with the increased presence of streetcars and automobiles in cities, she adds, "Streets were not only physically dangerous, but socially inadequate; the proper place for a 'sacred' child was a protected environment" (52). During this period, reformers identified child abuse and child labor as social ills, and changing views on corporal punishment reflected this transformation. The emphasis on the protection of child life was thus largely bound up with the moral and affective construction of the child as innocent (Ticktin 2017).

This history of child protection, however (and unfortunately), is largely and ostensibly unraced, or in other words, white. As Robin Bernstein (2011) notes in her study of the historical intersections between innocence, race, and childhood, "The connection between childhood and innocence is not essential but is instead historically located . . . This innocence was raced white" (4). Bernstein uses the term "racial innocence" to describe "the use of childhood to make political projects appear innocuous, natural, and therefore justified" (33). She notes that until the Civil Rights Movement, black children did not call for protection in the same way that white children did. However, the transracial adoption home study is an example of how the contemporary imagined black child is included in the quest for protection, at the same time that those poised to adopt her are ascribed a measure of innocence denied to her birth mother.[13] Prospective adopters get checked up on, but social worker surveillance is far from marginalizing or absolute.

These historical developments in the valuing of children and the structuring of families coincided with the professionalization of social work. At the turn of the twentieth century, the development and maintenance of family case records—of which the adoption file is a type—was central to the development of social work as a profession (Carp 1998: 61). Brian Gill (2002: 161) identifies a "new selectivity in adoption practice" during this time, which "was consistent with the interests of agency workers, who hoped to raise their professional status by demonstrating particular expertise in the creation of adoptive families."[14] By midcentury, the focus of adoption social workers shifted from a singular goal of harm prevention, to the creation of the "best" families, which conformed to the aesthetic ideal of the time, namely white, middle class, heterosexual, and nuclear (Gill 2002). However, in the several decades since the 1950s, norms for adoptive families have expanded immensely to include transracial adoption, LGBTQ+ families, and single parents. It was within this expanded field of possibility, and under fee-for-service economic conditions in which it was in the agency's best interest to approve as many families as possible, that social workers at First Steps labored to ascertain which families and homes would provide "a protected environment" for their precious unborn clients. As kinship brokers, they did this through a combination of audit and inspection, which prompted a certain racialized performance of parental fitness.

PRODUCING PREDICTIVE KNOWLEDGE

At First Steps, several contract social workers carried out home studies, and (not unlike anthropologists) each had her own personal style of methodology, analysis, and interpretation. There were typically three meetings. Often, the first two consisted of visits by the prospective parents to the agency, where they were interviewed in-depth about numerous aspects of their lives, including early childhood, education, relationships, employment, financial situation, hobbies, pets, religious views, experience with children, as well as their expectations for the adoption (Would they be open to a child with special needs? What level of contact with the birth family did they anticipate? How many children were they hoping for, and what ages?). The third meeting consisted of a home visit by the social worker. For example, Annette's 2013 home study included a brief introductory meeting with Stella, as well as a three-hour interview at the agency and two-hour home visit, both conducted by Barbara.

Corinne, another of First Steps' contract social workers, did things a little differently, preferring to visit the home twice. As she told applicants Jack and

Brielle, "So yeah, the next two meetings will be in your home. The second meeting I'll do a tour of your house, just to make sure that everything looks safe and appropriate, and that's when we'll also check for the smoke detector." In explaining to Tim and Erin what the home visit would entail, Barbara said, "So then what that meeting consists of is really checking to see if the home meets the licensing standards, and we will go over what I'm looking for." The purpose of the home visit is to assess the "look" of the home. Does everything look safe? Does this look like a good place to raise a child? Does anything look amiss? Certain standards for compliance were objectively set by the state of Illinois, such as hot water temperature and square footage per child, but for the most part, social workers used visual observation skills to subjectively define qualities like "safe" and "appropriate." And they never arrived unannounced.

Taken together, these three meetings, along with intense review of the adoption application and required documentation, constitute an imperfect form of risk management and social control through intermittent monitoring. It is by *looking at and through* that the agency, under the authority of the state, determines who is fit to parent and who is not. A great deal of power is exercised by social workers through these monitoring practices, relying on a dynamic in which the social worker is elevated above the adoptive family by virtue of "a purposeful and contextual asymmetrisation of visibilities" (Brighenti 2010: 150). In the popular imagination, social workers are imagined as those with the power to take children away; for prospective adoptive parents, they become those with the power to give a child, to grant one the status of parent, rather than to strip that title away. In fact, for prospective adoptive parents deep into the adoption process, it is the expectant / birth mother who is perceived as the one with the power to take a child away. Never mind that until the surrenders are signed "the child isn't yours yet," as social workers constantly remind prospective adopters, in an effort to reduce their emotional investment in a match.

In 2013, Monica Jones, a self-proclaimed "adoption assessor," published *Homestudy Boot Camp: A Step-by-Step Insider's Guide to Preparing for the Event Every Adoptive Applicant Must Pass before Adopting*. The back cover of the book exclaims, "Get whipped into shape for the most intrusive and exciting experience of your life!" and one of the chapters is titled, "So, What's a Homestudy Anyway?: From the Bedroom to the Bank Account." The book's Amazon page provides the following summary:

Adoptive applicants are required to pass a homestudy before being approved to adopt. Up until now applicants have faced the homestudy process with feelings of vulnerability, intimidation and uncertainty. Not anymore! Revealing "Insider Secrets" never before disclosed—the country's top adoption professionals discuss how to reduce anxiety, boost your confidence and pass your homestudy effortlessly.[15]

The home study process has become so "invasive," to use the phrasing of one adoptive parent, it is a source of anxiety and vulnerability worthy of attention from the literary genre of self-help. This language of intrusion and invasion reveals that these experiences are out of the ordinary, rather than part of a normalized and daily structure of state surveillance as experienced by poor women of color.

There is a long list of required documentation presented to applicants upon their initial meeting with their home study worker, which includes bank statements, tax returns, background checks, fingerprints, FBI clearances (for every state in which the applicant has previously resided), medical forms (including letters from psychiatrists, psychotherapists, and other mental health professionals, if applicable), and letters of reference from both relatives and nonrelatives. The home visit involves a lengthy "checklist of compliance." Are the smoke and carbon monoxide detectors within fifteen feet of the child's room? Is the child's room at least forty square feet? Are there thirty-five square feet available for each additional desired child? Are there guns in the home? Where is the medicine stored? Have child locks been purchased for low cabinets and drawers? What about outlet covers? Are any open stairwells adequately gated off? Have the parents picked out a crib? Is the dog properly vaccinated? Is there a permanent grate over the fireplace? How do the windows open? Is the hot water heater set so that the temperature does not exceed 115°F? Is there a park nearby? How "diverse" is the neighborhood?

The home, once made the target of a social worker's "observing gaze," Lars-Eric Jonsson (2005: 169) argues, "is a far cry from the private space or place of refuge from public life that the middle-class home is often described as being." One adoption trainer offered the following rationale for the home study process to a group of prospective adopters dismayed by the impending invasion of privacy: "Somebody's looking out for our kids." The tense and temporality of this statement is instructive; the trainer speaks as if the children are already "ours," a speculative fiction. Additionally, this statement demonstrates that through the home study process, social workers are looking in, looking around, looking for, looking through, and above all, *looking out.* They look with the primary goal of ensuring the future safety and happiness of a child-to-be. At the same time, they labor to produce kinship, to make others' children "our kids."

During the home study process, social workers leave few stones unturned. They interview couples separately and together, and questions cover vast ground, from early childhood experiences to current health status. If there are already children in the home, social workers interact with and assess the children. Pets are also "interviewed." For example, when Barbara visited the home of Tim and Erin, a lengthy conversation ensued about their two cats, Louise and Jo, and two dogs, Max and Claire. When, upon venturing into the partially finished basement, we did not see either of the cats, Barbara's first question was, "So are they pretty feral, is that it?" When Tim and Erin responded that they were "just shy," and did not really like people, Barbara's next question was, "So have they ever been around kids?" After Tim and Erin explained the cats' generally withdrawn and antisocial response to guests of any age, Barbara, satisfied, responded, "Well, clearly they're not going to be a threat to kids." Here the language of threat points to the function of the home study as risk management. After listening to Tim and Erin discuss Max and Claire's love of snacks and cuddles, Barbara assessed, "Affectionate dogs." She asked again about their behavior around children. Tim and Erin noted that both animals were patient and "sweet-tempered."

Barbara also gleaned information about possible future parenting styles from this conversation. She made sure to ask how Tim and Erin divided the labor of caring for and disciplining the dogs (equally), and what methods of discipline were used ("scolding first" and then "time-outs"). To all this, Barbara replied, "Well, I don't like to liken animals to children, but clearly if you know how to discipline an animal, you'll probably be fine with kids."[16] This future-tense if/then equation gives Tim and Erin the benefit of the doubt in a huge way. Toward the end of the conversation, Barbara asked, "Okay, I don't think this is true, but are there any pets here that might be classified as a breed that is associated with fighting or other crimes." "No," answered Tim, and Erin giggled over him, "Just Tim." "Alright," said Barbara, "I'm going to say 'no.' We're supposed to explain the presence of high-risk pets [that] could place children and other family members in danger. You know that, right?" At this point, Max and Claire, presumed innocent and plied with treats, were dozing at our feet under the dining room table. Tim and Erin nodded, and Barbara worked her way through the last few questions about potential interactions between the dogs and the future child.[17] This entire conversation unfolded in the service of producing predictive knowledge for Barbara about how a child would fare in this particular home environment, with not only Tim and Erin, but also Max, Claire, Louise, and Jo as potential future kin.

Barbara's quests for verification demonstrate that omniscience was of course beyond the scope of First Steps social workers' abilities. During the adoption process, the construction and evaluation of "fit" parents and a protected environment required applicant transparency. When a couple or individual began the adoption process, they were given a thick packet of forms to be completed for their home study. One form was the "Duty of Candor," the domestic version of which is reproduced below:

Duty of Candor for Domestic Adoption

We, (I), _____ and _____ have been informed by _____, a representative of First Steps, on _____, that based on Hague regulation (8 CFR 204.311 (d)), we, (I), have a duty of candor with First Steps.[18]

This duty is regarding ourselves and / or any adult member of our household. We, (I) are aware that we (I) must give true and complete information to the home study worker or placement worker, of any arrest, conviction, or other adverse criminal history in the U.S. or abroad, even if the record has been expunged, sealed, pardoned, or the subject of any other amelioration, and disclose other relevant information, such as physical, mental, or emotional health issues or behavior issues. We, (I) understand and have been informed that this duty of candor is an ongoing duty and continues during the adoption process until finalization is completed through the courts. We, (I) have been informed that we, (I) must notify First Steps if any new event or information might warrant submission of an amended or updated home study.

_____   _____

Parent   Date

_____   _____

Parent   Date

_____   _____

First Steps Representative   Date

All prospective parents, regardless of whether they were adopting domestically or internationally, were required to sign a version of this form, attesting to their trustworthiness. As Power (1997: 136) notes in his study of the social contours of audit practices, "good clients are those that can be trusted." Bad clients, on the other hand, are those that cannot be trusted, such as the always already lying "scammer," for example. In addition to mandating transparency, the form itself hails applicants as "parents," even though at the time of signing, they may be childless. In addition, the form notes that candor is "an ongoing duty" that governs interactions between applicants and social workers not only at the time of the home study, but into the near future until the adoption is finalized. Duty of candor, therefore, is not a singular event, but a continuous process of disclosure.

During a home study interview with Jack and Brielle, a white couple adopting from Haiti, Corinne reviewed a list outlining the home study process: "Yes. So there, you will find that there's a lot of paperwork involved." The couple reviewed the list and nodded in agreement. Corinne continued, "Which is fine for some people and daunting for other people, so, we'll just, we'll get right into it, and I will give you guys this too." She slid another sheet of paper across the table, adding, "You guys can make notes on this as I kind of explain what's needed for each of these things, but this is going to be your checklist of the things that are going to be needed in order to make your home study complete." Brielle readied a pen, while Corinne explained, "So the first one is the Duty of Candor for International Adoption, so this is one that you guys will just sign, and it's basically saying that you guys are going to be up front and honest with us about any criminal activity in your backgrounds, and if anything comes up throughout this adoption process, too—" Jack nodded, as Brielle sketched brief notes on the checklist. "That you need to be up front with us," Corinne finished. "Got it," replied Brielle. "Because it's much better if you report it to us rather than us finding out . . . in other ways," said Corinne.

Barbara had a similar conversation with Tim and Erin, who were hoping to adopt domestically:

> So, all right. So, Duty of Candor. This is really telling us that you agree to keep any changes that go on that might affect legally, our responsibility terms as the guardian of a child, that you're not going to withhold things from us if there's something that occurs, such as an arrest, or, only one I can think of offhand is arrest for, what do they call that? Not road rage? Road rage, yeah. We had a family, the day the child was supposed to go into the home, we get a call from the referring agency: "Oh, a hit just showed up. Your family had an incident of road rage where they got arrested because they got out of their car and beat up somebody."

Here, Barbara alludes to the function of the home study also as a legal tool of indemnity, offering future protection to both agency and child, a hint that the home study had goals beyond child protection. "Oh, geez," sighed Tim. "So try to control yourself," Erin teased. This is a situation in which potential criminality is so unimaginable, it serves as the punch line of a joke. Barbara continued, "Yeah, well, it was like, okay, the baby was supposed to go home the next day and they didn't tell us." "That sounds quite bad," Erin interjected, now serious. "So thank God we heard," said Barbara, ". . . and we had to say, you know what, not only are we not placing, we are never working with you again because you weren't honest with us." Here, the lack of candor forecloses the possibility for future adoptive kinship. Duty of candor firmly establishes, evaluates, and *produces* transparency as a value sought in "good parents." In these examples, more troubling to the social workers than the transgressions themselves, was the fact that the transgressions were not disclosed. Barbara finished, in the hypothetical voice,

> You know, had an incident occurred and you were remorseful and you said, "I'm going to get help. This has never happened before," we could have probably worked with you. But you didn't tell us, so, it's a bizarre example, but it's just letting you know that you're going to keep us informed.

"This has never happened before" is a statement of underlying innocence. The transgression is an anomaly, assuaged by remorse. Dishonesty only compounds the offense.

These transparency practices are visual, moral, and racial. During the home study process, social workers are looking *through* prospective adoptive parents with the goal of gathering enough information to make decisions about future kinship outcomes. There is also a sense that prospective adoptive parents are being looked *into,* checked out. They are being observed, monitored, supervised, and evaluated. Literally studied. Transparency and openness are not simply expected, they are required.[19] When I asked Kimberly, the adoption attorney, about the home study process, she responded, "I've said publicly many times—even though I think politically, it would be political suicide—I wish that it was a requirement that everybody had a home study before they had a child, by whatever method." She proposes here a sort of risk-averse blanket form of child protection, to prevent "bad" outcomes. She continued,

> Thereby rooting out some really bad parents as far as I'm concerned. But I have adoptive parents who have favorable home studies, they're wonderful

and have good backgrounds, but they still, still have a lot of resentment over the fact that they had to be studied and the rest of the world didn't.

From this perspective, "wonderful" people with "good backgrounds" should be trusted. A favorable home study verifies inherent goodness (or at least a convincing performance). Connoting openness, frankness, and transparency, the word "candor" literally (and also, perhaps, illuminatingly) is derived from the Latin for "whiteness."

In my conversations with adoptive parents and those hoping to adopt, the "unfairness" of the home study was often alluded to, as parents self-consciously compared adoptive family-making to its biological counterpart, which was perceived to be relatively free of outside intervention. This, of course, is a highly race- and class-specific perception: while middle- and upper-class biological parents experience a relatively low level of outside intervention in their family planning, this has never been the case for poor parents, particularly poor women of color (Roberts 1997, 2002).[20] Still, the notion—particularly among couples who had experienced infertility—that "if we had just had a biological child, we could have avoided all this hassle" was pervasive. At one informational session, a prospective adoptive mother lamented that she and her husband were "loving people who just wanna be good parents." "Why are there so many rules?!" she asked, visibly and audibly exasperated. When juxtaposed against the experiences of potential birth mothers in the previous chapter, the repeated insistence by prospective adopters that the home study was invasive, intrusive, unfair, and humiliating almost suggests that they resented being treated like the poor black women who were gestating their future children.

HOME INVASIONS

Prospective parents understood the "good" of child safety to be the goal of the home study, but this did not lessen the perceived marginalizing effects of invasive observation. Although I had contacted Jeanine about being interviewed months earlier, while she was in the throes of her home study, she had requested that we postpone our conversation until the home study was complete and she and Mark had been approved. When I asked her later why she did not want to do the interview until the home study was complete, she explained, "I was worried we wouldn't pass," echoing the language of examination used in the description of Jones's book. She went on, "And I'm sorry, if it's not adoption-friendly. That is how the adoptive parents feel. They don't know if they're going to *pass* this thing or not. I know that sometimes you get a fail." Frowning, she sighed and shrugged, as if to apologize for what she was about to say. "You get the red light. I didn't have any reason to think of, like, what it would be, but I was scared. I just wanted this to be completed," she finished.

Similarly, another prospective adoptive mother had described her own home visit as "the big final exam." Examination can be understood here as having a double connotation, implying both evaluation and inspection. Superstitious myself, I asked Jeanine if she was worried our interview might somehow adversely affect the home study outcome, and she replied, "I don't know, I was just worried—would anyone at the agency ever read something that you wrote? Not like what I said? And then use their power. It is *incredible* the amount of power that these counselors have." Jeanine was worried that my own observations might be discovered by someone charged with evaluating her.[21] My very presence—and observing gaze—thus served as a potential threat to Jeanine's imagined future. This was a remote possibility, given that she was not working with First Steps, but with another small agency in the area, but her anxiety about being scrutinized and the possible negative outcome of that scrutiny is telling. The stakes for her were very high. Her future—as well as her future parenthood—was at risk. The home study is a process that makes otherwise privileged white middle-class American subjects *feel* markedly disempowered.

When we began the interview, I asked Jeanine to walk me through the home study process. Her home study was broken into three meetings, similar to the way home studies were conducted at First Steps. The first meeting she described as an "interview" that was "more playful and fun." It lasted two-and-a-half to three hours and took place at the agency, she recalled. She and Mark had been asked about the "fun parts" of their relationship: how they met, their expectations for adoption ("what we're looking for"), and so on. She described the difficulty in discussing infertility and her and Mark's differing approaches to privacy: "They did ask us about our fertility journey, and that part was hard, to kind of, talk about. Particularly because I tend to sort of be an open book, and my husband is very private." Here, the process of the home study reveals competing notions of public and private with respect to reproduction. Jeanine went on, "So this has been an interesting dance that the two of us have been doing from the beginning of all of this. 'Cause

I would go and tell everybody if I could about what was going on, and he wants to say nothing." I nodded, and she continued, "And so, in this meeting, when they're asking about our fertility journey, I just kinda looked to Mark, 'cause I'm like 'How much are you gonna say?' So that was a little uncomfortable." There is no complete "true" story; the home study results in a narrative shaped by these tensions.

Jeanine and Mark had had two social workers, one who was very experienced and another who was in training. "So the second meeting," continued Jeanine, tucking her feet beneath her and holding her mug with both hands, "was hard . . . So let's see, that second meeting, we were just discussing our childhoods. And my husband had such a nice, kind of—you know his parents are still married, they live in the same house that they pretty much raised the kids in. And you know, the parents had dinner every night together." She painted an idyllic picture of a normative (white, middle-class) American family. For Jeanine, this was "healthy" and "clean": "I mean everything they say, like statistically, for like a healthy family life—check, check, check, you know? They completed it . . . And then, it was my turn. And, I did *not* have this kind of upbringing." She chuckled uncomfortably:

> It wasn't horrific, but it was *not* squeaky clean. Definitely not something you could show, on like, an after-school special kind of family. And so, um, it was *really* painful to go after my husband. So that was one thing. The second thing that was really upsetting to me was, you know I've started a business, and you know it takes a while for things to take off, and it's very intertwined in my personal life and my professional life. And I'm not making a ton of money doing this yet, you know, or maybe ever. This really is work that I do from my heart, and my husband is really the main breadwinner. They didn't ask me at all about my work. It was absolutely a blow to my ego. It's so much a part of my identity and who I am.

Norms of kinship and gender were played out and reinforced in these encounters. Jeanine's statement reveals the gendered logics of a process designed to determine her fitness as a mother, and how absence of monitoring and review in an area where it has come to be expected can be as injurious as the presence of the gaze itself. At the same time that sharing the details of her "not squeaky clean" childhood caused her to feel vulnerably exposed, Jeanine acutely felt the erasure of not being seen professionally, of not being looked for.[22] She finished, "So I left that room, like a deflated balloon." She added, referring to the written report of the home study, "You know they've given us a copy now, and I will not read it. I have *no* interest in going back there, that was *such* a painful day for me." Even though she and Mark "passed" the home study, for Jeanine, the finished document constituted a narrative of her own disempowerment.

Without missing a beat, Jeanine launched into a description of the third and final meeting: the home visit. "And the third visit was in our house. And so you know, it's funny, in the beginning," she paused to take a sip of tea, "I felt like, 'Aw, this one's gonna be so much better, because it's in my house! It's *my* turf.' You know, so I was feeling a lot more confident." This claim to private property was quickly challenged, however: "And you know, I'm telling you, these social workers are *so* nice. It's just that this is such sensitive stuff, I don't know if Mother Teresa could have walked in that door, and I might have still been so hurt from this experience." Jeanine went on to explain the walk-through of the house: "So she walks into my house, and suddenly that feeling of feeling that deflation again, came over me. 'Cause she just totally took charge of the whole thing. You know, she didn't want any drinks. I couldn't like—I'm a nurturing person." "Mmhmm," I nodded, gripping the mug of tea she had offered (and I had accepted) upon my own arrival at her house. "I just—it wasn't my house anymore. I just wished she could have relaxed a little with me." The house was no longer private. In a separate interview, one prospective adoptive mother, when speaking about her experience with one of First Steps' contract social workers, concurred: "You know, she's not warm and fuzzy, right?"

Jeanine continued:

> So she's here at the house, and she's calling all the shots. And we went over some paperwork, and she would actually read us questions from a list, I think from DCFS [Department of Children and Family Services]. Then we had all the paperwork, you know, like the Fire Escape Plan. And then I think we went around the house, and that part was more fun, in a way, 'cause then you definitely feel more kind of, in control. But of course I overanalyzed *everything*. Like in one room alone, I could tell you five possible hazards that someone could pick up on. But really she was very lovely about the experience, and would just kinda glance.

The social workers were intrusive in certain ways, but remained "lovely" and "nice." She continued:

> Like even in our bedroom, she didn't even—just kinda looked. Didn't even look in our bathroom, I don't know. Maybe just kinda turned her head, and then went to the other rooms. Spent *much* more time like in the nursery room

and in the baby stuff. That felt really good to me, 'cause it's really uncomfortable having really *anybody* in your bedroom, first of all, but second of all certainly, someone who's writing up a whole study on you.

The parallels between my visit and Jeanine's pre-adoption home visit were becoming sharply apparent. Given her anxiety, I felt indebted to her for allowing me into her home. Here, Jeanine describes the differential application of the gaze to various spaces within the house, a telling example of the "fractal" nature of the public / private distinction (Gal 2002); in this example, the bedroom remains private, but the nursery becomes a public space within the private home, appropriate for visual consumption by the social worker.

Also in this example, Jeanine distinguishes between a glance in her bedroom, which seemed less invasive, and the time spent scrutinizing the nursery, but a glance can also be violent. The glance, Foucault ([1963] 2003: 149–50) notes,

> strikes at one point, which is central or decisive; the gaze is endlessly modulated, the glance goes straight to its object . . . If it strikes in its violent rectitude, it is in order to shatter, to lift, to release appearance . . . The glance is of the non-verbal order of *contact,* a purely ideal contact perhaps, but in fact a more *striking* contact, since it traverses more easily, and goes further beneath things.

Although the glance feels cursory, it serves the broader purpose of the home visit by providing visual confirmation of the condition of the home, while allowing social workers to efficiently mark all spaces of the home as inspected, thus fulfilling the requirements of audit. At the same time, the glance preserves a sense of respectability and decorum between the white middle-class social worker and her clients. These visits occur within a social milieu in which it remains inappropriate to simply go rifling through another (innocent, white) person's space and belongings.[23] But the glance touches without touching, all in the service of the protection of a future child.

"ARE YOU THE STATE?"

As highlighted by the case of Jeanine and Mark, the tension stemming from the home study process is partially a product of prospective adoptive parents' notions of public and private, not just in terms of space and information, but also in the role and reach of the state as a public entity within private agency adoption. Prospective adoptive parents experienced both confusion and intrusion, respectively, as a result of finding themselves subject to a combination of state and agency regulations *and* having their private lives and spaces invaded by social workers in the latter's quest to determine parental fitness and predict future adoption outcomes.

Berlant's theory of the "intimate public sphere" (see also Anagnost 2000) is particularly useful when thinking about the formation of adoptive families. She observes, as opposed to life before the Reagan era, "Now everywhere in the United States intimate things flash in people's faces: pornography, abortion, sexuality, and reproduction; marriage, personal morality, and family values" (1997: 1). This visual and political assemblage fuels "a familial politics of the national future" (ibid.). Berlant argues that these intimate issues, including family formation and sexuality, are vital to definitions of America, Americanness, and American citizenship. For Berlant—as for Jürgen Habermas ([1962] 1991) before her—the contemporary United States lacks any cohesive public sphere. What she proposes in its place is the intimate public sphere, which "renders citizenship as a condition of social membership produced by personal acts and values, especially acts originating in or directed toward the family sphere" (1997: 5). Adoption is one of many routes by which the family becomes an object for public scrutiny. The home study is central to this process, with the audit functioning as "public performance" (Pels 2000: 161).

Writing about the American child welfare system, Jennifer Reich (2005) describes in detail the contradiction between public and private notions of normative American family life. Reich explains how through public intervention into private life (most often by Child Protective Services), "the therapeutic state serves to reinforce dominant definitions of family life" (5). She continues, following Habermasian logic, "As a historically private institution that was imagined to provide refuge from the outside world, families are believed to be free to nurture their unique traditions without external intervention" (8). However, Reich argues that the state, rather than private citizens, plays a significant role in determining what constitutes successful parenting. Although Reich's object of study is the foster care system, the same trend can be seen in contemporary forms of private adoption, in which prospective parents, even those who adopt through private agencies, must meet a rigorous state standard in terms of their estimated ability to be successful parents.

As is clear from the preceding ethnographic examples, in order to adopt, agency applicants had to comply with certain "licensing standards." To understand where these "standards" originate, it is necessary to examine the workings of private agency adoption as both public and private—or quasi-state—practice. A blurring of public and private at the institutional level had implications for the ways that monitoring practices were carried out on the ground. The role of "the state" in private agency adoption was not always clear to clients. In an initial interview with Corinne, one puzzled applicant stuttered through the following: "I guess my question is, what, are you, are you the state and she's the, I, I honestly, I'm not sure, like, I thought, I've, I figured we were going to a state building, to a state thing right now." Corinne replied, "Oh, sure. So First Steps, we do home studies for families, so that's what you, what is going—this is the assessment process. For you guys to be able to be approved to adopt." The applicant confirmed, "You report back to the state." "Yes," responded Corinne. "So the state will take a look at your home study once I'm finished with it, and they need to approve it as well." In another interaction I observed between a different social worker and a single woman hoping to adopt, the prospective mother sought clarification: "Your representation is, of course, you are helping me as well, but you represent the state, right?" Her reference here to the "helping" nature of social work reveals the complicated brokerage function. She went on, stumbling verbally, "Ultimately, to make sure that it—not represent them, but you're the face to the state in terms of making sure that a foster parent, because it's that licensing process, and an adoptive parent is, is able, right ... ?" Confusion is reflected in the halting cadence of the prospective mother's speech, and her repeated requests for clarification: right? The social worker interjected, "Theoretically. I mean, I am recommending the license." "So it's your name, exactly," finished the prospective mother. The social worker replied, implicitly referencing her moral duty to child protection, "So anything I write and submit to the state, I have to be sure that, okay, this is a good situation, or I'm not going to recommend the license." As Strathern (2002: 2) observes, "procedures for assessment have social consequences," and social workers were acutely aware of the risk.

The answer to this question—"Are you the state?"—is complicated. There is no national American adoption system, and adoption is regulated by individual states. In Illinois, the state (of Illinois) regulates certain aspects of the private agency process, such as final approval of licensing and accreditation and various standards for training and interactions between social workers and clients. Social workers are thus accountable to both the agency and the state. This was particularly evident in First Steps' use of guidelines developed for the state-administered (public) foster care licensing process: in Illinois, private agency adopters must be licensed first as foster parents, even if they are not adopting through the public system. So, First Steps borrowed heavily from Illinois's Department of Children and Family Services (DCFS) in its efforts to determine parental fitness, because the state had to approve any request for a foster care license before a private adoption could proceed. Thus, the social worker gaze and the state gaze were deeply entwined, as social workers facilitated this private process with moderate public oversight.[24]

Notions of public and private life are intimately linked to understandings of child protection. The family, Reich (2005) argues, becomes public through its duty to reproduce social norms sanctioned by the state and its public institutions. As noted by Berlant (1997), children are viewed as America's most vulnerable citizens (literally, the future of the nation) in need of protection, and the state's duty to protect individual citizens often supersedes the privacy of the family unit.[25] The vulnerable status of children, Reich (2005: 13) contends, "encourages the view that abused or neglected children are prisoners trapped behind the shrouded walls of the private family in need of rescue." The rescuers, however, must be vetted to ensure that subsequent rescue will not be needed in the future. This is true of both public and private forms of adoption, although the level and depth of scrutiny and assessment varies across a range of contexts and situations.

American adoption presents a complex web of privacy, intimacy, and publicity that is intricately bound up with the realities of social inequality and kinship. Class, as it becomes intertwined with power, plays a prominent role in American child welfare and adoption, with upper- and middle-class parents having the ability to opt out of public services and resources as they see fit, whereas parents of lower socioeconomic status are given much less choice due to their lack of social and economic capital, and are thus much more often put under state surveillance through their participation in public programs (daycare, schools, assistance, etc.) (Gilliom 2001; Reich 2005; Roberts 2002). Privacy in terms of family life, therefore, hinges on racial and class inequalities that are deeply ingrained in American history and contemporary society. However, class operates slightly differently in the case of adoption, as it is more often than not middle- and upper-class white parents who find themselves subjected to brief periods of invasive state assessment of their private lives—audit as "coercive accountability" (Shore and Wright 2000)—in order to adopt from a private agency. Their bristling under this abnormal scrutiny illustrates how adoption is the exception that proves the rule.

Within this private-public sphere of adoption then, what does it mean "to be studied"? As Jeanine's example in the previous section illustrated, the home visit, in particular, blurs the line between public and private by rendering certain parts of intimate family life hypervisible, and by making possible an external determination of who can have access to a particular kind of future, and who cannot. The home visit therefore constitutes yet another practice of intimate speculation. Embedded within larger structures of neoliberal governance and racialization, it is a mechanism upon which adoptive kinship is contingent. This contingency prompts a particular performance of parental fitness, which at times can seem subversive. Like the ultrasound in the previous chapter, this form of speculative inspection ("proof") has limits (just different ones).

PERFORMING FOR THE PENETRATING GAZE

Not every nook and cranny was rendered visually accessible to social workers. At one pre-adoption training, in an attempt to positively frame the home study process, the trainer asked prospective parents, "What's the positive part of the home study?" and an attendee replied bluntly, "A much-needed housecleaning." Prospective adoptive parents often negotiated what they perceived as intrusive scrutiny by manipulating objects and space within the home. While often speaking from a position of relative powerlessness in the face of intense observation, prospective parents had various strategies for producing homes and subjectivities specifically tailored for social worker consumption. These strategies enabled them to affect desired home study outcomes, and had implications for the subsequent unfolding of the adoption process and eventual granting of adoptive kinship.

Social workers use the home study in part to assess the future performance of potential adoptive parents. As Power (1997: 119) contends, "auditing and the development of concepts of performance are mutually constitutive." Performance can be conceptualized here in two ways: (1) most simply, "the doing of an action or operation," as it is used in performance reviews and most audits of something called "performance" (the way Power employs the term), but also, (2) "an instance of performing a play, piece of music, etc. in front of an audience" (*Oxford English Dictionary* 2014c). This second connotation also includes "a difficult, time-consuming, or annoying action or procedure" and "a pretense, a sham." Even Power's (1997) analysis blurs the line between these two versions of the concept: "Auditing has the character of a certain kind of organizational script whose dramaturgical essence is the production of comfort [for the auditor]" (123).[26] When he argues, "the power of auditing is therefore to construct concepts of performance in its own image" (119), it becomes clear that "performance" in the case of audit is always shaped by the observation itself, so that the performance being measured (in the former sense of capably carrying out an action) is always already a performance (in the latter sense of putting on a show). In the case of the home study, the future is in part what links the two. Since social workers cannot assess actual parenting of the imagined child, prospective adopters must perform their future fitness in the present. This is how the home study not only observes prospective adopters, but produces a certain kind of parenting subject.

Drawing on Foucault, Shore and Wright (2000) concur, linking notions of self-management with power and compliance: "a major feature of audit is the extent to which it reshapes in its own image those organizations that are monitored. What is required is auditee compliance with the norms and procedures demanded by inspectors" (72). Through the home study process, prospective adopters become "self-managing individuals who render themselves auditable" (58).[27] Strathern (2000: 2) notes that practices of audit create "new ways of practising, or performing, 'accountability.'" The following ethnographic examples demonstrate how the home study as audit prompted a certain production and performance of parental fitness through strategic concealment.

As suggested in previous sections, the home study sits at the nexus of mis / trust, surveillance, and race and class power dynamics. Power (1997: 135) notes, "Assumptions of distrust sustaining audit processes may be self-fulfilling as auditees adapt their behavior strategically in response to the audit process, thereby becoming less trustworthy." The potential for manipulation and subversion of social worker supervision is built into the very structure of the home visit itself as a site for the mobilization of the observing gaze. These visits were always scheduled and announced, so in preparation, applicants cleaned and rearranged their homes to match social worker expectations. This allowed prospective parents to carefully craft the image they projected. As a social worker explained to one prospective adoptive couple near the end of their second interview at the First Steps office, "So the next thing we're going to be doing is scheduling our visit to your home. And so what I like to do is kind of forewarn you what we're going to be looking for." This kind of coaching scripted a certain performance of fitness among prospective adopters.[28] "Because here's our goal," she said, narrowing her eyes. Before she could finish, the couple answered, almost in unison, "You don't want to come back." "That is exactly right," said the social worker. The prospective adoptive mother, laughing, responded, "Not that I don't love you guys, but I don't want you to come back either." Another facet of the speculative nature of the home study is revealed: through forewarning and preparation, a successful home visit circumvents both its own failure and the necessity for its repetition.

I attended several meetings, interviews, and follow-up home visits over a period of about seven months with Annette, a white, childless widow in her mid-forties, earning a six-figure income and living in a trendy Chicago neighborhood. At a two-month monitoring visit in Annette's home, Barbara explained the nature of pre-announced home visits. Sliding a piece of paper across the dining room table, Barbara said, "This is the monitoring record, which we typically fill out for every monitoring visit, which is what this [visit] is." Annette reached for the form, "Got it, this is a monitoring visit, okay." Barbara continued, "So as long as you keep the license open, you're required to have monitoring visits. Now, what can happen is if you refuse to let us in here to do a monitoring visit, we could potentially have reason to revoke your license."

To this mention of compulsory compliance, Annette nodded, "Got it." Barbara went on,

> Over the years—I've been doing this for so long, and the DCFS [foster care] workers that come through, they'd say, well, do you do unannounced visits? No. Our agency has never done unannounced visits. Um, partly because you never, really never have foster children in the home.

"Right," Annette affirmed. "I mean, the only children you're going to have are the adopted children," Barbara clarified. "Right," Annette repeated. "And are they foster children for those first six months [before the adoption is finalized]? Yes they are." "Yes," Annette confirmed. "And we're already doing pretty periodic visits during that six months anyway, so to do an unannounced visit would just seem crazy. I think the reason they put that in there is for families that have lots and lots of kids."[29] "Right," Annette repeated, nodding. "They want to be able to walk in and make sure that everything's in compliance," Barbara said. She went on,

And again . . . I get that, especially, we're talking about NPR [stories of child abuse], all the news and everything, they're looking at scrutinizing children, things that have happened to children in DCFS care, you know . . . This is like, they're under scrutiny. And if they don't do those periodic spot visits, they're not going to catch a lot of stuff.

"No, a planned visit is pretty easy to . . ." Annette trailed off. *Rehearse, subvert, prepare for, preempt,* fill-in-the-blank. "Well, and I am pretty good about giving you a little notice, you know. I mean, I didn't give you much notice this time, but I—" Annette cut Barbara off, "You gave me [scheduling] options; I could have done the following week." Social workers were not necessarily interested in exclusion or deterrence; they wanted approvals, happy families. As Power (1997: 126) insists, "where audit arrangements emphasize the production of comfort, this reflects an institutional need for auditing not to be too 'successful' in finding problems and in producing discomfort by reporting these problems."

Four months after the conversation about unannounced visits, upon visiting Annette shortly before Barbara returned for her six-month home study update, I noticed a large collection of unopened bottles of wine on the floor in her kitchen. Following my gaze, and without provocation, Annette self-consciously explained:

And she's going to come on Wednesday to make sure nothing's changed and, as you can see, nothing's changed. But I was really, really freaked out about it [the first home visit]. Like, I just didn't know. Because I am a single person, so I'll have holiday parties or barbecues and people will always bring—see? I still have them, bottles of wine, and I always tell them, "Don't bring it. Don't bring it, because I always have my own. I've got it all picked out. I've got a white. I've got a red. I've got it all sorted out." And they always bring it, and I literally will have cases of leftover wine that I don't like to drink because it's usually not even good. So, I was like, oh, I have to clean all this stuff, I can't have all this alcohol in my house, this whole thing.[30]

Anxiety cut into her speech. When I returned two days later with Barbara, the wine had disappeared. Annette's strategic removal of the wine demonstrates one way prospective parents resist the exposure that the visual logics of the home visit require of otherwise privileged white middle-class American subjects, and perform good, clean, healthy, fit future parenthood. These actions might fall under adoption scholar Stevie Larson's (2018: 11) notion of "whiteness as strategy": "the pursuit of viable life and promising futures primarily through commitments to tactics, mechanisms, ideas, and desires that preserve domination."

Prospective adoptive parents' subversion of the social worker gaze is not without limits, of course. When Barbara returned to Annette's home for a follow-up visit, Annette confessed to concealing the alcohol, buckling under the pressure of duty of candor. Barbara dragged her index finger down the assessment checklist. "Okay, liquor, didn't ask for that [yet]." Annette nodded and glanced toward the kitchen, "Uh-huh. Under the cabinet." "I have to be honest," she continued, over Barbara's muffled "Okay," "It used to be here. It's not there anymore." Barbara commented, "Oh, it used to be in visual—" Annette stated quickly, "It was in visible—it was in view." "Okay, okay," Barbara hardly glanced up from the checklist. "So it is no longer . . ." Annette continued. "So it's in the kitchen, in a cabinet," Barbara clarified. "Correct," Annette replied, "which has a lock on it." "With a lock, okay," repeated Barbara, satisfied with the arrangement. "I can show it to you if you like," Annette offered. The power that Barbara held over Annette's hoped-for future family arrangement, along with the pressure of her penetrating gaze and quest for transparency, coaxed forth the uncomfortable exposure of invisible things, now safely locked away, out of reach of a child that still had not been born. Indeed, this confession was a way to demonstrate both honesty and safety: there was wine here, but I have control of it now. See?[31]

Power (1997: 13) notes, "New motivational structures emerge as auditees develop strategies to cope with being audited; it is important to be seen to comply with performance measurement systems while retaining as much autonomy as possible." Jeanine recalled a practice of hiding and rearranging similar to Annette's in preparation for her own home study, minus the self-conscious confession to her social worker. She described her bedroom:

And that's like such a sacred space. You know, I'm a very spiritual person, so a lot of my space has little knickknacks, you know with angels and crystals and feathers from Native American—you know I like—whatever background, I'm like, I'm open to expressing from that place. Buddha, you know, Jesus, I've got it all covered. And, so, I put all that stuff away. 'Cause I just, I didn't want anyone looking at my—that, that's just such a sacred special part of myself. You know I made a vision board of what I want my future to look like, with the baby. And I just put all that way. And she probably (a) wouldn't have even noticed it, and (b) wouldn't have thought anything of it, but it's very private. And so all that stuff went away. And so I felt like a lot of the house looked really bare.

As Jeanine spoke, her spine curved, collapsing her shoulders. She made a cave of herself as she described a world she sought to protect. Through the "putting away" of "private" objects, Jeanine (the self-proclaimed "open book") practiced her own form of anti-surveillance politics (Gilliom 2001), her own form of self-erasure. She even hid her vision board, an effort to protect from prying eyes her own literal attempt to visualize an imagined future. While certain forms of privacy were not possible within the frame of the home study, with its obligatory "duty of candor," Jeanine did find ways to produce a particular version of herself for the consumption of the home study worker, a less vulnerable self. Annette too admitted to making small changes before the home visit: "You know, I took it very seriously. I changed some of the configuration of the house just to kind of accommodate a lot of—you know, I just didn't want anything to go wrong." These seemingly minor adjustments were important performances of parental readiness, at the same time that they represented resistance to the home study process.

As illustrated by Annette's example, a series of follow-up home visits was scheduled to make sure that approved home conditions were maintained while prospective adopters waited to be matched with a child. At Annette's first home visit, Barbara warned, "Now, I do have to tell you that we are going to have to come back here in sixty days after we license you. And . . ." "Make sure that I wasn't—I didn't go back to my bad habits?" asked Annette, at once anxious and playful. Her joke reveals the open secret of the performance, the potential for relapse into some underlying "badness." However, like Erin's teasing about Tim's potential for road rage, Annette's question functions as a joke because she is taken to be innocent. She alludes here to the disciplinary power of the home study, the way that it produces the very "good" parental subjects it seeks to evaluate, but also the limits of that discipline. Barbara answered, "We have to come back and make sure everything's still in compliance." For prospective adopters, the potential for continued state and agency scrutiny progresses along a predefined schedule into an indefinite future, at the end of which, hopefully, waits a child and a return to the normative privacy and intimacy of family life, a short six months after placement. While the vast majority of home studies, like Annette's and Jeanine's, were approved, failure—that red light Jeanine mentioned—was not an impossibility, and failure helps to illustrate the role of the home study as a particularly intimate form of risk management.

FAILURE

Since the continued existence of the agency was premised upon successful adoptive placements, it was in First Steps' interests to approve as many families as possible. But what happens when, during the home study process, prospective adopters are found not to be in compliance? Jack and Brielle raised this question with Corinne one night in the office toward the end of a long interview. Corinne asked if the couple had any final questions before ending the meeting, and Brielle ventured, "Right. I can't imagine that we wouldn't get approved, I mean, I don't know if we'd go onto this, but what happens if you don't get approved by them? You're done, or do you apply again, or what do ..." The unimaginable imaginable. "You know, it depends—" answered Corinne. "What happens?" asked Jack, speaking over her. Corinne finished, just beneath the rising inflection and emotion of his question, "on what would be the reason for why you're not approved. If there's something in your background that, you know, is just a bar for adoption, then there's no way you can approve. You can't adopt." Jack and Brielle both nodded. Corinne continued, referring back to duty of candor and the need for transparency from both sides, "There's no getting around that. If there's something—you know, it's something that we would be talking about throughout this process. So you wouldn't just be totally surprised and say, 'Oh my gosh, I had no idea.'" She went on, noting the potential for future fallout from a failed home study:

> But, you know, I would be bringing up concerns to you guys. So it can be something where, you know, if you weren't approved, then occasionally what would happen is that an actual home study would be written that says that you were not approved, and then, you know, if you were to look to another agency or something like that to do your home study, after we'd be all that ... You would have to reveal that you've had a home, you know, a home study ...

It was almost as if she could not form the words. "Unsuccessful," Brielle interjected, to which Corinne replied, "Yeah. So." Brielle continued, turning from Corinne to Jack, "No, I just, I can't imagine why we wouldn't, but, like, what if she doesn't like us? Like, is that a reason?" Corinne chuckled, "No, that's not a reason, just because I don't like you." "Okay," Brielle said, sitting back in her chair, still nervous.

Corinne had fresh memories of a home study that had not been approved. During my fieldwork, I was only privy to one failed home study, for a family with five biological children that was hoping to adopt a child internationally from Ethiopia. In the late summer of 2013, Corinne was confronted with a challenging case in which the notion of child protection was at once complicated and crystallized. Although I was not able to sit in on Corinne's meetings with the family, I gained a great deal of insight about the case from listening to Corinne and the other social workers reflect on strategies in a series of staff meetings. The failure of the home study hinged on the family's planned future use of corporal punishment. In initial meetings with Corinne, the applicants reported use of only one form of behavioral discipline: spanking. In the staff meeting, she noted that in the autobiographies that the prospective adopters had to write as part of their homestudy, "they were, I wouldn't say vague about discipline, but just used the word 'discipline,' so saying 'discipline' rather than saying what they *do* for discipline. And you know, 'Then the discipline would be . . . carried out . . . blah, blah, blah, blah.'" Not only is there vagueness about the form of discipline used, but a passive construction of who carries out said discipline. Corinne continued, "I asked them, 'What does discipline look like?' And it turns out that they do use spanking. And they had also turned in the form to me that says they agree not to use corporal punishment with their child, with their adopted child."

As part of the initial placement paperwork, all of First Steps' prospective adoptive families had to agree to the following by signing form CFS 452–3—the "form" alluded to by Corinne:

> *Rule 402.21(c) No child shall be subjected to corporal punishment, verbal abuse, threats or derogatory remarks about him or his [sic] family.*

> The use of corporal punishment upon any child, who is served by, or under the care of a licensed family foster home, constitutes a violation of State Licensing Standards. Corporal punishment may herein be defined as any type of physical punishment, discipline, or retaliation inflicted upon any part of the body of a child. This would include such actions as slapping, hitting, punching, spanking, shoving, pinching or any other type of action geared toward inflicting pain or body discomfort upon a child. Violation of this licensing requirement may result in the revocation of a license to provide care for children.

In this regime of child protection, care and corporal punishment are set in stark contrast to one another. The adoption process attempts to discipline applicants into parents who discipline in particular ways.

In the staff meeting, Corinne continued her report, explaining her continued questioning of the applicants.

> I explained, you know, "Is this something that you would plan to use with your adopted child as well, because there's harm in that with attachment," and you know all of that. And they said, "Well, we were under the impression that we only had to not use corporal punishment until we were no longer foster parents," which they're never going to be foster parents, because they're adopting from Ethiopia. And I said it's something that we ask our families— it is a foster care requirement, but it's something we ask of all our families just because of the harm that it can have in attaching to your child.

The public again becomes confused with the private. To clarify, during the first six months after placement, the adopted child (in domestic cases) was technically in the custody of First Steps. Only after six months had passed with satisfactory post-placement visits by a social worker could the adoption be finalized. After six months, the child would attain equal status (legally, at least) to a child conceived biologically by the adoptive parents. During the six months between placement and finalization, the status of the child would be closer to that of a ward of the state, and in the case of domestic adoption, corporal punishment by the adoptive parents was forbidden by the Illinois Department of Children and Family Services (DCFS). In the case of international adoption (of which Corinne's predicament is an example) DCFS was uninvolved, but as she notes, First Steps followed their mandate against corporal punishment as agency policy for all families.

Exasperated, Corinne finished her case summary: "And they said, 'Well, we're open to not using corporal punishment in the beginning, but we cannot commit to never using that. We believe that that's a Biblical form of discipline. And . . . so . . . we can't commit to that.'" As she spoke, the other social workers in the room looked at each other and shook their heads. But Corinne was hesitant to give up or "fail" the family based on this interaction. She was hoping her colleagues could counsel her on how to proceed. She went on, "And so, I said, 'Okay, well why don't I give you some resources that you can look through for some other recommended forms of discipline for adopted children. You can read through that and see what you think. And we'll talk more about it, you know, at a later date.'" She furrowed her brow: "So because it sounds like this is their only form of discipline, is, spanking."

The ban on corporal punishment was instituted by DCFS. A stated goal of DCFS's work is "to protect children by strengthening and supporting families," and as part of its mission the entity aims to "protect children who are reported to be abused and neglected."[32] Similarly, the vision statement of First Steps included a statement that the agency "protects and enhances the lives of children." In the summer of 2013, when the mission and vision statements were both revised, an earlier draft of the vision statement submitted by a member of the board of directors read, in part, "First Steps aims to cultivate resilience in the world by protecting the lives of surrendered children through adoption." Protection, then, was an integral part of how both of these organizations viewed their responsibility to the children in their care and custody. The ban on corporal punishment was part of this mission of child protection, and First Steps policy rendered social workers beholden to it.

As Scherz (2011) argues in her work on social workers in Child Protective Services, this discourse of protection is rooted in a belief that the child is in some form an embodiment of the future—one that is always potentially at risk. She observes, "In the United States, Child Protective Services (CPS) social workers are responsible for deciding whether or not to recommend state custody of children thought to be at risk of future abuse or neglect" (33). Describing assessments carried out by CPS social workers after an allegation of abuse, Scherz argues that the decisions social workers make about how to proceed "are particularly challenging as they largely concern the prediction of future events in the life of an individual" (37). As the other ethnographic examples in this chapter have demonstrated, adoption social workers performed very similar work when carrying out home studies. They were tasked with gathering evidence in order to produce accurate predictions about the future health and safety of adoptable children. Above all, the future well-being of these children, or children-to-be, was the responsibility of these social workers. For all of adoption's inherent uncertainty, during the home study process, social workers needed to produce plausible speculations about the future in order to protect the children-to-be in their care.

After Corinne first introduced her case at the September meeting, lively conversation ensued among the staff members, and continued in subsequent meetings spanning the next five months, as her case unfolded. In response to Corinne's predicament, Holly voiced concerns stemming from recent scandals in the media involving abuse and international adoption:

> The other point is that the adopted child might present with much more . . . spank-worthy behavior. And much more frequently, to the point where it could get out of control, whereas when you have a biological child that's just saying "No, Mommy," or throwing a spoon or something. But

I think that's where what we've read and kind of those horror stories that you see in articles and things—it is like that, and it starts off as calm and then you have a child that's *really* defiant, then what do you do? Do you spank harder? Do you spank more? You know, and it's the elevation [escalation] of it. I believe that they're not getting out of control now, you know, but it also seems like they're handling very minor behavioral issues. So I guess maybe that's another point.

Holly's concern about this slippery slope roots the problem in its own future unfolding. Corinne's case came in the wake of a massive Reuters expose of "re-homing" practices among international adopters in 2013: the illegal (i.e., without state or agency oversight) transfer of adopted children from their adoptive parents to other guardians, often located through the internet. These transfers of guardianship were often precipitated by behavioral issues stemming from trauma or difficulty adjusting to the new family arrangement. Many of the re-homed children featured in the report were physically and sexually abused by their new guardians. The story of re-homing, argues Reuters journalist Megan Twohey (2013), "illustrates the many ways in which the U.S. government fails to protect children of adoptions gone awry. It shows how virtually anyone determined to get a child can do so with ease, and how children brought to America can be abruptly discarded and recycled." Twohey's position reflects the notion that part of the government's responsibility is the protection of child life. But what is the responsibility of an organization? Of a broker?

At the September staff meeting, Barbara, alluding to the proper disciplinary tactics of fit and desirable adoptive parents, asked, "And you said that they *only* use that form of discipline? There's no other form of discipline used? No timeouts, no. . ." Corinne responded, "They don't like timeouts." Barbara tried again, "No sending [to their rooms] or taking away privilege[s]?" Corinne responded, "No, it doesn't sound like it." Stella interjected, "That's the scary thing to me is that they keep—you know I love their honesty, I give it to 'em for that." The others sitting around the table nodded in agreement, and Stella continued, "But they keep coming back. They *really* can't latch on and say, 'We're never—'. That's what's really scary to me." Candor, although highly desired, suddenly became a problem—the thing that foreclosed, rather than allowed, the adoption. The prospective parents' inability to make promises about future actions was the root of the problem, and of Stella's fear. They honestly rejected future compliance, which put their future adoptive kinship with the child in question in serious jeopardy. They refused to perform.

At one point, one of the social workers suggested that perhaps a religiously affiliated agency with similar values would be a more appropriate fit for the family. Corinne explained to the family that she would need more time to think about how they would fare in the future if First Steps moved forward with attempted home study approval: "So we're kind of taking the approach of 'Well, we need to do more research into what this exactly looks like, how long you anticipate—what would make you feel comfortable using spanking especially one day, or . . .'" Another contract social worker, Louise, jumped in: "I'm sorry but this really makes me angry, that people twist the Bible and Christianity to, to their own, through their own looking glass. What, you know, what is the way to raise a child? And to say spanking is *it?*" Others in attendance nodded in agreement. "That's dangerous, I think," concluded Louise, employing language of risk and future threat. The social workers sitting around the table, however, were tasked with just that: determining "the way to raise a child," and predicting whether or not their applicants would be up to the task.

In February of 2014 Corinne shared that she would not be approving the home study. However, the rejection was not simply a result of social workers' inability to reconcile the parents' disciplinary practices with the agency's notion of protection. It was revealed late in the process that the prospective adoptive father had recently sought counseling within the church for a pornography addiction, stoking anxieties among the social workers about possible abuse.[33] Not only had the family expressed the possibility of future violation of the corporal punishment policy, they had now violated the vital tenet of candor. Together these two threats to an imagined child's future were simply too serious for Corinne to proceed with home study approval. She could not reliably predict the future safety and protection of the child. Her official denial of home study approval would follow the parents in any subsequent effort to adopt a child.[34] Failure echoes.

A conversation I observed during a home visit in November of 2013 illustrates the ways in which an unfavorable home study can follow prospective parents in their future attempts to adopt. White and upper-middle income, Tessa was a single adoptive mother attempting a second transracial adoption with First Steps. Tammy sat down on Tessa's couch, holding a stack of forms. I sat between them, perched on an ottoman, next to my tape recorder, quietly reading *The Hungry Hungry Caterpillar* to Tessa's toddler son, Miles. Tammy eyed the top page in the stack, apologizing, "I know these were asked the last time, but I have to ask again. I know you have completed other home studies, because I've seen them." Yet, as Annette had joked, the social worker needed to reconfirm the absence of any nasty habits. Tessa nodded in anticipation of the questions. Tammy read from the sheet, glancing up occasionally, "But have you ever begun a home study process in relation to adoption or any formal foster, other custodial care of a child that was not completed, or have at any time been rejected or denied as a prospective adoptive parent?" Tessa answered easily, first to Tammy, and then to Miles, who had offered her a treasured toy: "No. Thanks, sweetie." Tammy moved down the list. "Have you ever had your parental rights to any child restricted or terminated for any reason?" "No," Tessa answered. "Do you have any history of either a victim or perpetrator of any physical, sexual, emotional, child, or alcohol or substance abuse or domestic violence?" "No," Tessa repeated. "Even if it didn't result in arrest or conviction," Tammy clarified. Tessa shook her head and went to fetch Miles an apple. Tammy scribbled something on her form and then looked at Miles. "Before you eat your apple, can you show me around your house?" Tessa took Miles's hand. "Let's go, let's go show Tammy." "Can you show us around your house?" Tammy asked again. Miles refused, but Tammy was persistent, and armed with a magic word. "Please?" "Yes," Miles said, smiling. Tammy reciprocated this smile, saying, "I really want to see your room." And the three of them embarked on a tour of the house, with the "right" answers provided to the difficult questions. A "yes" from Tessa to any of these questions would have severely curtailed and possibly precluded the impending adoption. Each "no" reaffirmed her status as innocent, a "fact" Tammy already knew.

Corinne's corporal punishment case—as well as this brief interaction between Tammy and Tessa—highlights the work of social workers and prospective adoptive parents tasked with both the discipline and the protection of child bodies in the contemporary United States. These events are the reverberations of the sacralization of the American child, and reflect how social workers' modes of inspection are deeply implicated in the dual production of predictive knowledge and speculative kinship.

CONCLUSION: THE SOCIAL WORK OF PROTECTION, INSPECTION, AND PREDICTION

The home study as a form of audit is integral to intimate speculation. The modes of looking at and being seen that have been examined in this chapter highlight the underlying complexity of what appear from the outside to be relatively straightforward power dynamics. A home study and its accompanying visual inspection are perceived as constituting a humiliating invasion of privacy. Those who are generally imagined as empowered gazing subjects are instead gazed upon by others. By virtue of its myriad forms of monitoring and inspection, private agency adoption, in one sense, turns a powerful external gaze toward once unmarked subjects. For prospective adoptive parents, the adoption process functions as a speculum, necessitating an opening up of a once private space with immense implications for the kinship formations that result.[35]

These are high-stakes encounters, and adoptive parenthood hangs in the balance. The home study produces and affirms the performance of innocence, goodness, and fitness, contributing to "the production of assurance" (Power 1997: 11). Social workers as brokers and auditors use the home study to produce not only future kinship, but also certainty, promise, and guarantee. In this way, the home study both produces and alleviates anxiety about the future. As Strathern (2000: 1) contends, the audit is aspirational:

> [Practices of audit] determine the allocation of resources and can seem crucial to the credibility of enterprises; people become devoted to their implementation; they evoke a common language of aspiration. They also evoke anxiety and small resistances, are held to be deleterious to certain goals, and as over-demanding if not outright damaging.

For both social workers and prospective adopters, the anxiety produced by audit is linked to notions of risk. Power (1997: 121) notes that "the programmatic faith in auditing reflects wider social anxieties and a need to create images of control in the face of risk." Now that we have a sense of how expectant parents and prospective adoptive parents are constructed through intimate speculation, let us go back to the beginning, to examine the adoption *process* as it unfolds from start to finish. The following chapter charts social workers' affective labor of risk management in their attempts to mitigate and control the uncertainty and contingency of future adoptive kinship, and ultimately to avoid failure.

THREE

Temporal Uncertainties

MAL: I'll tell you a riddle. You're waiting for a train, a train that will take you far away. You know where you hope this train will take you, but you don't know for sure. But it doesn't matter. How can it not matter to you where that train will take you?

COBB: Because you'll be together.

—*Inception* (dir. Christopher Nolan, 2010)

IN THE SECOND-FLOOR LOUNGE of a large conference hall at a small regional college, I sat with about forty other adults, mostly first-time prospective adoptive parents, waiting for the workshop, "How to Adopt a Child without Losing Yourself," to begin. The lights dimmed and soothing flute music drifted through the room as the last few attendees took their seats on couches and metal folding chairs. A woman appeared at the front of the room and politely called us to order before playing a short video. The room quieted as our attention shifted to a large white screen displaying an image of a young girl, perhaps two or three years old, standing on the platform of a train station (see figure 3).

The camera zoomed in on her face, capturing her reaction to an approaching train. Her eyes widened. She could barely speak. A man (presumably her father) asked from off-camera, "What's coming?" "A traaaiiiin!" she responded with a grin, shifting from one foot to the other, unable to remain still. Her excitement was not only palpable; it was contagious. I noticed myself smiling, moved by her joy and wonderment, as I am sure the workshop leader had intended. I looked around to see others smiling and chuckling to themselves, perhaps recalling a time when they too were awestruck by something that later in life would seem so ordinary. A moment later the screen went dark and the woman at the front of the room—who would later introduce herself as Rosalind—explained that the video was meant to illustrate what she called, borrowing from Buddhism, "the beginner's mind," a

FIGURE 3. Film still from YouTube video "Madeleine + Train = Sheer Joy," used by Rosalind to demonstrate first-time adopters' affective orientation to the process. Filmmaker: Daniel Dubois.

mentality shared by those new to adoption. Rosalind's metaphor came from the notion, common in the adoption community, that expertise comes only from direct experience. But this language of beginning resonated in other ways. For many in the room, this conference was a sort of beginning. Following prospective adopters and social workers on the fraught quest for a child reveals how the complex contours of the adoption process produce contingency and futurity. On this journey, through modes of processing and being processed, contingency can manifest as a kind of a hoped-for arrival or, as we have seen, a missed connection.

Let us go back to the beginning. As Stella's diagram illustrates (figure 2 in the Introduction, and figure 4 later in this chapter), the expectant mother is one of two beginnings to the adoption process. She is a source. The other beginning is the prospective adopter(s), who is / are about to embark upon a journey with various possible destinations. In the summer of 2010, I asked Stella if she could estimate the percentage of planned adoptive placements at First Steps that failed or "fell through" before the baby was placed (i.e., the number of expectant mothers who decided to parent their children *after* making an adoption plan). "Ah, I would say, 60 to 70 percent," she reported matter-of-factly. While her figure was based on personal experience and intuition rather than hard numbers, this kind of folk statistic was indicative of the ways in which social workers attempted to prepare parents for the adoption process and strived to facilitate successful placements. The figure was also an attempt to transform uncertainty into calculable risk. The startling failure rate illustrates that while prospective adoptive parents have a great deal to gain through private agency adoption, the process is fraught with the impending possibility of immense loss as well as a pervasive sense of insecurity. This chapter explores the hopes and anxieties attached to those precarious imagined gains and losses, revealing how the temporal and affective unfolding of the adoption process, as well as discourses surrounding it, produce the imagined child as a highly contingent, precarious future. The affective labor of social workers, simultaneously working as brokers, therapists, fortune-tellers, and risk managers, was integral to the unfolding of this process. Adoption social workers' attempts to address contingency and uncertainty form a constellation of strategies for engaging with imagined futures. In particular, notions of risk—an important element of intimate speculation—shaped understandings of adoption for both social workers and prospective adopters.

KINSHIP WITH COMPLICATIONS

On a blustery November day, a six-hour pre-adoption training session took place in a small multipurpose room inside a Presbyterian church in one of Chicago's more charming suburbs. In attendance were six prospective adoptive couples, led by a social worker from a Chicago-area agency. This was a training that First Steps encouraged all prospective parents to attend as part of a sixteen-hour training requirement. I had arrived at 8:45 a.m., entered the church and followed signs to the training room, where I met Lynn, the trainer. I introduced myself and Lynn gave me a thick packet of assorted handouts, information, training materials, and slide printouts. I took a seat near the back of the room and watched as hopeful parents-to-be trickled in, Starbucks cups in hand. In the course of her introductory remarks, Lynn referred to adoption as "the ultimate blind date." "It's like a high-risk pregnancy," she said.

Parents and adoption professionals (scholars as well, see Howell 2006) often refer to the adoption process as akin to biological pregnancy, but to my knowledge Lynn was the first to explicitly add this element of risk to the analogy. It was an affectively loaded metaphor, particularly for the prospective parents in the room who were about to embark upon this risky endeavor.[1]

What exactly is a high-risk pregnancy? According to the National Institute of Child Health and Human Development, a branch of the National Institutes of Health, a high-risk pregnancy "threatens the health or life of the mother or her fetus" (NICHD 2012). It is "of greater risk to the mother or her fetus than an uncomplicated pregnancy." It "puts the mother or fetus at increased risk for poor health during pregnancy or childbirth." And it is a case "where complications are more likely than normal." Adoption therefore, in Lynn's assessment, becomes a form of kinship with potential complications.[2] The very contingency of adoption, within this context, is characterized by threat. But Lynn had shifted the directionality of the risk: in her analogy, she spoke not of risk to the expectant mother, but of risk to the prospective adoptive parents. Someone else was gestating (or had gestated) what they hoped would be their future child. "Modern society represents the future as risk," writes social theorist Niklas Luhmann (1996: 37). To engage with risk is to attempt to act on the future in the present.

Risk has been identified as the "central challenge for modern adoption" (Herman 2008: 14), but at the root of risk is a profound sense of contingency, "the precarious and perilous character of existence" (Jackson, quoted in Malaby 2002: 285). Contingency encompasses elements of indeterminacy, conditionality, and uncertainty (Schedler 2007). Uncertainty in the adoption process was produced and exacerbated by social workers' inability to predict outcomes. In the case of fall-throughs, social workers were confronted by prospective adopters who asked, invariably, "Didn't you *know?* Couldn't you tell?" Their attempted assessments of risk were always incalculable; they could name it, but they could not quantify it. There is threat in a future with no measure, so social workers labored, often without success, to make chance quantifiable (cf. Hacking 1990). Stella's soft fall-through statistic is one example of this.

At First Steps, prospective adoptive parents began the adoption process by having their attention drawn to the myriad risks they could encounter along the way. Social workers usually began an interview with a litany of questions and admonitions. "Sometimes the birth mother changes her mind, sometimes the birth father comes back and wants to parent." "Are you okay with a drug-exposed baby?" "What about a family history of mental illness?" "What will your family think about you adopting a child who doesn't look like you?" Prospective parents were asked about their expectations for openness—a future relationship with the birth family after finalization of the adoption—which was a normative practice at First Steps. In addition, their willingness to consider a variety of possible outcomes was encouraged. It was generally understood that neither social workers nor prospective parents could know the future, but in their interactions with prospective adopters, social workers laid out an array of possibilities that could be predicted with varying degrees of reliability. Social workers often employed the language of risk to mitigate uncertainty in an effort to prepare adopters for a range of contingencies. *We don't know what's going to happen, but here are some possibilities.* Or, *We have a sense of what will happen; we just don't know when.* This labor was meant to temper emotional investment in a child not yet one's own. As was evident in the discourse of legal risk surrounding putative birth fathers, the language of risk was one mode by which social work expertise was mobilized within the adoption process.

The openness of adoption at First Steps added to the production of futurity and uncertainty by encouraging ongoing contact between adoptive families and birth families after the adoption was finalized. Open adoption was one of the conditions of possibility for the fall-through and its accompanying sense of risk. In the twenty-first century, we have entered an era in which adoption is "coming out of the closet" (Herman 2008: 14; Weir 2003), and openness is the preferred mode of practice.[3] Adoptive parents are increasingly choosing (or encouraged to choose) to maintain some level of post-adoption contact with birth parents. Within the discourse of openness, domestic infant adoption in America is no longer about total "strangers" becoming kin (Melosh 2002; Modell 1994), but about building a connection months before the birth of the child. At the conference where Rosalind spoke, a prominent area adoption attorney gave a talk on the role of the internet in adoption— which has created the possibility of belonging to "an adoption diaspora that never before existed" (Herman 2008: 297)—noting that with the advent of social media, even international adoptions are "opening up." Adoptions are unfolding in new and interesting ways with the development of novel forms of connectedness and relatedness. At First Steps, for example, many adoptive parents met or at least spoke on the telephone with an expectant mother before the baby was born. These calls and meetings were always overseen by a social worker. As a result, at the conference where I met Rosalind, presentations were peppered with talk revealing a preoccupation with adoption "scams" and the risks inherent in these increasingly relational investments.

When a relationship, however brief or mediated, is initiated before parental rights are transferred, the potential arises for an increased sense of loss should the transaction fail. For example, one adoptive mother told me in

2009 about the experience of waiting six weeks for a father to sign the papers surrendering his parental rights:

> So, I mean, it was just meant to be. And then it was, like, six weeks of waiting for him to come home. He stayed at the agency while we went there, because the birth father wouldn't sign his parental rights away, and his birth mother did not want to sign her rights away until the birth father did, because . . . we were taking him or she was taking him and that was it.

These complications are not unique to domestic adoption; they also occur in the case of international adoption, but the difference is that prospective parents are matched with a waiting child rather than an expectant birth family. A mother who I met at a suburban "culture camp" for children adopted transracially and internationally explained her reasons for switching mid-process from Bulgaria to Russia because the adoption was taking so long:

> Before I even went on my first trip there was—they have to actually get the parents to sign off, kind of relinquish the child before you go through with your adoption. Before I made my first trip, there was a delay in getting it. You know, they got one parent, they didn't get the other, and I was really trying to be—the whole time—be very, kind of, you know, not, like, not become too attached to this child, always be prepared to say, "Okay, let's move on."

The choppiness of her speech perhaps reflects the difficulty of the situation she recounted, the hesitancy of her attachment to a particular imagined future. She continued:

> And actually, it came to a point where with three or four months, they were saying, "Yes," you know, "We're going to get it, we're working on it." And I kind of came to this decision. I said, "You know what, I don't want to wait, you know, a year and not be—and even then nothing may happen." I said, "Let's, let's start looking at Russia." So they went, I guess the adoption agency told the people in Bulgaria this. I don't know if they had lit a fire under them or who knows whatever it may have done, but then I was prepared to just say, even though, you know, it was a beautiful little girl, and I thought, you know, I can't—this may never happen. So I tried to kind of be—not, like, get my hopes set on something that may never happen. But then eventually it worked out, but I do feel—I don't know if that has anything to do with what you're doing, but to me, I think some, I, I, I really tried to not be the parent who, like, hung on for three years and then it still fell through.

A flurry of smaller risks accompanies the looming possibility of a fall-through: two prominent examples are biomedical / psychological risk (a child born with unforeseen special needs, for example, or a child exposed to certain substances *in utero*) and legal risk (an unknown biological father returning to claim parental rights, for example). The fall-through, however, forecloses the only current possibility of adoptive kinship, inherently necessitating a starting-over. In the beginning stage of the adoption process, prospective adoptive parents attend a series of meetings with their home study social worker, who lays out several scenarios in an effort to inform and prepare parents for these possible futures. Specific technologies have arisen to mitigate these risks, with mixed success. The "beginners" in Rosalind's audience at the conference most likely found themselves in this early stage—"freaking out" about the experience of being in a crash-course in risk management and contingency planning.

Early in 2014, an adoption attorney related the following to me, employing a discourse of legal risk:

> Because prospective adoptive parents have to be, not only honest with the adoption agency, but also with themselves about what is okay and not okay. If they have a birth mom who is actively using alcohol and drugs, or has a mental health history, or is clearly not telling the truth about the birth father, those are all issues that can be legal issues and can lead to heartbreak. Clients can take a risk or not take a risk. I see my job as making sure that they know what that risk is and knowingly making a decision.

Prospective adoptive parents invest in imagined future children, monetarily, temporally, and emotionally, from the initiation of the adoption process onward. As one adoption trainer observed, much of the anxiety around adoption stems from a perception of loss of control among prospective adoptive parents, and there are precious few ways to intervene in the uncertain future that looms on the horizon. Social workers and prospective adopters came up against this lack of control at every stage of the process.

The experience of time—particularly the temporal distortions inherent to waiting, delays, and expectation—is central to the process of private agency adoption in the United States. Adoption at First Steps entailed a great deal of anticipating, forecasting, and sequencing and ordering of events; it was by no means a process characterized by smooth continuity. This dynamic stemmed from adoption's structure as a highly contingent process with a number of volatile moving parts. Rosalind spoke of the "beginner's minds" in her audience, a direct reference to adoption's specific temporal unfolding characterized by a beginning, middle, and end. Beginners found themselves

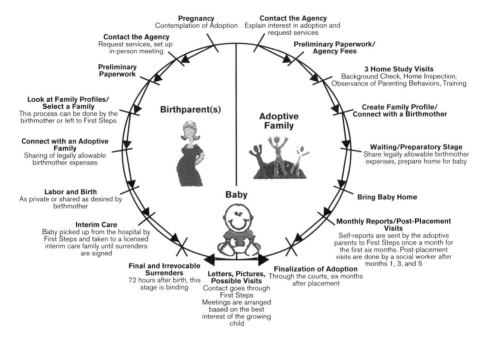

Pregnancy
Contemplation of Adoption

Contact the Agency
Explain interest in adoption and
request services

Contact the Agency
Request services, set up
in-person meeting

Preliminary Paperwork/
Agency Fees

Preliminary
Paperwork

3 Home Study Visits
Background Check, Home Inspection,
Observance of Parenting Behaviors, Training

Look at Family Profiles/
Select a Family
This process can be done by the
birthmother or left to First Steps

Birthparent(s)

Adoptive
Family

Create Family Profile/
Connect with a Birthmother

Connect with an Adoptive
Family
Sharing of legally allowable
birthmother expenses

Waiting/Preparatory Stage
Share legally allowable birthmother
expenses, prepare home for baby

Labor and Birth
As private or shared as desired by
birthmother

Baby

Bring Baby Home

Interim Care
Baby picked up from the hospital by
First Steps and taken to a licensed
interim care family until surrenders
are signed

Monthly Reports/Post-Placement
Visits
Self-reports are sent by the adoptive
parents to First Steps once a month for
the first six months. Post-placement
visits are done by a social worker after
months 1, 3, and 5

Final and Irrevocable
Surrenders
72 hours after birth, this
stage is binding

Letters, Pictures,
Possible Visits
Contact goes through
First Steps
Meetings are arranged
based on the best
interest of the growing
child

Finalization of Adoption
Through the courts, six months
after placement

FIGURE 4. "Adoption at a Glance" diagram used by agency staff to explain the adoption process to clients.

at the start of something. The boundaries between these three ordinal stages were often porous—and the "middle" was by far the most difficult and lengthy part for prospective adopters. In order to think through the adoption process as a temporal journey, let us return to Stella's "Adoption at a Glance" diagram (see figure 4).

That day in the conference room, Stella had sketched out the large bisected circle, explaining, "And so yeah . . . for somebody that, where you wanna break down, or show them where they come in on the process, it's good to know—beginning, middle, ends." She placed her hand flat on the table emphatically with each word, three times, underscoring the narrative and temporal unfolding of the process. Her pluralization of "end" is instructive; it reveals the fact that the adoption process creates different and separate outcomes, different and separate futures, for birth parents, adoptive parents, and child. Adoption is thus a means to multiple and uncertain ends. The smooth circularity of the diagram obscures a series of liminal spaces of waiting and apprehension, with invisible dead-ends and detours winging off in disparate directions. In American adoption, the most potent examples of human engagement with uncertainty through the experience of anxiety, hope, and anticipation materialize in these unmapped, invisible, liminal temporal frames, the in-betweens of the adoption process, constituting a(n always potentially) near future "punctuated" (Guyer 2007) by specifically anticipated—as well as undiagrammed and thus unanticipated—events.

Anderson (2010: 794) observes that "desired futures can be made present through multiple ways of anticipating, welcoming, waiting for or otherwise relating to the future." In particular, paying close attention to the stages of the adoption process reveals how adoption professionals, through their interactions with prospective adoptive parents, construct the process as one characterized by inherent and enduring uncertainty, while at the same time, always forecasting a hopeful and certain endpoint, even in the face of impending failure. Social workers struggled to keep stressed and disillusioned prospective parents *in the process*. The chief desired product of their labor was kinship, after all.

BEGINNING: BATTLING UNCERTAINTY WITH WILL AT THE "FRONT-END"[4]

The daylong conference, "Parenting through Adoption 2013," was coming to a close. Weary adoptive parents and adoption professionals, many of whom had arrived before 8 a.m., had assembled in various rooms for the day's fifth and final round of breakout sessions. Those in the lounge had chosen Rosalind's session over five others covering topics as disparate as civil unions, childhood trauma, raising responsible children, diversity and education, and international adoption homecoming. According to the conference program, this session would equip attendees with mindfulness strategies useful in navigating the adoption process. "Tools will be shared," proclaimed the program, "on how to look beyond the logistical marathon of papers, trainings and appointments to the emotional journey within."

The room quieted as Rosalind introduced herself. She was petite with a slim build and commanding presence, the result of a very dedicated yoga practice. Among her many titles (social worker, counselor, adoption doula, fertility coach) was certified yoga instructor. She wore a blonde bob framing her expressive face and energetic eyes. One could imagine that she was the grown-up version of the little girl in the video clip we had just watched, ebullient and hopeful. After years of infertility treatments, she had recently begun her own adoption journey; she was a prospective adopter herself. After introducing herself, Rosalind spoke briefly about the origins of the workshop, noting that "the terrain of adoption" had become more rugged, which could be discouraging to prospective parents. Countering this atmosphere of despair and projecting a slightly more utopian future, Rosalind grafted certainty onto a landscape of insecurity; "Once your home study is complete, you *will* adopt . . . the child that's meant to be with you *will* find its way to you."[5] This *will*—literally, the future tense of the verb "to be"—has a double character of future temporality and want / desire.[6] The will references a sort of willpower, as if prospective parents, simply by persisting, can will the adoption into reality; it implies that they have some measure of control over the process, even though they will be told over and over again that they do not. This will implies certainty in a highly contingent process; it is the basis of adoptive hope, and its cultivation lies at the heart of much of social workers' efforts during the adoption process.[7]

Adoptive anxiety, on the other hand, stems from temporal uncertainty. Social workers tell parents over and over again that they *will* adopt. The one thing they cannot tell them is when. Rosalind's language, which identifies the child as the acting agent ("will find its way to you"), reflects prospective adoptive parents' perceived lack of control over the adoption process. To locate agency, power, or will in the child-to-be is to live in a speculative future, and to reverse dominant power dynamics. In reality, the (unborn) child does not have any control over the adoption process, as adoptee activists are wont to remind adoptive parents and adoption professionals. Later, Rosalind would relate to hopeful parents the sad fact that between finishing the home study and being united with that child, they may—indeed, were likely to—experience one or more failed attempts. Handouts were distributed with guidelines for several emotion-specific meditations that we would practice together during the session.

The explicit focus of the workshop was mindfulness, defined on a presentation slide by Jon Kabat Zinn, the developer of Mindfulness-Based Stress Reduction, as "the awareness that arises through paying attention, into the present moment, on purpose and non-judgmentally." Rosalind's goal was to help prospective adoptive parents to be more present-minded and "not worried about the past or concerned about the future." Rosalind briefly discussed the benefits of mindfulness, which, she insisted, "allows our anxiety levels to go down, and also helps with the intensity of our feelings." After a hiatus in her twenties, she reported returning to meditative practice in her thirties and forties, noting, "I am so much more calm."

The first meditation strategy we were taught specifically targeted anxiety. Rosalind grounded this emotion in the first meeting with an adoption professional. During this initial meeting, Rosalind noted, prospective adoptive parents are often filled with "tremendous anxiety." The adoption process can be long and arduous, and as Rosalind observed, "you just wanna race through" when it becomes uncomfortable. She stressed the importance of "being mindful and slowing down" at this early stage, and "acknowledging that you're anxious." This was a marathon, not a sprint. Pacing was prudent. "I'm freaking out! I'm *so* nervous," she said, voicing prospective parents. Together, we did a four-part breathing exercise. Rosalind led us, speaking softly:

> Inhale . . .
> Two.
> Three.
> Four.
>
> Hold.
> Two
> Three.
> Four.
>
> Now exhale.
> Two.
> Three.
> Four.
>
> Let's try that again.

The room itself seemed to expand and contract. Anxieties floated away, carried off by the rhythm of the flutes and our collective breathing, if only momentarily. We may not have been able to predict or determine the future, but Rosalind's lesson was that we could manage our own minds and bodies in the present. The adoption process was out of prospective adopters' hands, but the child would find its way.

Certainty projected into the future battles uncertainty, and even despair, in the present. I witnessed—or rather, overheard—another example of the hopeful *will* one day in the office when Stella answered a phone call from a prospective adoptive father who had recently been matched with an expectant mother. The expectant mother had contacted the prospective couple to tell them she would not be placing the baby. Below, I repeat the half of the conversation I was able to hear. The following are all Stella's words:

Hi Darren, how are you?

[Long pause]

Oh nooo. Oh, no . . . she was so definite.

[Pause]

I'm so sorry to hear that.

[Brief pause]

Oh no. Not at the moment, there's no one that's not linked up already. Now, it's been quiet for a while. But I am sure it will reawaken. People come in, so I know it will happen. You know I just don't know when.

[Pause]

Oh . . . I'm so disappointed.

Even things that seemed "definite" were rarely so. This did not prevent social workers from employing the will with conviction. Stella tilted her head to the side with each "Oh." She sighed audibly in response to something said on the other end of the line.

I think we need to look to somebody that's not a long wait. Not a long and bumpy road. I don't think we need to go through another three-month link . . . you've gone through some of those longer roads. If we could just find somebody with a short wait it would be a better fit. Let's just see who comes in the door. Keep that optimism. It is this kind of a process. And I know it's rough.

[Pause]

It is this kind of process, but we're going to get a child. It's gonna happen. We just have to get through the bumps, the potholes, the obstacles, the disappointments. That's part of this process. It just reminds us of how much we don't control, even when we do all the right things, sometimes it just doesn't happen for us.

[Pause]

It doesn't mean it's not gonna happen. Nobody that waits comes away without a baby.

[Pause]

Well you're back in, as of right now, you're in. I'm sorry that you had to feel this, I'm sorry it did not work out, but you are back in the queue, on my list.

[Pause]

There's about twenty-five families. I had thirteen placements in 2013.

[Pause]

We'll go back to the drawing board, and it's gonna happen.

[Pause]

Do not despair, it's gonna happen.

[Brief pause]

Alright, sorry about the news, Darren. Never good to hear that, I know.

The receiver clicked as she placed it back in its cradle with a sigh. Here, Stella uses the journey metaphor implicitly through mention of "bumps," "potholes," and "obstacles" in the road. Similarly, I heard one adoption trainer tell prospective parents, "Adoption is not for the faint-hearted, because you're probably gonna have some bumps in the road." The *will* of Rosalind's discourse shows up in Stella's repetitive reassurance, "I know it will happen." "We're going to get a child." Echoing Rosalind, the message is that if prospective parents wait long enough, an adoption plan *will* succeed. Laboring affectively, Stella revives hope for a future placement amidst devastation and anxiety about the loss of an imagined future. The will is a remedy for despair. A starting over—"back to the drawing board"—was inevitable. But these "bumps" were inherent to the unfolding of adoption. "It is this kind of a process," Stella conceded, repeatedly. This end sent Darren back to the beginning.

At another adoption conference later that year, Beatrice, a smartly dressed adoption counselor and adoptive mother from the Midwest, bluntly cautioned her listeners, "In the adoption process you are out of control. You have no control in this process." There was a sense that prospective parents were careening toward an outcome over which they had no power, in Rosalind's language, a journey with an unknown destination—one that Stella, over the years, had attempted to map with her diagram. "We [adoption professionals]," Beatrice admitted, "don't have that much control either." "I will not be surprised if you gain weight," she said as she discussed the stress of the adoption process.[8] "I will not be surprised if you ask unanswerable questions, because you think knowledge gives you power and control, but it doesn't in the adoption process." Her lack of surprise, however, revealed an enduring sense of certainty, predictability, and continuity within a highly contingent and uncertain process. Uncertainty was the only sure thing. With these words, Beatrice proceeded to lead us through the same breathing exercise Rosalind had used in her workshop ("four-square breathing"). In the contemporary moment, controlling anxiety—in the midst of a process over which one has *no control*—is an integral part of preparing for adoption. Calm, in the absence of control, was another product of social workers' labor, another service rendered. Adoption social workers employed future-oriented discourses of both risk and certainty in an attempt to mitigate the inherent unpredictability of the adoption process.

Social workers often alluded to this lack of control in early informational sessions with those hoping to adopt, in an attempt to shape expectations for the experience to come. Their discourses of certainty and uncertainty often contradicted one another. "Let's face it," said Dotty to a group of prospective parents during an evening informational session. "We don't have a lot of control over anything anyway. There's no guarantees here." Like Beatrice's contradictory comments above about the particular certainties of the process embedded within larger structures of unpredictability, Dotty's frank admission of a lack of guarantees flies in the face of Stella's and Rosalind's adoptive will. At one adoption training, after the trainer (an adoptive mother herself) admitted, "I didn't like not having a due date," a prospective parent in the audience said, "It's like an arranged marriage," referencing the lack of control over match and outcome. Prospective adoptive parents are entering into a social relationship with an expectant mother in the service of interests partially outside—perhaps even at odds with—their own. Social workers claim to orchestrate adoptions in the "best interest of the child," and power is perceived to rest with the social worker and the expectant mother. The will of adoptive hope, sitting at the nexus of time and desire, serves to provide a modicum of certainty and control in a process pervaded by uncertainty. As Stella struggled to assure Darren, "nobody that waits comes away without a baby."

MIDDLE: THE IM / POSSIBILITY OF PREPARATION DURING "THE WAIT"

As Rosalind's conference workshop progressed, attendees learned additional breathing exercises for dealing with stress during the home study process and impatience during the inevitable waiting period between completing the application requirements and home study and being matched with a child, natively referred to as "The Wait." Waiting, noted Rosalind, would be the hardest part. Like the little girl on the train platform, prospective parents would need to "let one foot dance, and the other stay grounded," thus tempering their affective engagement. Dreams of the future had to remain rooted in the realities of unpredictability. One strategy Rosalind presented for managing stress during The Wait was to get a journal, and "start communicating with your future child . . . How can I prepare for you?"

A contradiction began to arise between Rosalind's initial emphasis on mindfulness and being present in the moment, and the realities of the adoption process, which seemed to require an ever-present vigilance toward an uncertain future. Finally, Rosalind noted, these prospective adopters would "get The Call." A child would be ready. But would the prospective parents? A few months into her process, Annette received an unexpected call about a born baby available for adoption, but she turned down the referral—it was too soon. She had been preparing herself for a two-year wait, and she simply "wasn't ready":

> And then I got a call on basically Friday that she wanted to speak to me, and we had discussed that that might actually happen, and I was absolutely fine with that. So I spoke to her on Friday, the birth mom, at, like, four o—four in the afternoon, and I got the call back, like, five minutes later that said, "She's yours." And I'm like, "Okay. What does 'she's yours' mean?" She was alive, had been born. Um, "She'll be ready on Sunday."
>
> And I, I, I panicked. I, I couldn't, I just couldn't get my head around it. I was, I freaked out. Um, and maybe, you know, I know the other family—I couldn't get, somehow, you know, the other parents, the other adoptive parents were able to step right in, but I'm one person. I literally, like, I had just changed—I hadn't changed jobs, but my manager had changed. I hadn't even had communications really with anyone except for my family on that plan. Obviously I've fixed that now. Um, I, I just panicked. Um, it, like, literally I spent a week just kind of processing all of it. It was very hard. It was probably one of the hardest things besides, you know, deaths and things that are so permanent, one of those, I've worked so hard to get to that point, and then it came up, and I was, I couldn't, I couldn't do it.

Annette contrasts the permanence of death—she had lost her husband in an accident several years earlier—to the loss of a missed opportunity; this was an end, but it was not *the* end. "Nobody is prepared," said Rosalind to the workshop participants, indexing the futility of attempted preparedness. "What?!?! Today?!? Oh, God!" To end the session, we all practiced another breathing exercise. Rosalind handed out a flyer for a support group for "women growing their families through adoption." One of the sessions was titled "How to Thrive While You Wait."

Through trainings, conferences, and meetings with their social workers, prospective adoptive parents are armed for the battle against a perpetual sense of unpreparedness. Rosalind's admission that parents are never really prepared was echoed by Dotty, in an exchange we had while she was setting up for her adoption information session. She asked why I wanted to attend the session, and I told her that I was particularly interested in how social workers prepared prospective parents for adoption. She rolled her eyes emphatically and laughed, "They're never prepared! Never are they prepared. No matter how much training, they're never really prepared." There seemed to be a sense that one could only strive to be less unprepared. The future loomed so uncertain that preparedness was impossible to achieve. Drawing on her social work expertise and personal experience, Dotty offered, "I'm just telling you from decades of experience, you can be training forever, but you can't prepare people fully for what's going to happen, and we don't know what's going to happen." Experience became comfort with a lack of knowledge and control.

At Dotty's informational session, she spoke at length about navigating The Wait. She started the session by quickly listing the three questions that "everyone is secretly wondering": How long do we wait? What kinds of kids are available? And how much does it cost? "While you're busy and getting all your paperwork together, it's easy," she said. "It's when your paperwork is done and you're waiting. The mark of maturity is the ability to accept life's uncertainties . . . It's hard to wait. It's very hard," she said, shaking her head. "It can be anywhere between eighteen months and two-and-a-half years. You're not going to have a baby right away." Or perhaps you are, as in the case of Annette; that scenario creates its own problems. In general, prospective adoptive parents were told to prepare to wait a length of time equivalent to no less than two full-term pregnancies, and up to a little over three. As I mentioned above in response to Lynn's characterization of the process as high-risk, adoption is perceived by some prospective adoptive parents as a form of protracted pregnancy (Howell 2006). "You just need to, in your mind, say, 'It's going to be a year or two,'" Dotty finished, cautioning the prospective parents to temper their expectations with the certainty of a lengthy wait. At the end of the session, she reiterated, "The kinds of people who don't do well in domestic programs are the ones that really have problems with anxiety and waiting."

At this stage in the process, Barbara always cautioned parents against buying items for the baby. "Why?" she asked, quizzing the prospective parents. "Because they get recalled," she answered her own question bluntly. Parents were told not to buy a car seat or crib in preparation because it would probably get recalled before they brought their baby home. The temporality of product safety was out of sync with the temporality of adoption. Barbara and other home study workers routinely cautioned prospective parents against making unnecessary investments. She would often lay out a timeline of when it would be okay to tell relatives, paint the nursery ("but for God's sake, don't buy the crib yet"), throw a baby shower, buy diapers, and so on. Adamant about this form of preemptive minimalism, she told one prospective couple, "So if you think about it, newborns, they don't move around a lot. They need diapers and formula, buy a car seat, and a small place to sleep. So could be a pack-and-play, could be a bassinet. That's about it, with a few sleepers." This is a form of minimal preparation or nonpreparation; prepare as little as possible, to mitigate the risk of things not going according to plan.

At the end of Beatrice's conference presentation, a practitioner in the audience asked her for tips to help prospective adoptive parents cope with The Wait. Voicing one of these parents-in-waiting and referencing the temporal distortion embedded in the act and experience of waiting, she said, "We've been waiting one month and it feels like three."[9] Beatrice took this opportunity to reframe The Wait as an opportunity to prepare for parenting, suggesting that social workers treat The Wait as a period of productive anticipation—a way to regain some semblance of control over the process. Beatrice echoed Rosalind: prospective parents cannot control what might happen in the future, but they can control what they are doing *now,* in the present.

An interaction I observed during an initial home study meeting at First Steps further solidifies the cession of control required of prospective adoptive parents during The Wait. Corinne had spent nearly thirty minutes reviewing and explaining all of the preliminary paperwork for Jack and Brielle's home study. As she laid out a timeline of requirements and events, she sighed, "And, from this point on, so for the home study portion of it? *I* will be working at *your* pace." She paused seeking affirmation from the would-be parents. "Which is kind of the only time that you guys will really have control, over time, during this process," she finished. "Right," Brielle said. Corinne continued, "So if you guys work quickly, I will work quickly with you." Unfortunately for Jack and Brielle, once the home study was complete, so was Corinne's work, and with it ended any hope of timeliness. Timelines, process steps, and temporal reference points would also dissolve—in contrast to the neatly paced and marked-out picture drawn by Stella—as the couple entered the protracted stage of The Wait. The Wait did not end with a match either. One prospective adoptive couple, after being matched with expectant mother Fiona, wrote an email to Stella saying, "Now we are expecting and waiting with Fiona," echoing again the experience of adoptive pregnancy, and the multivalence of expectation within the adoption process. Another prospective adoptive mother told me that she had booked a trip to Europe but then wondered if it was appropriate for her to leave during this waiting period. "You never know when it might happen," she explained. "I guess I'll just fly back if I have to."

Another ethnographic example serves to illustrate the centrality of The Wait and its attendant uncertainties. In March of 2014, I attended a large adoption training conference in the San Francisco Bay Area. The keynote presentation consisted of three personal and artistic performances by members of the adoption triad: a birth mother, an adoptive mother, and an adoptee. The adoptive mother was Julia Jackson, a comedian and playwright who performed an act of her one-woman play about adoption, entitled *Children Are Forever—All Sales Final.* She performed the following piece, from the section "Amy in Group," to an auditorium filled with adoptive parents, adult adoptees, birth parents, and adoption practitioners:

> Hello. My name is Amy . . . and I do not like to speak in public—in groups. It makes me entirely too nervous. I've been coming here for six consecutive Thursdays, but I haven't spoken yet. I've been listening though. I'm more of an observer. My therapist gently suggested that I raise my hand and start participating more, so. I just wanted to introduce myself to the group.
>
> My week was good. My partner and I signed up at an adoption agency. It's a path forward.
>
> I *am* excited. I guess I'm just more of a cautious person.
>
> There actually are quite a few things to be cautious about. I didn't know that you don't get to choose the baby you want. The birth mother picks you and you just have to wait.
>
> It makes me feel like . . . Well, it's as if someone has taken you by the hand and led you out into the middle of nowhere and says, "Wait right here, do not move, there's a bus coming." And then they leave. And you don't know if that bus is coming in five minutes or five years. It might never come. This whole process just seems so loose.

Buses with uncertain arrivals and trains with uncertain destinations. Jackson's abbreviated performance (the excerpt above is only a small part) was received with laughter and thundering applause by those in attendance. Her fictional account, based loosely on her own experience as an adoptive mother, throws into sharp relief the sense of uncertainty and potential interminability that characterizes The Wait. It also references an awareness of possible failure: that the bus "might never come." Control is located in the expectant mother: "The birth mother picks you and you just have to wait." Structural and material realities of power and agency are skewed by individual experiences of relative powerlessness.

Jackson's bus metaphor was perhaps inspired by a scene from the Showtime drama *The L Word* (2004–09); if not, they surely share a common ancestor. Longtime lesbian couple Bette and Tina have one child by alternative insemination, and are hoping to adopt a second. In one episode, the couple meets with an expectant mother from Nevada and agrees to bring her to Los Angeles to live with them in the final weeks of her pregnancy. They await her arrival eagerly. At a bus station. Tina has a bouquet of flowers. The bus arrives. Passengers stream off. Marci, the expectant mother, is not among them. "Maybe she fell asleep on the bus," Bette offers, climbing aboard as the last few passengers disembark. Hope is slowly draining from the scene. The viewer already knows how this ends. Marci is not on the bus. So not only might the bus never come, it might arrive, but be empty. The absence of birth and expectant mothers—and by extension, imagined children—is not merely an ethnographic fact; it is a phenomenon that gets reproduced in popular portrayals of adoption. It is a feature, rather than a glitch, of the process. And a source of much anxiety among prospective adoptive parents.

As the examples above illustrate, the characteristic temporal mode of the American adoption process is waiting. And contrary to how it might seem, The Wait is only one—the primary one—of *several* periods of waiting. The rest of the adoption process is interspersed with smaller waits (indeed, wait with a lowercase w), the most difficult (but also usually the shortest) perhaps being the time that must pass between the birth of the child and the mother's signing of the irrevocable surrenders, 72 hours in Illinois. In addition, prospective adoptive parents faced with infertility may wait years to conceive before even considering adoption.[10] Some single individuals may spend years waiting for the "right" co-parent before deciding to parent alone, as was the case for several single adoptive mothers I encountered. Prospective parents wait, with time always running out—due to social factors, biology, and policy. At First Steps, for example, the sum of a prospective couple's ages could not exceed 100 if they were interested in domestic adoption.[11] Once the adoption process is initiated, prospective parents wait for their home study approval (normally 3 to 6 months), wait to be matched with an expectant mother or child (anywhere from 18 to 24 months—although occasionally much sooner, as in the case of Annette), wait for the birth (if applicable), wait for parental rights to be terminated (no less than 72 hours after the birth), and then wait for the adoption to be finalized (6 months after placement). The primacy of The Wait among prospective adopters was reflected throughout the adoption community, such as in the now-defunct online boutique Adoption Bug, which offered ladies' fitted tees (notably nonmaternity) for prospective adoptive mothers screen-printed with the phrase "Mom-To-Be: Just Waiting to Find Out When!," and onesies for adopted babies emblazoned with "Worth the Wait!"

This perpetual engagement with waiting is not unique to prospective adoptive parents. Newly pregnant, expectant mothers wait for the time they will feel able to make an adoption plan, wait for support, wait to be "pregnant enough" to be matched, wait for a suitable family, wait for social workers to deliver (money, paperwork, counseling, etc.), wait to go into labor (which entails its own micro forms of waiting—waiting to go to the hospital, waiting for the contractions to quicken, waiting for a predetermined dilation, waiting to be able to "push"), wait for the birth, wait for the obstetrician to proclaim the infant's health, wait for the surrenders, wait to say goodbye, wait for letters and updates, maybe wait for the day when they will see their child again.

While their waiting is built into the routine established by their bureaucratic position, and as a result perhaps carries a different affective dimension (Kaufman 2005), social workers also spend a great deal of time waiting. They wait for new potential adoptive parents to show interest (the existence of the agency depended, in part, on them), wait for pregnant mothers (who were not always readily available), wait for subsequent contact from expectant mothers, wait outside of houses and shelters for expectant mother meetings, wait to start paperwork until expectant mothers are ready, wait for prospective adoptive parent paperwork and payments, wait for the birth, wait for the signing of the surrenders. It is no surprise that the refrain commonly voiced by social workers at the completion of a home study was, "And now we wait."

One morning in the summer of 2009, Stella and I went to a neighborhood on the South Side of the city to obtain final and irrevocable surrenders from a new mother, Jenna. As mandated by Illinois law, Jenna could not sign surrenders until at least 72 hours had passed since the birth, revealing an implicit state-generated temporal logic of kinship dissolution that assumed rational decision-making could be accomplished only outside an arbitrarily determined temporal window. The 72-hour rule also functioned as a tool of indemnity, protecting the agency and new adoptive parents from a birth mother's claims that she was not allowed sufficient time to make her decision. Jenna had picked the baby up from the hospital the day before and spent the night with her at a shelter. When we arrived, she emerged from the shelter carrying a small bundle wrapped in a pink blanket. Stella drove us to a nearby McDonald's, where she bought Jenna lunch.

There was always an uncomfortable "settling-in" period at the beginning of a visit, when Stella waited for the appropriate time to suggest getting started on the paperwork. Filling out forms caused the interaction to feel more like an exchange. Documents and signatures had a way of stripping away a moment's intimacy. Jenna snuggled the newborn and kissed her face, cooing repeatedly, "Don't steal my kisses"—a phrase which could just as easily have been directed at Stella as the baby. Jenna held her daughter for the duration of the meeting, even as she signed away her parental rights, her left hand gingerly supporting the baby's head, her right neatly penning her initials and signature. Embracing the child that was finally in the world rather than her womb, as she completed in a matter of minutes the legal and symbolic action that had been in process for the last several months. Physically swiping ink onto paper, legally relinquishing her rights to parent the child in her arms, her signature on the binding forms thus dissolving her legal kinship tie to the child, even as her social and physical connections endured. Halfway through the signing, Jenna stopped to feed the baby, halting the process momentarily. Paperwork could wait—legal futures could be avoided, prolonged—babies, once immediate and alive, could not. Stella waited patiently. On our way to take Jenna home, we stopped briefly at a grocery store where Jenna picked out a pacifier for the baby, and then Stella dropped her back off at the shelter, this time childless. On the drive back to the agency, signed surrenders in hand and infant tucked snuggly into a car seat, Stella called the adoptive parents, who had been doing their own waiting, with the good news.

Waiting in adoption is a bureaucratic necessity, but also a function of supply and demand: at First Steps prospective adoptive parents were facing increasingly long wait times as expectant mothers willing to relinquish became more and more scarce, putting increasing pressure on social workers laboring as brokers.[12] Social workers' common references to—and prescribed correctives for—parental anxiety suggest that the waiting inherent to the adoption process profoundly shaped the ways in which prospective parents engaged with the process affectively.[13] My time at First Steps revealed the liminal states of adoption, between being a prospective parent and becoming a parent, and the central role of waiting in filling those liminal states. Kaufman (2005) explores the space between life and death, which she identifies as a "zone of indistinction," and the ways in which it is actively produced by processes of waiting. In the American hospital, anticipation of death and hope for recovery bring the future crashing into the present moment. Kaufman observes that for patients and families, waiting entails the layering of anticipation, hope, and dread. "The anticipation is born of incomplete understanding on a journey of uncertainty," she argues, echoing Rosalind's discourse of the journey, ". . . and they always hope while they wait" (148). Here, an inherent link between waiting and hope is established that mirrors the affective attachment to the future witnessed in American practices of adoption—particularly during The Wait. Upon committing to adoption, at once there is a feeling of immobilization and being thrust forward, in which hope is the positive face of anticipation and dread its negative. Prospective parents find themselves in one of Kaufman's "gray areas": between the birth of "their" child and a symbolic miscarriage.

For Kaufman (2005: 149), temporally and affectively, the moments of waiting are distinguishable from the moments after waiting, but in American adoption, the process is one largely characterized by different types of waiting, punctuated by these rare "moments after waiting," which almost inevitably bleed into another wait. It might even be said that in the adoption process, the moments after waiting are simply additional waits. The fall-through complicates this further, as a true zone of indistinction: there was no codified protocol at First Steps for dealing with a fall-through. As street-level bureaucrats (Lipsky 2010), social workers made the call of a failed adoption after waiting for a presumably "lost" expectant mother to get back in touch. How long would the social worker wait? How many times would she try to contact the expectant mother before notifying the hopeful adoptive family that their current arrangement had failed? In these moments of ambiguity (which were frequent at First Steps) hope often fought for life in the face of terrible odds and a lack of closure that left future possibilities at once painfully and hopefully open.[14] An affective attachment remained fixed to "the one that got away."[15] In American adoption, the common practice of waiting (while attempting to map certainty onto an uncertain future) exposes the affective reality of hope's entanglements with anticipation, through which the future is made present today. The affective experience of anticipation created through the common practice of waiting provides the context in which these parents-in-waiting actively "reckon" not only with risk (Herman 2008), but also with uncertainty and contingency.

Adoption professionals' framing of and attendance to prospective adoptive parents' anxieties are not confined to the beginning and middle stages of the adoption process. These anxieties extend into the future through (dis)placement and beyond. As I exited Rosalind's conference session, I passed through the exhibitor hall, where various area adoption resources (attorneys, agencies, therapeutic services, and other similar supports) were represented by booths lining the walls of the cramped lobby and a labyrinth of attached hallways. An area "adoption clinic," which offered pre- and post-adoption medical and behavioral services, had a booth, and visitors were greeted by a large glossy poster with a blue background and simple white text that read, "Keep Calm and Call the Center for Adoption Medicine." The poster mimicked a popular revival of a particular piece of British World War II memorabilia: a propaganda poster, first produced in 1939 to assuage anxieties caused by wartime disaster. The poster in question originally had a red background with simple white sans serif text reading "Keep Calm and Carry On" beneath the white silhouette of a metonymic crown. It was never actually publicly released, "intended for use only in times of crisis or invasion" (Barter Books 2012). In 2000, a copy of the poster was discovered in a used bookstore in Alnwick, Northumberland, called Barter Books, and since then has been taken up by popular culture, reproduced, disseminated, and parodied to the extent that it won a spot on *Huffington Post*'s list of "10 Décor Trends We're Done With in 2013" (Manetti 2012). Its resonance with the American public, to the point of oversaturation, illustrates a moment of widespread anxiety. During my fieldwork, Americans literally required—and enjoyed—posters in our offices, mugs in our kitchens, pencils in our hands, and throw pillows on our therapy couches urging us not only to calm down, but to march on toward an unknown horizon. By 2015, the slogan and its infinite variations could be found gracing stationary, mouse pads, Band-Aids, T-shirts, and iPhone cases. In early 2017, a Google image search revealed a resurgence of Keep Calm images referencing Donald Trump.

Upon seeing the poster, I was immediately reminded of a large bright orange sign about a block from my Chicago apartment. It read: "Take a Deep Breath. You're Here Now. Chicago Animal ER." The message of calmness in the face of grave emergency was clear in both signs, as well as in Rosalind's talk. *Don't freak out. It's going to be alright. Whatever you do, don't forget to breathe.* As if the adoption process were akin to an airplane's loss of cabin pressure, and the measures taken by social workers and other adoption professionals to allay parental fears were like metaphorical oxygen masks.[16] *Breathe normally, for even though the bag may not inflate, oxygen is flowing. Even though the process is long and arduous, and you may actually fail, if you keep at it, you will successfully adopt someday.* Oxygen won't save you, though, from the impending impact if your plane is actually falling out of the sky. When I asked Marlie, the adoption clinic's business manager, how she came up with the idea for the Keep Calm poster, she told me that "it just seemed to fit," since the clinic staff were planning to serve tea and cake at the conference, a nod to the poster's British origins. What she neglected to mention was another reason the message on the poster seemed so appropriate, one so well-known among adoption professionals that it seemed too obvious to state: the pervasive anxiety that the adoption process engenders in those who adopt. The clinic's Keep Calm poster at once diagnosed disease—the notion that "disaster is incubating" (Cooper 2006: 119), literally, in WWII Europe *and* in the bodies of what you hope will be your future children—and a kind of dis-ease (Rapp, Heath, and Taussig 2001), the anxiety against which Rosalind had just attempted to arm us. Just as British civilians were urged to press on in the face of fear and alarm, prospective adoptive parents were urged to consult expert resources and to breathe deeply, for a child—victory—waited at the culmination of the battle, if they could just survive the process. Rather than the physical threats of bullets or explosions, prospective parents faced the emotional threat of anxiety and heartbreak. The threat of the loss of future kinship.

As this chapter has illustrated, there are legitimate causes for all this anxiety. The constant reminders to "relax" and "keep calm" are necessary to soothe a range of prospective parent fears: that their home study will not be approved, that the child they receive will have some unexpected deficit or special need, that their decision to adopt will not be embraced by their friends and family, even that the adoption itself will fail or "fall-through" before it is finalized and that their wait will extend into a childless future. The potential for these negative outcomes, and participants' perceived lack of control over them, has contributed to the notion of adoption as a risky enterprise. Adoption conferences and trainings at times become anxiety provoking, even fear mongering, in their attempts to prepare prospective parents for these bumps along the road to adoption. At one particularly alarming training on fetal alcohol spectrum disorders (FASD), the trainer told prospective parents, "It depends on what day it was [that the mother consumed alcohol], what brain cells were developing, and what got dinked."[17] This trainer's pseudoscientific perspective reinforced a sense of uncertainty and lack of control, painting the effects of exposure as randomized risk. The rising anxiety associated with middle-class parenting has been interrogated at length, and helpfully put into context through an exploration of Beck's (1992) "risk society" in which solidarity arises from a shared sense of anxiety (Cucchiara 2013). But, we might ask, what about would-be parents? How might we characterize their persistent anxieties, not about *how* they parent, but *if* they *will* parent at all? Prospective adoptive parents constitute a very heterogeneous group, but they are united by a common end: a desired child. The fall-through threatened to foreclose this desired end.

. . .

end, n. An intended result of an action; an aim, purpose.[18]

. . .

The fall-through was a kind of disruption, one often precipitated by the absence of the expectant mother. In her study of "disrupted lives," anthropologist Gay Becker investigated the ways in which people make order out of chaos when unexpected events alter predicted life paths. "Such disruptions represent loss of the future," she observes (1997: 4). In adoption parlance, the term "disruption" refers to a situation in which an adopted child is removed from a family after placement. The etymology of disruption is conceptually useful here. It stems from the Latin *rumpere,* which means to break, with the prefix *dis-* (apart). So to disrupt is to break apart. The word shares its Latin root with terms like rupture, abrupt, interrupt, irruption, erupt (Ayto 2006). The Latin root has a Proto-Indo-European origin in *reup,* which means to snatch; it is where we get the English verb "to rip" (Harper 2018). From the perspective of social workers and prospective adoptive parents, in the case of disruption, something was snatched away.

A disruption was perceived by social workers as the worst possible outcome of the adoption process, the ultimate failure, a traumatic reversal of the permanency adoption aims to produce. But what happens when the adoption fails *before* the child is placed, or even before the child is born? The line between these befores and afters is anything but sharp. In these situations—which usually resulted from a mother's decision to parent, rather than place, her child—a future was also lost. To avoid confusion with post-placement disruption, social workers at First Steps referred to this pre-placement collapse as a "fall-through," but it was no less disruptive for waiting prospective adoptive parents and the social workers tasked with supporting them through the losses it entailed.

As was evident in the phone call between Stella and Darren, in the event of most fall-throughs, prospective adoptive families were left without closure, and social workers counseled them through the loss, akin to a social miscarriage, as they tried to understand and justify what had happened.[19] When Barbara first met with Tim and Erin, she attempted to educate them about the emotional risks of a fall-through:

> So obviously we have no control over a birth mom's decision, right? We can encourage her, support her, help her in any way we can, sometimes even financially, but in the end it's her decision. So if you're linked before a birth, what do you think happens? The minute you get that call and it's like, "Oh, she chose you. She liked your profile. She wants to meet you?" I mean, emotionally?

In the end it's her decision. This discourse of lack of control was common among social workers, as this chapter has shown. Barbara's reference here ties lack of control specifically to the expectant mother's decision, casting her as unpredictable at best, unruly at worst. This move is pedagogical. Barbara is teaching the prospective adopters what to worry about.

The couple nodded at Barbara's questions, and she continued, referring to a hypothetical emotional investment, "You've already started to bond with that child. It may already seem like it's really going to be—this child's going to be a part of your family, and you already start thinking ahead." The child does not exist yet; the adoption process produces the imagined child as a future, the product of "thinking ahead."[20] "Mm-hmm," said Erin. Barbara continued, voicing the couple, "'Okay, let's see, I'll let my boss know. I gotta take time off, gotta get the room ready.' Baby's born. You meet her. Maybe you're even at the hospital. She's got—is it 72 hours, Kate? I think it is. She has 72 hours to decide if she's going to sign." "Or longer," I offered, indicating that 72 hours was the legal minimum. "Or longer," Barbara agreed. "Minimum." Barbara's tendency to check in with me about these details indicated her distance from the processing of expectant parents, which was primarily handled by Stella. She went on,

And the baby's ready to go home from the hospital and what we do, if the baby's healthy and can go home the day after the birth, the baby goes into an interim care home for a few days. But during that time Mom could be home. She could still be in the hospital—probably not; I don't think they usually discharge the baby before the mom unless there's complications. But anyways, she still has that time, and you're waiting. You've gone out and got the car seat. Your family knows, right? And then she says, "I'm the parent." So it's—I don't know if it's—some people say, well, it's like having a miscarriage. I think it's almost worse than that, because you've seen her. Maybe you've seen the baby. You know, and it's like, the baby's not gone, it's still alive, right?

She still has that time, and you're waiting. Barbara's speech faltered in describing the loss; a sudden hypothetical disruption reverberated discursively. As Barbara mentions, during the time between birth and the signing of surrenders, newborns usually went into "interim care," the name of which indexes a particular type of liminal temporality, time intervening. An interim care home was simply a foster family that would care for the child until the surrenders were signed; this was a strategy for tempering further investment in a child who was not yet "legally free" for adoption. Barbara's miscarriage analogy—as well as her language around visibility and her use of the euphemism "gone"—reflects the stakes of these investments and exchanges, as well as the politics of erasure inherent to adoption.

Barbara was doing very important work to shape Tim and Erin's expectations around the potential ends of the adoption process. The prospective parents nodded, shifting in their seats, as Barbara continued:

But it's not going home with you, so that's a potential, and it can happen, and there's no guarantee to say at any point that we have a certain placement. Probably the only time I have to say that it's less likely that it will go the other way is if the mom's in the hospital, hasn't talked to anybody before, gives birth, and knows at that moment there's no way she's going to take that child home, because she can't. Usually we call those "born babies," now, they're all born, but it's a "born baby." We get the call, and that birth mom's probably going to place.

Barbara's language of potential and probability reflects the speculative nature of the adoption process. She echoed Dotty's discourse of certain uncertainty with the statement, "there's no guarantee."

We've had people, you know, have had—well, we call it a fall-through, if you planned on it and it doesn't happen, and we've had families say, after a fall-through, "I think I'll just wait for a born baby next time. I don't know that I can go through this build-up and this loss, it's too much, right?" And that's fine. I've had families that have gone through maybe two or three fall-throughs, and they still want to be linked before the birth. That's just their decision to do that. Um, I've had families that never had a link before a birth. They've only had a call.

Social workers found this type of explanation necessary to prepare prospective parents for the disappointment of a fall-through. No matter the outcome, the adoption process entails a going-through. As evidenced by Stella's phone conversation earlier in this chapter, as brokers, social workers have to be effective in counseling people through these situations, so that they "remain in the game," so to speak.

One mother, who had suffered a fall-through before adopting successfully, explained that she was at work when she got the call from Stella that the expectant mother with whom she and her husband had been matched had decided not to place the baby. She left work weeping, and when her coworkers—who had been following the process and were also emotionally invested in its outcome—found out later that day, they also left work for the rest of the day. Another couple, who—against the advice of Stella—had filled a nursery with items for the baby, upon hearing of their first fall-through (they had multiple), went away to Canada for several days to be alone and mourn. Stella wondered aloud how difficult it would have been to remain in the house with all of the baby things, material reminders of a hoped-for future, unrealized.

In August of 2010, when an expectant mother became unreachable, the prospective adoptive family waited in Pennsylvania, car packed, for Stella's OK to drive the twelve hours to Chicago. Several weeks later, the mother had not been located and her due date had passed. Stella's reluctance to allow the family to make the long trip to Chicago prematurely is an example of her practice of risk management. This type of travel by adoptive families involves a considerable emotional and financial investment (not unlike purchasing a nursery's worth of baby items), which if undertaken too hastily may not result in any kind of positive return. Quite the opposite in fact; it may end in loss. Adoptive families from outside the Chicago area, therefore, were only encouraged to travel after the surrenders had been signed, and the baby was made available for legal kinship. This policy, enforced by First Steps' social workers, helped adoptive families avoid the unnecessary expense of money, time, and emotional energy for a future that would never be.

The three days between the birth of a child and the signing of surrenders were often a very stressful and precarious time for agency workers and the prospective adoptive family. The tension present was akin to the apprehensive energy that slowly brewed over the last two or three months of a pregnancy compounded and condensed into three days. During this time, the baby was no longer a potentiality, but a real living being, a real daughter or son who, for the prospective adoptive family, was always haunted by the specter of a mother who "changed her mind." However, Stella had observed that more often than not, if the expectant mother stayed in contact with the agency up through the birth of the baby, she would continue on with the adoption process. These kinds of "odds" (and ends) were one way that uncertainty was transformed into calculable risk.[21] Notions of probability based on personal experience and observation allowed Stella to concretize in a sense the highly precarious and subjective experience of expectant / birth-motherhood and pre-placement.

Several international adopters cited the possibility of a fall-through and the failed emotional investment that came with it as a reason for choosing international adoption over domestic, a way to avoid the stress, trauma, devastation, and disappointment of a fall-through.[22] One adoptive mother compared a domestic fall-through to the previous unexplained death of her biological seven-week-old infant:

> We quickly chose not to do domestic because of all that we'd been through with our daughter's death. We were afraid if a birth mother chose us and changed her mind, which I absolutely think she has the right to, like, totally believe in that … But we felt like we couldn't go through the trauma of another loss, that this program—an international program—seemed more predictable.

Despite an awareness of a mother's "right" to choose to parent her child—a sentiment echoed by many prospective adopters—this adoptive mother locates the unpredictability of contingency in the domestic expectant mother. In comparing the hypothetical fall-through to the trauma of her daughter's death, she gestured toward the kind of preemptive kinship that begins to form between a match and the final outcome of the adoption. When asked how she narrowed her search to China, another mother responded:

To China? Well, we decided against domestic adoption because we felt that it was more of a competition, you know, and we would put ourselves out there and then if the birth mother decided that, you know, it chose us, and then it would just be too stressful for us if she decided at the end, which is her right, you know, to say "No." We just felt that that was too much of a stress for us. We felt that China was pretty straightforward, and we knew after the process that, you know, at the end we would have a child, you know, and we would be able to build our family.

At the end we would have a child . . . our family. A mother adopting from Guatemala voiced a similar rationale:

I think that more importantly, after going through fertility for four years, just being devastated time and time again, like, with all the fertility treatment, a couple miscarriages, like, I don't think we could handle maybe being picked by a birth family, getting close to her and then maybe having that fall through. And we would never blame a birth mom for making that choice because that has to be—I can't imagine a decision harder than that. Really, you know, I mean, that is, we're so grateful to our children's birth parents for having that courage. But we couldn't blame her for changing her mind, but we just were not prepared to deal with that. You know, and, um, so that was probably the key factor in, in making that decision. We just, mainly because of all the disappointments we'd faced in the four years before that, we just couldn't handle any more than that.

This mother's repetition of maybe—"maybe being picked by a birth family," "maybe having that fall through"—reflects the "looseness" of the process to which Julia Jackson referred. There is so much uncertainty. This mother's account also highlights the ways in which contingency in adoption mirrors contingency across other modes of reproduction, such as assisted reproductive technologies.

Many prospective adoptive parents, particularly first-timers like those who attended Rosalind's mindfulness workshop, are on a quest to fulfill the culturally sanctioned American Dream of a "happy family." The "happy" in this happy family is premised upon the existence of a child or children. According to this common cultural narrative, childless couples or individuals (due to infertility, choice, sexual orientation, or other reasons) constitute a portrait of an unhappy family—indeed, no family at all—as well as a threat to a national future.[23] In his seminal cultural analysis of American kinship, David Schneider (1980) observed the necessity to reproduce as being at the heart of American family formation, and more recently, scholars have commented upon the heteronormative drive of "reproductive futurism" (Edelman 2004) and the "unhappy queer" who fails to continue the family line (Ahmed 2010).[24] Lee Edelman (2004: 4) critiques the "pervasive invocation of the Child as the emblem of futurity's unquestioned value," whose origin lies always in the specter of heterosexual conception.[25]

For Sara Ahmed (2010), happiness is ends-oriented; like hope it is an affective orientation toward the future. As she points out, etymologically, the very "hap" in happy is the hap of contingency, chance, fortune, fate, and luck (30)— the same "hap" of happenstance, haphazard, and hapless (not necessarily adjectives common in the mainstream discourse of American family planning). Happiness for Ahmed is also intentional, that is, it is directed toward an object. Stressing the temporality of happiness as future-oriented affect, she contends:

> If objects provide a means for making us happy, then in directing ourselves toward this or that object we are aiming somewhere else: toward a happiness that is presumed to follow. The temporality of this following does matter. Happiness is what would come after. Given this, happiness is directed toward certain objects, which point toward that which is not yet present. When we follow things, we aim for happiness, as if happiness is what we get if we reach certain points. (34)

For prospective adoptive parents, the imagined future child is a happy object—both in the sense that the child is imagined to be happy to be adopted, happy to have new parents, but also in the sense that through the child as an end, the prospective parents imagine they will be made happy.[26] A problem—disappointment—arises for would-be parents, however, if an imagined future is not fulfilled; indeed, as Ahmed suggests, disappointment requires an imagined future happiness. In this way, happiness and disappointment in the adoption process can be seen to map onto hope and despair as affective states that are mutually, dialectically constituted, but not always in opposition to one another. Complicating this affective portrait is the fact that prospective adoptive parents so often derive happiness from a(n) object / subject—the child—that at the same time may be a source of despair for a(n) expectant / birth mother. One's utopia is another's dystopia. Anxiety stemming from childlessness has an *other*: anxiety stemming from being *with* child.[27] Adoption is a singular end for both of these anxieties. Brokerage is sustained by this dynamic; fulfilling both ends of the transaction seems like a win-win. The affective stakes are high in the adoption process where imagined futures are in constant flux and inherently at-risk.[28]

CONCLUSION: "BECAUSE YOU'LL BE TOGETHER"

As a form of intimate speculation, the adoption process moves ever forward, with its attendant fits and starts, toward a future with or without a child, like a train rumbling down the tracks. As I listened to Rosalind talk about trains and time and destiny, I was reminded of a scene from Christopher Nolan's 2010 sci-fi heist film *Inception,* from which this chapter's opening epigraph is borrowed.[29] In the scene, Mal (played by Marion Cotillard) is recounting a memory in which she and Cobb (the film's protagonist and her husband, played by Leonardo DiCaprio) became lost in a dream world, with suicide as the only escape back to reality. In the scene / dream, the couple lie together, their heads resting on cold metal train tracks, and in an effort to allay Mal's fear and anxiety over their impending "end," Cobb recites the riddle quoted at the beginning of this chapter, in which the uncertainty of the future (i.e., the train's—and characters'—final destination) is mitigated by intimate connection: "We'll be together." Indeed, Cobb spends the length of the film trying to reunite with his young children—a final attempt at the "happy family"—after being framed for Mal's murder (in reality, suicide). We are reminded of Rosalind's divine prognosis: You *will* adopt; the child that is meant to be with you *will* find you. You *will* be together in the end(s). Rather than waiting for death as a new awakening, prospective adoptive parents (as well as expectant mothers and social workers) wait for birth, as both an end and a new beginning.

In adoption discourse, the adoption process is often likened to a journey (one that must be mapped, whether by Stella or another professional), a metaphor that, like the train, references space, but which in reality refers to a temporal voyage, from the mindful here-and-now into an unforeseen future. However, the difference between American adoption and the filmic example I have cited is that the anxieties and hopes that surround becoming a parent do not end with placement of the child (or the arrival of the bus / train). They extend into a distant future, often, through the end of a parent's life. Indeed, one is ideally a parent for the rest of one's life—the popular term "forever family" has a particularly strong sort of purchase here. As Julia Jackson insisted, children *are* forever, all sales final.

An analysis of the many ways in which the unique unfolding and contingent qualities of the adoption process required participants to engage with risk and uncertainty reveals complex emotional and temporal investments in an imagined future child. These anticipatory logics of family formation can be read in prospective parents' and others' practices of risk management, preparation, and waiting, practices through which the future is at once folded squarely into the present while remaining a distant horizon, forever receding out of reach of even the fastest bullet train. Building upon these notions of temporal and emotional investment, the following chapter interrogates adoption as an economic transaction wherein the imagined child is variously conceptualized as a gift, a commodity, and a future.

FOUR

────────

Kinship's Costs

IT WAS A WARM AUGUST day in 2009, my first summer at First Steps, and Stella and I were out in the field, "tooling around," as she would say. On this particular day we had several stops to make (collecting paperwork, delivering money, checking in with expectant mothers, stopping by a hospital to see a new baby), and our fourth or fifth stop was a four-story walk-up, Valerie's building. We were coming from a suburban Wal-Mart, where Stella had purchased a $300 gift card for Valerie, using funds provided by the family that would adopt her baby, to help offset her living expenses. Money for housing, utilities, food, and clothing was deemed "legally allowable," meaning that prospective parents could cover these expenses without charges of coercion or child-buying.

Valerie's building was flanked on one side by a similar brick walk-up and on the other by a grassy vacant lot. The area was mainly residential; we passed a currency exchange and a small mini-mart / liquor store as we approached her street. Access to amenities such as fresh produce, household goods, or general retail outlets was clearly limited; this neighborhood was located on the far West Side of the city, an area of "advanced marginality" (Wacquant 2008: 2).[1] The majority of the expectant mothers who approached or were referred to First Steps in need of adoption services resided in neighborhoods such as these. By 2014, many of the poor neighborhoods on the South and West Sides of the city had "vacant housing percentages" between 13 and 34 percent (Newman 2014). Food deserts have also been an enduring public health issue in Chicago's low-income neighborhoods, disproportionately affecting African American residents (Gallagher 2006).

Stella parked along the street and we went up to the third floor. A stout and noticeably pregnant African American woman answered the door with a smile and invited us inside. She exuded openness and calm, but also exhaustion. We sat on the couch and I took in the surroundings while Valerie and Stella talked. The carpeted living room was small, and somewhat crowded with a matching couch and loveseat, a set of glass-topped coffee / end tables, a small flat-screen television, and a laptop and printer. Valerie told us that her fiancé—the primary financial support for her and her existing children—had recently been shot and killed, and that after the pregnancy she expected to go back to work. Making matters worse, her mother had just been diagnosed with cancer. Sharing this sad news, Valerie kept her voice steady.

Stella expressed sympathy and explained to Valerie how the adoptive family she had chosen had experienced a difficult fall-through earlier in the process: they had given an expectant mother $1,000 for living expenses and she had gone to another agency and chosen a different family without telling anyone. Valerie responded by telling Stella that she had been keeping in touch with the family by e-mail, sending ultrasound images, asking if they had bought anything for the baby yet, and so on. She said that something just felt good, "felt so right," about being able to give a child, an indescribable "miracle," to someone who could not carry their own. The feeling was so strong that she even expressed interest in becoming a surrogate. Her main concern genuinely seemed to be bringing a healthy baby into the world for the adoptive family. Several weeks later, however, Valerie's phone number was disconnected, and Stella never heard from her again. As far as Stella knew, she never placed the baby. She had effectively exited the adoption process in advance of its planned conclusion.

At First Steps—where more than half of planned adoptions fell through—a fall-through was often accompanied by not only the loss of a temporal and affective future, but also the loss of a particular kind of monetary investment—what social workers referred to as "legally allowable birth mother expenses" and what state law referred to as "reasonable living expenses"—which further complicated the transfer of the imagined child. The fall-through broke hearts and broke banks. It was a(n) (anti)climax in the adoption process that threw conceptions of the child-as-future into stark relief. It was a strange kind of end.

Examining the complicated exchange of money for the idea or potentiality of a baby in the months leading up to the birth illustrates additional forms of affective labor that social workers, prospective adopters, and expectant / birth mothers carried out in order to protect themselves—and the institution of adoption itself—from the necessary overlap of intimate and economic concerns. In using the term affective labor, I refer not only to the emotional work that tempering expectations and soothing loss entails, but also detective work and moral maintenance, two forms of protective labor. For social workers, this labor is a defining characteristic of their role as the brokers of these transactions. Some scholars have theorized affective labor as "*the* hegemonic labour of twenty-first-century global capitalism" (Thomas and Correa 2016: 11). Here, I am decidedly not classing this form of labor as "immaterial" or in opposition to industrial labor (Hardt and Negri 2000).[2] Indeed, the affective labor required by adoption is intimately connected to the embodied labor of birth and reproduction, as well as the capitalist logics that create the class inequality that renders these adoptions necessary, at the same time that "fee for service" discourse erases the human transaction inherent to adoption. This convergence of intimacy and economy is most clearly glimpsed in the event of a fall-through, in which questions invariably arose about reimbursement of funds given to the mother. I use the word "given" here intentionally: this money was necessarily conceptualized as a gift, as I will detail below. It was also an important investment in an imagined future. Attending to these transactions provides insight into what Sara Dorow (2006: 17) has described as "social relationships of exchange, meaning, and value that are both caring and consumptive."

In this chapter, I follow these exchanges to one possible end—an end in which the imagined future of the adoption is left unfulfilled, and an end that necessitates a starting over—in order to examine the practices carried out by social workers, expectant / birth parents, and prospective adoptive parents to cleanse the adoption process of its perceived morally problematic confluence of love and money. The economic loss produced by the fall-through is a product of two social forces: (1) the class dynamics of adoption, and (2) the interplay of ideologies of the adopted child as a commodity and the funds paid to the mother as a gift. The commodification of the imagined child is brought to the fore specifically through the disavowal of that very commodification. As a mode of intimate speculation, the adoption process entailed risky economic exchanges that linked high investment, stark inequality, and ambiguous morality within the adoption process.

"DO YOU WANT YOUR BIRTH MOTHER NOT TO HAVE FOOD IN HER BELLY?"

I shielded my eyes from the morning sun and peered across the table at Melodie—an adoption attorney who worked with First Steps—as she nursed a steaming cup of black coffee. Melodie self-identified as biracial, and had recently adopted an African American newborn as a single parent. She was interested in issues of race and diversity, and often led trainings for transracial adoptive parents. On that particular morning, Melodie was describing how the socioeconomic conditions of adoption in Chicago differed from the post-WWII "Baby Scoop Era" (the decades prior to *Roe v. Wade*), and succinctly articulated the role of poverty as contemporary adoption's primary impetus. "I don't think in the sixties poverty was the issue," Melodie opined. She took a long swig of her coffee, and continued, referring to the middle-class women who were often forced to surrender children born out of wedlock due to the stigma of illegitimacy, "I mean, it might have been if they went out on their own, but it wasn't like they were like 'Oh my God, how am I going to feed myself?' because they were still sixteen, living in their parents' house." Shifting her focus to contemporary expectant mothers in Chicago, Melodie noted, "Now it's an issue of 'My food stamps run out before the end of the month and I already have two kids to feed.'" I nodded in understanding. We were sitting in a booth at a sparsely populated McDonald's on the gentrifying Near West Side. She continued, "Poverty is the issue, and so they are in more need of assistance, truly in more need of assistance, and there is something, you know, different states balance it differently, and yeah, adoptive parents really don't want to spend the money because they're afraid of scams–" She paused and shrugged, leaning forward slightly. "But the reality is, *do you want your birth mother not to have food in her belly when she's carrying this?* We know that poverty affects, you know, or malnutrition or lack of nutrition affects a fetus." Melodie clearly framed the provision of particular resources for expectant mothers ("food in her belly") in terms of investment. Her use of the possessive pronoun in the construction "your birth mother" reflects the politics of the matching process. Not only is the woman prematurely categorized as a birth mother, but she belongs, always already, to the prospective adoptive parents. Of course the fall-through is conceptualized as a failure, a disruptive "change of heart," when the language of adoption professionals predetermines an imagined outcome.

Melodie drew attention to the potential effects that poverty can have on the future of the child; economic intervention in the form of money from prospective adoptive parents functioned as an investment in the future health and well-being of the child. By literally putting food in an expectant mother's belly, prospective adopters were investing in the future of the child she carried. Before the child was born, the well-being of the expectant mother was strongly tied to the future health of the child in such a way that to ensure one was to ensure the other. Stark economic inequality between those relinquishing children and those seeking to adopt formed an underlying structural component of this category of investment. The adoption process was always haunted by the specter of the "scam," which was only rendered thinkable by the potential for monetary exchange.

While the racial and cultural dynamics of domestic transracial adoption have constituted a popular area of interest among social scientists and lay audiences alike, these dynamics are further elucidated by an examination of how class inequity forms adoption's social base. The transracial adoption of black infants from poor neighborhoods by middle- and upper-class white parents is profoundly intersectional, a product of forces inflected multiply by gender, race, and class (Ducre 2015). Adoption in the United States is deeply entwined with the development of gendered notions of social class and illegitimacy, the impact of which extends through the present day as class identifications, poverty interventions, and possibilities for upward mobility continue to change over time, affecting the social locations of both those who relinquish children and those who adopt them. In an era in which single motherhood is—and has been for some time—gaining increasing social acceptance, poverty most often structured the transfers of children that First Steps facilitated. By the time First Steps closed, adoptive families, who were predominantly white, were paying upwards of $25,000 in fees to adopt babies from low-income neighborhoods on the South and West Sides of the city. The pregnant women approaching the agency to relinquish their babies, many of them already parenting one or more children, cited repeatedly the fact that they simply could not afford the costs associated with raising a child, simply could not feed another mouth. They very often sought financial assistance from prospective adopters for essential everyday expenses, such as food and shelter. One of the first questions Stella would ask new expectant mothers was always, "What do you need?" And she took care in only presenting prospective adopters who could meet those stated needs.

Melodie repeated, referencing shifting demographics, "So the women today who are placing, I would say poverty plays a high factor. Not always, but often it's that threshold of, 'I'm trying to keep my child, child or children I'm already parenting out of poverty and one more is going to break the bank,' right?" We were seated by the window and I could feel the pre-winter chill coming off the wide expanse of glass. I nodded, listening intently. "So they're trying to balance making sure none of their kids really get raised in poverty or another kid doesn't get raised in poverty," Melodie continued, describing a dynamic I had witnessed at First Steps. "But I think you do have a higher group of birth mothers, you know, now middle-class women who are single and have the resources, they don't make this decision anymore. In fact, there's a line of single middle-class women wishing to adopt and be a single mom, right?" she asked, or perhaps insisted, the rising inflection at the end of her sentence mirroring a rise in her right eyebrow. Indeed, Melodie was one of these single middle-class women who had chosen to adopt solo. From her perspective, the stigma of illegitimacy had all but disappeared for single women perceived as having the economic resources to raise a child. "Common wisdom today insists that children deserve parents with appropriate bank balances," historian Rickie Solinger insists (2001: 221). These socioeconomic patterns highly influenced the shape of adoptions at First Steps, particularly where "legally allowable birth parent expenses" were concerned. Melodie's rhetorical question, "Do you want your birth mother not to have food in her belly?" at once points backward to a long history of strategies for addressing surplus reproduction among the poor, and forward to the ways that contemporary adoption commodifies this reproduction. But this commodification is strongly disavowed by those who participate in the adoption process. Expectant mother poverty created a condition in which the transfer of money became both investment and incentive, but a great deal of work had to be done to minimize the uncanny resemblance of these exchanges to a market in (future) babies.

MORAL MAINTENANCE

As a graduate student, I once attended a dinner event for Chicago-based alumni of Stanford University, my alma mater. I was seated next to an older white man, a Stanford alum and current college professor. We exchanged pleasantries and brief summaries of our scholarly work. He was an adoptive parent—I have encountered several fellow academics over the years who take a special interest in my work because of their own experiences as adoptive parents; fewer adoptees, not a single birth parent. When I told him of my interest in the circulation of money entailed by the adoption process, he straightened in his chair and insisted, "In our experience, it wasn't really about the money."

· · ·

ends, n. *slang.* Money, likely from the proverbial phrase **to make ends meet,** to live within one's income.[3]

· · ·

My aim has never been to suggest that adoption is all about money; intimate speculation illuminates additional forces that work in concert with the economic. What I find anthropologically interesting, however, are the social forces at play that prompted this new acquaintance, and many others I encountered, to tell me—often emphatically—that it really wasn't "about the money." As Elizabeth Raleigh (2017: 30) observes in her analysis of the market forces of adoption, something about the language of business, markets, and supply-and-demand just "doesn't sound right" when applied to adoption. I refer to this discursive denial as moral maintenance, and an exchange I overheard between Stella and a birth mother named Mallory helps to illustrate how it functions as disavowal of commodification.

One afternoon while Stella drove us back to the agency from a hospital in the suburbs, her cell phone rang. She answered it with her usual sing-songy, "Hello, this is Stella," and from the passenger seat I could hear a raised voice erupt on the other end of the line. Stella's eyes widened and she held the phone a couple of inches away from her ear. Seconds later I heard her say, "Okay, Mallory, okay, put her on the phone." Soon she was reassuring the party on the other end that Mallory had not "sold" her baby, that she had "chosen" an adoptive family "very carefully" and "placed" the child with them. Her measured and patient tone revealed that this speech was practiced. Audible distress emanated from the phone and I saw Stella roll her eyes. She repeated herself: Mallory *did not sell* her baby. "Okay? Okay, you can put Mallory back on." A few more seconds passed. "You're welcome, Mallory. Okay, bye bye now." Mallory had just called requesting that Stella tell her sister that she had not sold her baby. The audible argument on the other end of the phone was their heated debate over the link between adoption and baby-selling. Even in the event of a "successful" placement, Stella's work to protect Mallory as well as the institution of adoption itself from the fallout of this common cultural association was evident.

Sara Dorow (2006: 18) contends, "Difficult contradictions form around the child; to count fully as family, she and the bonds with her adoptive parents must be protected and distinguished from the very market forces of adoption in which parents and agencies are increasingly implicated." Social workers at First Steps practiced a complex amalgam of detective work and moral maintenance in order to protect all parties to adoption, as well as the institution of adoption itself, from the negative effects of commodification. Within the broader context of clinical social work, case managers pass moral judgment on a daily basis, and moral dilemmas often revolve around money (Floersch 2002: 126–28). This is also very true of the social work carried out at First Steps. Part of Stella's job was to mitigate the complex effects of the two-pronged question of money and morality, which was most amplified in the moment at which a mother decided definitively whether or not to place.

The tension present in the office during the last couple months of a given pregnancy was almost tangible. Stella would field calls from increasingly stressed and apprehensive prospective adoptive parents, seeking some sort of reassurance that the process would be completed. Every day that passed put the family one day closer to the birth of what they hoped would be their child, and every day Stella half-expected an expectant mother's unexplained disappearance, which was almost always indicated by the first of several unreturned phone calls or missed meetings. In the event of a fall-through, staff at First Steps made moral judgments in order to proceed with the adoption process and to make sense of the event for the prospective adoptive parent(s). One of those moral judgments involved trying to determine whether or not a "scam" had taken place, and in the case of expenses, whether or not financial remediation was possible or "right."

Examining the role of monetary transfers between prospective adopters and expectant mothers (always mediated by the agency) reveals an ideological conflict between notions of intimacy and economy. In the United States, mentioning money and adoption in the same breath often leads to intense feelings of discomfort caused by the specter of child trafficking or economic coercion.[4] There is a tendency to avoid thinking of the economic and the intimate as deeply entangled, when in reality that is precisely what they are. At First Steps, the taboo of mixing money and kinship was particularly strong because exchanging money for a black child uncomfortably called forth America's history of slavery. But how can we make sense of the role of money in the adoption process? And how does money complicate (and sometimes motivate) instances of fall-through?

Viviana Zelizer (2005) argues against theorists who employ "separate spheres / hostile worlds" and "nothing-but" models of intimacy and economy, insisting instead that "people who blend intimacy and economic activity are actively engaged in constructing and negotiating 'connected lives'" (22).

Among the examples she provides of this blending of intimate and economic activity is the fact that "adoptive parents pay money to obtain babies" (27). Igor Kopytoff (2004) contends, employing Zelizer's language of sacralization:

> In the modern American and general Western perspective, then, there is a *moral threat* in the commoditization of children and, by extension, of human reproduction; the threat lies in the possible invasion of the human and sacralized world of kinship by economistic principles deemed appropriate only to the world of things. (272; emphasis added)

Morality then, becomes the node at which Western notions of the economic and intimate realms intersect. Kopytoff (2004) goes on to argue that economism (including commodification) in kinship relations is "natural" and widespread, but that in Western society the two realms often come into cultural and ideological conflict, especially in recent history in the face of capitalism and industrialization. Within adoption, intimacy / economy proves a false binary; these social forces are mutually constituted.

Some anthropologists have put forth theories in which gift and commodity are not fixed statuses of people and things, but instead temporal phases through which subjects and objects pass (Appadurai 1986, 2013; Kopytoff 1986).[5] In adoption, the idea of a future baby contains what Appadurai (1986: 13) has referred to as "commodity potential." Helpful here is his borrowing of Marquet's notion of "commodities by diversion," defined as "objects placed into a commodity state though originally specifically protected from it" (16). Appadurai clarifies Maquet's distinction between the processes of enclaving and diversion: "The central contrast is that whereas enclaving seeks to protect certain things from commoditization, diversion frequently is aimed at drawing protected things into the zone of commoditization" (26). Social workers in adoption play the role of brokers and mediators, but they are also protectors and law enforcers. Enclaving, then, is an example of moral maintenance, a type of discursive and regulatory labor in which certain children and children-to-be are specifically and actively protected from the commodification implied by the transfer of money. In adoption, these exchanges are emergent, always on the brink of some kind of moral transgression.

Diversion, on the other hand, involves the entrance of these specifically protected items into the economic realm through commodification, while often hiding or obscuring that very commodification. "Diversion," writes

Appadurai (1986: 25), "is frequently the recourse of the entrepreneurial individual." Perhaps then, an expectant mother's desire (or need) to switch families or agencies mid-adoption in order to secure more money in exchange for the placement of her child—or in the case of a "scam," simply the hope or idea of future placement—is a type of diversion. Appadurai acknowledges the moral issues wrapped up in the process of diversion, arguing: "The diversion of commodities from their customary paths always carries a *risky* and *morally ambiguous* aura" (27; emphasis added). Disavowal of commodification was key to understanding the moral and economic implications of fall-throughs and how social workers navigated them.

In the example of the phone call with Stella, Mallory performed moral maintenance by refuting her sister's claim of child-selling and enlisting Stella's authority in that refutation, and Stella did so by explicitly clarifying the terms of the adoption so as to set it apart from child-selling. Dorow (2006) discusses a similar kind of moral maintenance at length in the case of Chinese adoption. She describes international adoption facilitators who "protect" adoptive parents from "signs of a commodified child" (74):

> A complex intersection of economic, political, cultural, and emotional labor by the formal facilitators of adoption buffers the production of kinship from the raced, gendered, and classed excesses of marketized relations that would make parent and child into consumer and consumed. (72)

In a similar vein, Goodwin (2010: 2) argues, "The free market in children, as a concept, is rejected based on what it symbolizes, including its argued resemblance to slavery or the auction block." A sort of discursive money-laundering, moral maintenance is involved in the disavowal of adoption as being in any way economized. When I asked Stella to differentiate adoption and child-buying, she argued that several aspects of child trafficking were absent from legitimate adoption: spontaneous or unexplained fees, working with noncertified facilitators, and absence of paperwork. In Stella's view, the line between adoption and illicit trafficking was marked by a lack of regulation, a defining trait of what Goodwin (2010) has termed "baby markets" (see also Raleigh 2017).

State regulation of adoption—in particular, the restrictions placed on "legally allowable birth parent expenses"—constitutes another form of moral maintenance in which the state intervenes in order to prevent the sale—or the appearance of the sale—of children. Take, for example, the following excerpts from Illinois law regarding these expenses:

Birth Parent Expenses Allowed
(Comp. Stat. Ch. 720 § 525/4; 4.1)

The provisions of this Act shall not be construed to prevent the payment by a person with whom a child has been placed for adoption of reasonable and actual medical fees or hospital charges for services rendered in connection with the birth of such child, if such payment is made to the physician or hospital who or which rendered the services or to the birth mother of the child or to prevent the receipt of such payment by such physician, hospital, or mother.

The prospective adoptive parents also are permitted to pay the reasonable living expenses of the birth parents of the child sought to be adopted. "Reasonable living expenses" means those expenses related to activities of daily living and meeting basic needs, including, but not limited to, lodging, food, and clothing for the birth parents during the birth mother's pregnancy and for no more than 120 days prior to the birth mother's expected date of delivery and for no more than 60 days after the birth of the child.

The adopting parents shall be permitted to pay the reasonable attorney's fees of the birth parents' attorney in connection with proceedings under this Act or in connection with proceedings for the adoption of the child.

Birth Parent Expenses Not Allowed
(Comp. Stat. Ch. 720 § 525/4.1(a))

The term "reasonable living expenses" does not include expenses for lost wages, gifts, educational expenses, or other similar expenses of the biological parents.

Allowable Payments for Relinquishing Child
(Comp. Stat. Ch. 720 § 525/4.1(d))

Payment of their reasonable living expenses shall not obligate the birth parents to place the child for adoption. In the event the birth parents choose not to place the child for adoption, the adopting parents shall have no right to seek reimbursement from the birth parents, or from any relative or associate of the birth parents.[6]

The law carefully delineates what constitutes an acceptable transfer of funds, and separates—enclaves—the exchange from traditional forms of buying / selling by removing the possibility of reimbursement. Temporal limits (four months prior to the birth and two months after) function to bound the acceptable exchange of money, suggesting also a bounding or transformation of kin relations between expectant / birth mother, child(-to-be), and prospective / adoptive family, in particular by stipulating a window of financial support. Unreasonable targets of exchange are listed, limiting the ways this particular money can be used by the expectant / birth parent(s). In practice, the money would enter the agency in the form of cash or a check from the prospective adopters, and it would then be transformed into grocery store gift cards, money orders made out to landlords, or actual goods, in order to restrict the ways in which it could be spent. The language in the statute negating obligation and reimbursement acknowledges and attempts to mitigate the coercive potential of these funds. Economic moral maintenance is practiced at the individual, institutional, and state levels at all stages in the adoption process, but the role of morality in the transfer of (imagined) children is further complicated by the notion of fraud or "scam," stemming from the temporal dynamics inherent to the adoption process. The exchange of money for "reasonable living expenses," however, is the very thing that creates space for the so-called "scam," wherein notions of investment, morality, and economic inequality become increasingly imbricated.

"SCAM" DETECTION

The character and circulation of money paid for expectant parent expenses enabled what social workers referred to as "scamming," or posing as a potential birth mother in order to obtain funds without actually placing a baby. To refer to an expectant mother as a scammer is to participate in a long discursive tradition of racializing and criminalizing poverty in the United States. Although Jenny, First Steps' business manager, insisted that "scam is a harsh word," it remained a term used fairly often in the agency office, and one expectant mother was even referred to as a "big scammer." As in the American notion of the welfare queen, the problem of the scam is that intimacy and economy overlap in ways that are perceived as problematic by social workers and prospective adoptive parents.

In the 1980s and 1990s, as the image of the welfare queen proliferated, instances of welfare fraud or "cheating" were used to convince "the public that the welfare program wasted their tax dollars on financially secure, manipulative criminals" (Kohler-Hausmann 2007: 338).[7] Solinger (2001: 143) adds that, in the 1980s, many Americans associated the welfare queen "with the figure of the prostitute: she had sex for money—the money she got from the government for having children." Wahneema Lubiano (1992: 338) describes the political equation of poor black mothers with larger-scale economic drain:

Within the terms specifically of, or influenced by, the *Moynihan Report* and generally of the discourse on the "culture of poverty," "welfare queen" is a phrase that describes economic dependency—the lack of a job and / or income (which equals degeneracy in the Calvinist United States); the presence of a child or children with no father and / or husband (moral deviance); and, finally, a charge on the collective U. S. Treasury—a human debit.

The figure of the welfare queen has an unpayable debt. Similar to how the welfare queen is demonized for having sex / children for money, the adoption scammer is demonized for using her unborn child—or in rare cases, faking a pregnancy altogether—to get monetary resources. Resources that can never be paid back. She is an end that causes an end, to make ends meet.

The problem with the "scam," in the case of women confirmed pregnant, was that it was almost always uncertain, because its identification was tied to the expectant mother's intentions, which remained inaccessible to social workers. This contributed further to the profound sense of uncertainty and risk that characterized the adoption process for social workers and prospective adoptive parents faced with the looming threat of a fall-through, and social workers carried out a measure of precarious policing within this space of uncertainty. Complicating matters further was the difficulty of disentangling a "scam" from a "change of heart," two attributions with vastly different moral implications.

Adoption attorney Kimberly insisted, "If disappointed adoptive parents immediately jump to the conclusion that they've been scammed, I don't think that's accurate either." The two of us were sitting in a cavernous wood-paneled conference room in the office of her Chicago law firm. She continued, leaning forward, "I mean, it certainly happens, but that isn't usually the case." I nodded, and she went on, "More often, you know, and I—it's so hard for people to understand this. Birth mom can be a hundred percent set on adoption and have the baby, and after that physical and emotional experience, decide, 'I can't do this.'" Here, she frames the decision to parent in terms of inability to relinquish, a sort of weakness, rather than affirmative ability and willingness to maintain legal kinship. Kimberly sat back in her chair, shaking her head almost imperceptibly. "That doesn't mean it's a scam," she finished; "it means that she's had a change of heart and can't do it." Verification of a scam was exceedingly rare; suspicion alone was more often the case. The ambiguity of the scam challenged attempts to make sense of the fall-through. Although theoretically the "scam" and the "change of heart" are more accurately conceptualized as overlapping in their logics and motivations (and the "truth" is always inaccessible), the temporal, economic, and affective demands of the adoption process often prompted social workers to try to distinguish between the two. They did so with varying degrees of success. The "scam" became an explanatory mechanism for behavior perceived at once as deeply flawed and completely logical, producing an outcome that was difficult to digest.

One mode of "scamming" was to keep one's options open, by linking up with more than one prospective adopter (via multiple agencies) simultaneously. Illinois adoption law states that one of the responsibilities of expectant / birth parents is "to not accept financial support or reimbursement of pregnancy related expenses simultaneously from more than one source" (Comp. Stat. Ch. 750 50 / 10). One day, as we were driving back to the agency after meeting with an expectant mother on Chicago's South Side, Stella told me that she could remember three separate occasions on which she discovered an expectant mother "working" two agencies simultaneously and collecting money from both. "It takes some mastery to uncover it," she admitted, alluding to her own investigative skills. Like in the case of the home study, here the logic of detective work is that it should produce predictive knowledge, and therefore mitigate risk by allowing social workers to identify "scammers." Early detection was key. Stella continued, "And there is a fine line. Who really knows if it's a scam? It's set up so that you can take money and walk away. And that's the right thing; nobody should be able to force you." Stella often verbalized her belief that expectant mothers should be able to change their minds about placement. Her use of the term "right" in this example references her own moral stance, which is at odds with her use of the verb "take" in the previous sentence.

"But the line can blur so easily," Stella continued, speeding us down the freeway; "And adoptive families will say, 'Well didn't you know? Can't you figure it out? Weren't there signs? How do you screen them?'" The reactions from prospective adoptive families to which Stella alludes indicate an expectation that social workers carry out a certain amount of protective detective work in order to evaluate their level of risk. As Stella lamented, the successful "screening" of expectant mothers was simply impossible given the myriad conditions that determined the outcome of a pregnancy and adoption plan, in addition to the heterogeneity of expectant mothers. In terms of "signs," Stella often listed "red flags," or warning signs that made her suspicious of scams. I once went along with her to meet a new expectant mother, Jamie, who lived on the far South Side of the city. After the meeting, Stella related several red flags to me including Jamie's desperation about money, the almost complete lack of furniture in the house, and the high rent, the first two of which, notably, could be interpreted as symptoms of poverty in addition to red flags. Even in the face of these red flags, Stella always continued to work with the mothers until her suspicions were confirmed, or she lost contact. Stella's suspicion alone that an expectant mother might be scamming never served as a rationale for terminating the adoption plan. Successful brokerage required this mix of hope, vigilance, and persistence.

Particularly illustrative of Stella's system of red flags is her return to the situation with Valerie, whom she suspected was working in tandem with another expectant mother named Angeline. We were having lunch in the agency's multipurpose room, and Stella was catching me up on her work with various expectant mothers. "The red flag for me," she said, picking at her leftovers, "was that I had been to that same apartment building [Valerie's] for another birth mother, and they both described their own mothers as having cancer." Stella went on, describing her suspicion that Valerie was somehow related to another expectant mother she had worked with, "Based on confidentiality I didn't want to ask one or the other, 'Whoa, is Angeline your sister?' So I never asked that, but that seemed very strange. And Angeline had not placed two kids, and had taken a lot of money for both of those kids. So I had a big red flag about Valerie." Again, Stella's use of the verb "taken" rather than "received" begins to reveal a moral positioning toward Angeline's (and Valerie's, by association) orientation to money offered by the prospective adopters. Stella continued, "And at first it seemed to me she didn't want money, and then she said she couldn't manage without more money, and if she had to she would change families. And we did because she said she needed help with her rent." "So she took the money," Stella said, matter-of-factly, again using the language of taking, calling to mind the imbalance implied by give-and-take absent the giving. "Her mother died of cancer, at the same time Angeline's mother died of cancer. Angeline fell through, and Valerie eventually fell through," Stella finished with a sigh.

Stella went on to tell me a series of stories about situations she later identified as fall-through "scams." Again, she references the "taking" of money:

> I had one birth mother that took a lot of money, and was again this kind of desperate person, texting texting. And I put a lid on how much she was gonna get. No more rent, until—that was the agreement that we had—until the baby's born. I remember going down, taking fifty dollars out of my pocket and bought her food. She called me and did a long set of texting, saying that

the cord had wrapped around the baby's neck, wrapped around the baby's shoulder, taken the baby's arm off. And um, never said the word "died," but obviously, and I think we talked about "passed," and when this happened, and she was very upset and she said, "Of course, well you didn't get what you want, so you're done with me, right?"

The expectant mother's response to Stella in this instance references the underlying—though often disavowed—reciprocal logic of these exchanges, the fact that the relationship between social worker and expectant mother is premised on the eventual delivery of a baby. Stella offered no comment on the woman's assessment of the implications of the unfulfilled exchange, but instead continued the narrative:

> I called that social worker at that particular hospital, and said, "I would really like to verify that there was a death, of a child, for closure for the adoptive family." And she of course told me about confidentiality, and I said, "I have, in the record, an authorization for medical records signed by the mother that I can fax you." Upon faxing that and going through her hierarchy, there was never a record of a baby that was dead at that hospital in that time period.

Neither was there a record of one born to this particular woman. Was there ever a baby then, or just the idea of one? During my time at the agency I heard this story from Stella multiple times.

As with the example above of Valerie and Angeline, Stella was distressed by the placement of this particular fall-through within a pattern she had observed. "And this came in a grouping of birth mothers in the past three months. There were like five or six. There were three at one time," she sighed, exasperated. She went on, "Several of them shared stories of rapes and assaults. And several of them were [at] Mount Sinai [Hospital]. And the social worker was very disturbed to hear that." The notion that expectant mothers might have been colluding to "work" the system was particularly upsetting to Stella, but she conceded, acknowledging the material realities of the class inequality that undergirds adoption, "If anybody is going to fit in the slot or the role of thinking about giving up their child, well, what would one expect?" Here, she specifically references her own expectations of fall-throughs and scams, a potential future that is always threatening. She continued, emphatically, "If you're going to be considering that at all, you know you're going to have some pressures and some needs. Or you wouldn't be there! And that's part of the adoption process." It is telling that her explanation does not actually allow for a true "scam"; it requires the expectant mother to be sincerely contemplating adoption, to be "thinking about giving up" her child as a necessary precursor to the ensuing "taking" of money. This is an interesting twist to adoption's central quandary: the fact that the expectant mother is always already constructed as unfit. Here, she is always already constructed as sincere, even within a discourse of "scamming." These relations are slippery. By this reasoning, there is no such thing as a pure scam.

Whether or not certain expectant mothers truly were working in tandem or alone with the goal of "taking money" without placing a child will never be known. Their actions and decisions, however motivated, did have moral implications for the ways in which adoption proceeded at the agency, including the difficulty faced by social workers of distinguishing adoption from baby-selling—and striving to protect the former from the immoral encroachment of commodification—as well as deciding how to proceed with a prospective adoptive family that had invested, and then lost, thousands of dollars at the mere idea of a baby, perhaps multiple times. It is telling that the actual moral dilemma most often faced by social workers concerned the fall-through as an unfinished exchange, which was not an act of baby-selling, but baby-keeping. Each time a fall-through occurred (whether as the result of a scam or not) and a prospective adoptive family lost money and the hope of a child, social workers were pressured to be even more vigilant in spotting potential fall-throughs and / or "scams." Social workers' detective work was deeply speculative, trying to ascertain the difference between a fall-through, sparked by circumstance, and a scam, which was premeditated.

Another example of Stella's work to uncover a scam involved Dawn, the expectant mother we had taken grocery shopping in the northern suburbs. Stella had described Dawn as "a perfectly likable, adorable, cute, chubby little faced girl." "She reminds me of my kids," she said, "trying to pull fast ones right and left." Transference all the way down. Stella gave me a lengthy account of Dawn's story one day at the agency. The first red flag occurred when Dawn was filling out the preliminary paperwork. Stella told me, "Some people fill it out like they've seen it before. And I did get that impression." Dawn had been located by an agency in Ohio that had completed the home study for the couple with whom she was matched. In interstate arrangements like this, Stella carried out the casework with the expectant mother, while the agency in the other state handled the process for the prospective adoptive parents. Stella was initially suspicious because the referring agency had mentioned that Dawn had two children. The children were not living with her, and she did not disclose their existence in the paperwork she completed for Stella.

Stella was also concerned because she had given Dawn money to buy groceries, furnished by the prospective adoptive parents, but Dawn had called to tell her that her freezer had broken and all the food was spoiled. This had necessitated the trip to take Dawn grocery shopping, an effort to monitor and control her spending. Stella recounted:

> Three days later, or a day and a half, "My freezer broke, all the food from the grocery money was in there. It's all spoiled, and I lost everything." I said, "Well, there's a freezer outside permanently, and, you know, it usually takes a little while for food to get to the point of spoiling, and you had everything you bought in the freezer?" "Mm-hmm, yeah, yeah, yeah, yeah." So then we went by again, bought the—we took her shopping.

After telling me about Dawn's account of the broken freezer, Stella said, "I think she made it all up." "Spent the money on something else?" I asked. "I think she blew the money. Totally . . . so this time, I said, I'll take her shopping for a minimum amount of things. I don't necessarily think she's drugging. I think she's just a young woman that doesn't have any money, and so when she got some, she just, boom!" Stella's strategy in this instance was an increased level of supervision. She went on:

> She weaseled out more money from me for laundry. House was empty; we didn't see what was behind the hidden door in the bedroom. Um, okay. [Prospective adoptive mother's] husband returns from a trip, he must be a traveling person all over the world. Gets on the phone, "Well, you know, I don't mind giving somebody rent, but is this looking legit?" I said, "Well, there are some signs, it's not looking good." "Do we have any medical records?" I said, "Well, I took her there [to the clinic]. She took the pictures for the ultrasound; we didn't get them that day. She said she went back, but I don't know, I don't have them, I should have asked her for, specifically for a copy, and I didn't.

This weasel analogy is another species of Dotty's slippery little eel, an extractive and cunning mammalian counterpart. At this point, the prospective adoptive parents were beginning to worry about the "legitimacy" of the arrangement. Stella went on to recount additional warning signs:

> She didn't volunteer them [the ultrasound photos]. I said, "I have the release for medical records. So I'm going to get the information. I have her clinic, but information from her, and I'm going to sit and get the medical records." So we did that, took a while. I think they paid another full month's rent.

The more red flags Stella identified (omission of information, empty house and closed doors, reluctance to share ultrasound photos), the more wary she became. Suspicion can be a form of speculative affect, an uncertain sense that something is about to go horribly wrong. A troubling sense of the outcome before it occurs. The unsettling feeling: "I know how this will end."

In these situations, the recourse was often to withhold money from expectant mothers as a way of tempering potential financial investment and loss among prospective adopters, and also to encourage compliance from the expectant mother. An attempt to create reciprocity. "I need to see those medical records / ultrasound photos / prenatal care forms / et cetera, or no more money," Stella would say. She went on:

> So, I spent the night looking at this and think, this does not bode well. Don't think we should send that rent. Then she called and said, "The furnace is broken, I need a heater, I need another—" I said, "That's the landlord's responsibility." Oh. After a lot more blah-blah about that, she said, "Um, you know the time when they helped me before with the rent? The landlord reminded me about the fifty-dollar late fee." Uh-huh. So by now, and she had adjusted the due date. And I said, "Where'd you get that information?" "From the ultrasound tech." I said [to myself], "She adjusted the due date to tell us it's over."

Intimate speculation is encapsulated in this kind of (fore)boding. Dawn reported a new due date, about ten days after the original due date. An arrival deferred. Stella interpreted this as a signal that Dawn had no intention of placing a baby, and that the adoption plan had failed. She told me,

> The baby will be born, I bet you, on the due date, but she's going to connect with us on the twentieth. The baby's born on the ninth, or whatever the due date—there's nothing in these records anywhere that indicates. And she didn't follow up. She's missed appointments. I confront her with that. She wasn't liking me very much. I was feeling pressure.

She shook her head, lamenting, "I didn't want to have Ohio think that I'm not doing well with their birth mother." The brokerage function surfaces. She continued, "The family is frustrated. I said, 'You know, what can you say? I just think we—no more money until . . .' Oh, meanwhile she's texting me: 'Where is the rent? Where is the rent? Where is the rent? Where is the rent,' right?" Stella's words reference the relative powerlessness that the adoption process creates. Those in possession of racial and class-based privilege feel as though they have no control over the outcome of this process, even as they possess the power to withhold precious resources from the resource-poor. Pressure mounts, frustration builds, desperation bubbles over.

Stella went on, relating to me how she outlined the terms of the exchange for Dawn, "So, then she texted me, 'I'm feeling—' I talked to her. 'I'm feeling very overwhelmed. What do I have to do to get this rent help?'" Like the mother who Stella discussed earlier, who predicted that Stella would be "done" with her in the absence of a baby, Dawn's text message references the reciprocal nature of these exchanges. This is not how adoption is supposed to work. To get the rent assistance, Dawn needed to do something in exchange. This reality undercuts the notion that this money is anything other than payment—or at the very least, an investment—for a specific future child. Stella's response to Dawn further illustrates the central place of reciprocity:

> And I said, "Well, first of all, did you have the baby?" And, she said, "Yes." I said, "Well, I don't blame you for feeling overwhelmed. It's a very tough decision. If you're going to keep your baby or place your baby, either one is a tough decision to make. But what you would have to do [to get the rent money] is sign surrenders. I would pick up the baby and take the baby to the family and then we would make arrangements to help you with your rent." And she said, "Thank you. I'll get back to you." The end.

Surrenders for shelter. The equation is clear-cut. When faced with this calculus, Dawn removed herself from the cycle of exchange. Perhaps this was always her intention. Either way, the price—her parental rights—was too high.

· · ·

the end. *fig.* and *colloq.* Of persons and things, a term to express the extreme in disparagement; the "limit": the "last straw."[8]

· · ·

By 2014, there was an online group hosted by Yahoo in which area social workers and agency staff alerted each other to possible scams. After losing contact, Stella listed Dawn in the group, and referenced correspondence with the hospital where she delivered: "I don't think she ever intended to place. So, we at least picked up on it early. And then I got a call from St. Mary's [Hospital] that she had bumped around over there. And they said, 'We talked to you before. Mm-hmm. When you were pregnant the last time.'" Expectant mothers' movements through this system are often cyclical, a series of bumpings around. Knight (2015) calls these "institutional circuits." Stella continued, "She never called them back. Because I posted her on Yahoo! So that's when they got back to me on her. So I think it was a scam, but we caught it." "I *think* it was a scam": the intention remains uncertain. Stella finished, again referencing her position as broker, "So I think they felt terrible in Ohio. I said, 'It happens.' But I don't have to feel like I let the ball drop. Client was happy that we had gone as far as we could go and they didn't just get royally reamed." Stella's language suggests that the true clients in this exchange were the prospective adopters, not the expectant mother (nor the child). I asked her how much they had paid in legally allowable expenses. "Six-fifty, one-fifty, and the food she made," Stella responded, referencing the cooler of premade meals we had delivered to Dawn. Having been around the agency when prospective parents were losing thousands, I responded, "That's not too bad." Stella replied, "Mm-hmm. It's really not too bad. So they felt happy with us." Throughout my fieldwork, rarely did a mother considered a "fall-through" contact Stella with an explicit explanation (the text message that opened the Introduction is a rare example). Even so, absent multiple "red flags," Stella tended to give fallen-through mothers the benefit of the doubt, acknowledging the courage required to come forward and admit a "change of heart."

The fall-through "scam" phenomenon, as I have described it, is not uncommon in American adoption. Pertman (2000: 246–47) relays the following extreme example:

> [A] California woman in her last days of pregnancy was charged with fraud and grand theft after she allegedly told six different couples and one single woman that they could adopt her baby. The indictment said that Kimberly Ussery, 21, and her boyfriend had received a total of about $16,000 during the previous months from the parental hopefuls, each of whom had thought they were the only ones providing assistance for housing, medical care, and other legally allowable expenses.

The legacy of the welfare queen is starkly apparent when comparing this description to a passage from a campaign speech delivered by Ronald Reagan in 1976: "She used 80 names, 30 addresses, 15 telephone numbers to collect food stamps, Social Security, veterans' benefits for four nonexistent deceased veteran husbands, as well as welfare. Her tax-free cash income alone has been running $150,000 a year" (quoted in Edin and Schaefer 2015: 15). However,

Stella and Dotty, for all their investigating and detective work, rarely uncovered what they felt comfortable calling a *real* "scam" (despite their posting of women on online watch groups, tightening of purse strings, or discussions about the ethics of reimbursement), or for that matter an *insincere* expectant mother. For in this world of intimate decision-making there is no pure, no authentic, no sincere, at least not in any tangible or accessible sense. As institutional and highly regulated as the social work carried out at First Steps may have been, at its core it was deeply subjective and highly contingent, just like the work of brokerage more generally.

The loss of money paid to an expectant mother entailed in the fall-through further complicates efforts to enclave adopted children from the realm of commodification. One wonders which situation is more ambiguous from a moral standpoint: a completed adoption that—through the placement of an infant—enables a birth mother to pay "reasonable living expenses," and thus more closely resembles the sale of a child; or a fall-through in which the expectant mother accepts money without placing, thus keeping her kinship relation with that child—assuming a child exists—intact, while breaking a socially constructed, but unspoken, financial contract with the prospective adoptive parents.

. . .

to keep one's end up (also **to keep or hold one's end**), n. To sustain one's part or bear one's share fully in an undertaking or performance.[9]

. . .

When conceptualized as an investment in future kinship, money paid for legally allowable expenses begins to render adoption a sort of risky and intimate form of futures trading.[10]

FROM COMMODITY TO FUTURE

In the analysis of domestic adoption fall-throughs and possible (but never certain) expectant mother "scams," it is difficult to conceptualize the unborn adoptee as anything more than an idea, potentiality, or future, which as such may be *more* powerful than a living, breathing child. Much of the difficulty in reconciling Western notions of the economic and intimate realms lies in the distinction between human beings and "things."[11] Kopytoff (1986: 85–86) insists on a "natural continuum" between person and thing:

> The conceptual unease of conjoining person and commodity renders, in most modern Western liberal societies, the adoption of a baby illegal if it involves monetary compensation to the natural parent—something that most societies have seen as satisfying the obvious demands of equity. In the modern West, however, adoption through compensation is viewed as child-selling and therefore akin to slavery because of the implicit commoditization of the child, regardless of how loving the adoptive parents may be.

The difficulty here lies in defining and deciding what type of "thing" an unborn baby is. Within the frame of adoption, I argue that an unborn baby is an array of possible futures.

The idea of baby as future or potentiality requires a great deal of emotional and financial investment, which in turn puts the prospective adoptive family at a great deal of perceived risk. Risk of losing hundreds, even thousands of dollars. Risk of losing what they have already come to think of as their child, even before the baby is born. Adoption carries an incipient similarity to futures trading, at the same time that it transcends the speculative practice's financial implications. "A futures contract," writes Caitlin Zaloom (2006: 19), "is a contract between individuals to provide an agreed amount of commodity at the expiration of a 'delivery' time." In the private agency adoption process, an agreement is made for the literal delivery of a future child.[12] As can be gleaned from the preceding ethnography, this futures-trading metaphor can be further extended by comparing the social workers at First Steps to brokers on the trading floor:

> Brokers are traders who accept orders from outside the market and complete these transactions in the pits in exchange for a commission on each trade . . . Brokers are the link between outside market participants and trade in the pits, the conduits for orders from traders outside the pit to the speculators inside. (Zaloom 2006: 61–62)

Social workers were links, conduits. In much the same way that brokers link traders to commodities, social workers at First Steps linked prospective adoptive parents to expectant mothers, and by extension to imagined future children. Guided by state and agency policy, they set the terms for these exchanges. Adoptive parents then made good-faith agreements—futures contracts, on the other hand, are indeed binding from the start—with the expectant mothers, which may or may not have included a transfer of money, concerning the future delivery of a baby. As a potentiality, the imagined child becomes a site of immense investment and risk. To compare adoption to futures trading is an explicit and intentional move of conceptual financialization, "the explicit application of particular financial market values to new domains, fracturing illusions that capitalism is separate from multiple, intersecting sites of production, such as the household, corporations, or education" (Bear et al. 2015).[13]

I gazed out the frosty McDonald's window and across the street. The little Cuban sandwich place where Melodie and I often met for breakfast was unexpectedly closed, and we both lamented a morning chat absent crusty bread and molten guava paste. Continuing our conversation about the role of "reasonable living expenses" in adoption, and employing a bit of speculative algebra, Melodie outlined the problematic role of monetary investments in the adoption process: "I think there is a higher risk financially for adoptive parents [now]." She rested her elbows on the table and clasped her hands, adding, "In the past, you would go to an agency and you'd write your check. You knew what it was. Right? Whatever it was, obviously cost of living and everything else has gone up, but it was, it was y." I listened and started scribbling an equation on my notepad. Y as a known quantity, a constant, something predictable. An unvarying number of dollar signs ($13,000 for most of my time at First Steps, before an increase to $27,000 in 2014). Voicing prospective adopters, Melodie continued, "I'm going to write a check for y, and I have to jump through all their hoops and get the home study and whatever, and then I go home and I sit, and then one day I get the phone call and they say we're going to bring by your daughter, right?" I instinctively nodded at her rising inflection. "But you knew it was y," she finished. Write a check. Jump through hoops. Wait. Receive a child. She narrated a fairly straightforward, linear progression from payment to kinship.

Here, Melodie alludes to the notion that before the introduction of "reasonable living expenses," which were often quite flexible and varying, the amount of money paid for an adoption was static, dependable, expected. In my first couple of years at First Steps, adoptive parents paid a series of fees, and payments to expectant parents often presented a financial unknown. Melodie noted that when the total amount required was no longer a known quantity, the calculus shifted:

These days, so much of adoption is piecemeal, so for the adoptive parents, there is a huge financial risk to move forward, because not only do they have to pay *y* to the agency, but instead of the agency eating the cost, or figuring it out in their general *y* cost of helping a birth mother out with rent, food, maternity clothes, whatever, they pass it on to you.

Melodie blew on her coffee, and pointed out that underlying the dynamic created by money paid to the expectant mother is its conceptualization as a free gift:

And because it's a gift, you know, different states have different restrictions on how much you can do, but it's still a gift. You can never ask for that back, at least not in our state, and in most states, you know, unless there's fraud and you catch her catching it, you know, two different adoptive parents or something like that, which is pretty hard to catch, number one. Number two, if she's doing that, she probably still doesn't have anything, so the best you can do is put her in jail, it's not like you're going to get your money back, right?

The notion of these payments as a gift came up again in my discussion with Kimberly, First Steps' other adoption attorney. She concurred: "The problem is intention and, under Illinois law, when you pay living expenses, they're a gift." The attorneys echoed a common discourse and legal definition that positioned both the child and money paid to the expectant / birth parents as gifts, building from an ideological notion of gifts as circulating outside the market and thus free of the moral stigma of mixing money and intimacy, and reflecting a long-standing theoretical binary in anthropology between gifts and commodities.

In an (unsuccessful) attempt to escape the uncomfortable commodification of human life, the child too is frequently imagined as a gift (Layne 1999; Ragone 1999; Rapp 1999).[14] Several mothers who had completed their adoptions explicitly described their adopted children as gifts:

I mean, again, the whole pedestal thing, you know, people think, what a gift these children get? I don't think these children get a great gift. They were surrendered by their biological families, I don't think that's a gift. The gift is to me, I made the choice to adopt.

I cannot even imagine my life without my son. He is the joy of my life, and he's just, I mean, he's a gift, and he was meant to be with me, I didn't give birth to him, but he was meant to be my son, and I know that—I believe that.

My three kids are the light of my life. I mean, I'm a happily married lady with a very successful career, but my kids are the ones who make me laugh the most and make me remember not to take myself too seriously. They are really a gift, that we were able to join and form a family with them.

You know, it's amazing to be given a gift basically from somebody else as huge, as miraculous as a child.

A child is the kind of unpayable debt that Harney and Moten (2013) and Chakravartty and Ferreira da Silva (2012) describe—that which can never be repai(re)d. As noted by Mauss ([1950] 1990), our most seminal theorist of credit and debt, the gift locks the receiver into a social relationship with the giver. The gift is a form of intimate speculation.[15]

In contrast to Maussian notions of reciprocal gift exchange, what renders money paid for expectant parents' living expenses a gift is precisely the built-in freedom from obligatory reciprocity. The reciprocal gift of the child is not guaranteed, nor is reimbursement in the event of a failed transaction. The free gift does exist. As Melodie noted, "You can never ask for that back." I listened as Melodie laid out a hypothetical scenario, prompting more equation-scribbling on my part:

Anyway, so now you're going to help this birth mother out. She's got rent at seven hundred dollars a month; add in, you know, food, utilities, whatever. You're paying a thousand dollars a month for three months, so now I got y plus three thousand dollars for, we'll call her Expectant Mom #1. Expectant Mom #1 has the baby and legitimately decides, "I can't do this, I want to parent."

Melodie's language of legitimacy here calls forth its opposite, the possibility of an illegitimate fall-through, or scam. The investment stands at $y + \$3000$. The lesson continued, "Now I go on to Expectant Mom #2. Well, Expectant Mom #2 has a little higher expenses and it's $1500 dollars a month. She chooses to parent and now I'm out, you know, $4500, plus the $3000, plus y. Right?" $(y + \$3000) + \$4500$, and still no baby. Melodie went on,

So then I'm like, all right, here's one, we really connect, we're going to go to California.[16] California allows me to pay not just three months' expenses, but I get to pay eight months' expenses at a thousand dollars a pop, so now I just paid $8,000, and she backs out, right? And so all of a sudden my y is y times two. So I think there's a lot more financial risk.

$(y + \$3000) + \$4500 + \$8000 = 2y$, and still no baby. As Melodie notes, the class inequality undergirding modern domestic adoption further complicates the role that money plays in the exchange. As fall-throughs accumulate, the financial investment rises steeply. Social workers are often left to solve for (wh)y.

In 2009, on the eve of a series of fall-throughs that social workers speculatively attributed to the Recession, First Steps allowed prospective adopters to provide up to $3,000 to an expectant mother for legally allowable expenses, and applicants were individually responsible for supporting their matched expectant mothers. However, not all adoptive families that experienced fall-throughs also suffered financial loss, because not all expectant mothers requested coverage of legally allowable expenses before the birth of the child. This dynamic allowed the agency to move to a system in 2014 in which every adoptive family paid $675 to a central "birth mother fund" from which all expenses were paid. Thus, "reasonable living expenses" were absorbed into the total static y, or agency-set cost of adoption, to use Melodie's formulation. In order to mitigate the financial risk of fall-throughs, First Steps had effectively instituted an insurance program, which spread the financial risk evenly among prospective adoptive parents. Under the old system, one family might pay $2,500 in birth parent expenses, while another might not pay anything. Under the new system, everyone paid the same premium. This insurance-like system also helped to further distance the money given by adoptive parents from a specific child—parents were contributing to a fund rather than financing a specific infant. "Fees are for *services,* not a baby," social workers would stress, in order to further differentiate adoption from child-selling. This refrain could be construed as another example of moral maintenance, cleaving the child off from the dangers of economic exchange.

Insurance is a strategy for rendering an uncertain future actionable in the present (Lakoff 2007). In thinking about insurance as a modern form of risk management characterized by an attempt to mitigate future losses through present action, the question arises, *Is there a form of insurance that protects against the fall-through or the other risks attendant to adoption?* Enter the mysterious case of adoption disruption insurance, or ADI. This form of insurance was once available to prospective adopters, but it disappeared sometime in the late 1990s. It is very difficult to find any information about this insurance, and no company or lawyer seems to offer it anymore. I asked Melodie if she knew anything about ADI or how it functioned. Her first e-mail reply was brief, asking why I was interested and musing, "I can ask lawyers but so many adoptions are risky now not sure if anybody offers it. I believe it is legal." Like a chronic and pervasive preexisting condition, adoption threatens potential financial losses so great that it is considered uninsurable. I responded that I was working on a research paper about adoption and risk, and Melodie, after forwarding my inquiry to her colleagues nationwide (none of whom responded), replied with her own "dissertation," excerpts from which follow and reveal the social complexities wrapped up in the idea of insuring adoption, particularly the requirement of risk (financial and emotional) and the passage of time—especially the act of waiting:

> What I see is a lot of angry / sad / disappointed / scared / defeated PAPs [prospective adoptive parents]. The risk of financing adoption (if not foster care) has shifted to the potential parents in recent years despite the price of adoption going up. I see this as a problem for many reasons including it prices many people out of the possibility of adoption.
>
> PAPs usually take on all birth mother expenses risk (if the expenses are allowed) but to even process the expenses requires a professional be hired to assess the situation, give counseling, deliver check (in some states as PAPs can not pay directly). For example, in IL all birth mother expenses must go through an agency (must hire agency) or through a court approval process (must hire lawyer) in order to help with birth parent expenses. (Which, by the way, are almost always asked for at the last moment causing timing problems.)

Here, Melodie alludes to the unpredictability of the adoption process: "timing problems" are inherent to the circuitous ways in which adoptions often unfold. She insisted that the financial risk entailed by agency adoption is often quite high, and the agencies themselves no longer fully absorb it. As she mentions below, however, the risk is also emotional and temporal. Prospective parents risk dollars, hearts, and years. She concluded:

> Finally, the best insurance is the adoption tax credit (currently a little over $12,000 and thankfully renewed with no sunset clause in 1 / 2013) as it is applicable for failed adoptions. However, for failed adoptions it cannot be taken until the year after the failure (i.e., long wait). And many people are waiting to take the failed adoption as a tax credit to get money back to start over again.

The process was rarely linear from start to finish. Melodie offered, "In any case, the risks regarding finances (not to mention hearts) are there and very much a huge concern for PAPs. Many are scared to start, can't afford to start, choose alternative routes to parent (ARTs / foster care), give up, etc." Starts are both ends and beginnings. So as prospective adoptive parents begin the process and begin to weigh the risks involved, the closest thing to insurance against economic loss is the Adoption Tax Credit. In 2017, the maximum credit allowed to cover "reasonable and necessary adoption fees" and other related expenses was $13,570 per child (nonrefundable), subject to income limits for those making over $203,540.[17] In the "timing rules" section of the IRS policy, it is noted that one of the determining factors for which tax year the credit shall apply to is "when, if ever, the adoption was finalized." The credit cannot be claimed until the year following the payment, requiring prospective parents to continue waiting—and what little financial relief it provides is an ineffective remedy for the heartbreak and time lost that results from a fall-through.

About a month after Stella and I met Valerie—before the institution of the central "birth mother fund"—she switched families because she needed more money than the first family with whom she was matched could pay. When this happened, the agency leadership was split down the middle on what steps to take next for the prospective adoptive family Valerie had left. She had originally been matched with a family in Germany, and Stella switched her to a second family in the Chicago area who could more adequately meet her financial needs.[18] The problem was that the German family had already paid some of her expenses. The dilemma Stella confronted was whether or not the second family should have to reimburse the first family, since the baby would be theirs in the end.[19] In August of 2009, Stella presented the case to the staff in the office, believing the second family should indeed reimburse the first. Dotty, the agency's director at the time, adamantly disagreed. Rita, an intern, reported that the whole situation made her "sick."

Stella later told me, "I think it [reimbursement] is the right thing to do if they accept placement. I think it should be brought up. I don't think you can make them, but you can strongly, strongly encourage." In Stella's reasoning (which goes against the notion that the funds are a gift to the mother rather than payment for or investment in a particular child), it was only rational that the original family be reimbursed in the event of successful placement, since technically, the second family would have received something for which the first paid. Stella's use of the qualifier "right" signals her moral stance. This is part of the "moral discourse" of adoption: "the emergent, experience-near commentary on the rightness and wrongness of clinical action" (Brodwin 2008: 130). Stella continued, "I had one mom who took money; the following day another agency called me to say they were now working with this woman. And I asked for reimbursement for the family and they said well they would see. And they never did. That's not right. That is ethically not right." This was the same family with whom Valerie was originally matched, and this marked their second fall-through. Social workers at First Steps occasionally guided adoptive families through *multiple* fall-throughs before a placement was achieved. If a family had experienced one or more financial fall-throughs, they would often be placed into a special category only considered for expectant mothers not asking for money, or placed into a queue waiting for "born" babies, for whom an adoption plan was only made *after* the birth. It was through the mother's erasure—the removal of her needs from the equation—that these problematic "fall-throughs" were avoided.

It was not uncommon at First Steps for certain mothers to place multiple children. Occasionally, an expectant mother would fall through and then return months or years later with another pregnancy, wishing to place. To one mother who successfully placed one baby, had a fall-through, and then returned, pregnant again, Stella said, "Call me when you go into the hospital if you still wanna do this . . . no more money." The agency was only willing to work with this placement as a born baby, a *real* child rather than a potentiality that simply carried too much risk. This particular type of risk management serves to bridge the gap between baby-as-future and baby-as-kinned-entity-in-the-world. Stella continued, "And Angeline called me a third one too, and I said, 'Just call me when you're in the hospital, because we just can't do this.'" The high rate of fall-throughs, some but not all of which appeared to staff to be "scams," forced social workers to take measures to protect prospective adoptive families. For example, Stella told me the following about a white mother named Celeste:[20]

> She had received money for several months . . . I think it was about $300 per month, which Leslie [the prospective adoptive mother] could afford. Right before she was about to deliver, she was due more money but I put a halt on that until we had some medical confirmation. She made arrangements to get me this from the doctor's appointment that day and never showed up or called again. She had also during this time agreed by phone with Leslie and her sister's arrangements to fly here. So who knows what ever really happened? I told Leslie she was not to fly until we had this documentation.

Most fall-throughs occurred without warning, before the birth of the baby (while it remained an idea or potentiality), and the primary indication—aside from occasional "red flags"—was lack of contact. In these situations, invested money was lost and irrecoverable, along with the imagined child and the future kinship she encapsulated.

Many of the adoptive parents I encountered were offended by the question from strangers, "How much did s/he cost?" in reference to their adopted children. They often lumped it in with inappropriate questions about abandonment and adoption stigma. When asked if she had received offensive comments from strangers about her family, one adoptive mother said, "I've had one person ask about money, which was just a totally—" "Really?" I cut her off without meaning to. "Yeah." "Like, like if you bought her or something?" I asked. "Like, how much. Like, how much," she clarified. "You know, how much did she cost? And I said, just, 'priceless.'" Another adoptive mother, complaining about similar questions, said,

> I don't get it too much, but I got, oh, "Isn't it expensive?" and "Did their mothers abandon them or they didn't want them?" and you're like, "Do you have to say this in front of them?" Yeah. "Save your questions for—" Yeah. Sometimes people just, they don't have boundaries. They just feel they can come up and say whatever they want to you.

She went on, "How much, yeah, how much did they cost?" before retorting, "Well, okay, did you have kids? Obviously you have to pay for your insurance and pay for the birth of the child, yeah." Adoptive parents' anger and discomfort stems from the ideological notion that children are priceless (Zelizer 1985) and therefore exist outside the realm of commodity exchange. The question "How much did x cost?" is appropriate only for things. The contested role of money in the adoption process illustrates how morality represents one node through which the economic and the intimate are co-constituted. Strategies to mitigate the effects of this "immoral" overlap are built into the very fabric of the adoption process, which involves a temporal lag between the circulation of money and the delivery of an infant.[21]

Stella said she often felt like a mother to struggling young expectant mothers, but that after a fall-through or even after a successful placement, her role often converted uncomfortably to "the person who took away the baby." In a wider professional schema, social workers in general are given *immense* power as they are legally mandated to remove children from their biological parents. However, adoption is complicated by the fact that expectant mothers also retain some power until the surrenders are signed. The baby is theirs until they relinquish parental rights, and the system is designed—rightfully so— such that they may simply vanish (from the perspective of social workers and prospective adopters) along with the idea of that baby, with no legal consequences (unless a scam is discovered, of course). For many prospective *adoptive* families, this is akin to losing a child through death or state action, regardless of the fact that the child was never theirs to begin with. Indeed, other factors exist that determine the power differential between Stella (white, middle class, institutional agent) and these expectant mothers (most often African American, low income, unstably housed on occasion, and sometimes living with mental illness), and these social inequalities further complicate an already-fraught relationship. The choices and judgments that expectant mothers and social workers make during the adoption process are highly conditioned by a number of factors, and subjects practice a complicated form of discursive and regulatory moral maintenance to defend this intimate form of futures trading from the perceived cultural and ideological contamination of commodification.

Fall-throughs were perceived as problematic by social workers and prospective adoptive parents not only due to the financial difficulties they presented, but also—perhaps more so—because of their affective implications. This is part of the reason that futures, rather than gifts or commodities, provide such an apt theoretical frame for the adoptable child. Futures can be invested in monetarily, but also affectively and temporally. Adoption as a form of intimate speculation carries the risk of multiple forms of loss. Adoptive parents were reluctant to discuss the loss of money in the event of a fall-through, emphasizing instead the sense of emotional devastation. This is perhaps further illustration of the cultural taboo of mixing intimacy with economy. As this chapter has demonstrated, adoption professionals, such as Melodie and Stella, certainly discussed the economic difficulties of fall-through scenarios more freely, perhaps because they did not have kinship ties to the children in question, ties put at risk by the acknowledgment of money's role in the adoption process.[22]

The cultural logics of kinship formation as a form of intimate speculation are crystallized in the failure of the adoption process to create new forms of kinship, even when aided by gift and commodity logics. The fall-through, whether "scam" or "change of heart" or something else entirely, as a sort of premature and preemptive end, negates adoptive kinship in advance of its emergence, and often prompts substantial losses. However, the fall-through is rarely an example of "failure as an endpoint" (Miyazaki and Riles 2005), but rather a launch-pad for fate and future possibility. The end makes possible a new start, even in the case of institutional collapse, as the next chapter will show.

FIVE

———

Closure

Well, that's why Ecclesiastes was so popular and has worn the
centuries. There's a time for everything. And I believe that.
Nothing is forever.

—STELLA (March 28, 2015)

"I AM JUST HANGING IN, and I will continue to hang in," Stella told me
the last time we spoke. Contingency requires a sort of hanging. She went on,
"Life puts curves in everybody's way. There could be many worse things happening than this." Contingency is much more than an individual position. It
can also be an institutional state of being. In March of 2015, First Steps closed
its doors permanently. On the eve of the closing, Stella told me, using the
same language she had used to describe fall-throughs, "This is a bump in a
road for everybody, and this, too, will pass, so I will greet people with a smile
and a blessing, and that's the way it is." In the summer of 2016, after being
away from Chicago for a year, I returned to the absences and presences that
were left in the agency's wake. By this time, Stella had moved to another state,
but I gathered accounts of the closing from fifteen of her former colleagues
and clients, a mix of staff, board members, and adoptive parents. Their
accounts chart a turning tide at the twilight of First Steps' institutional life,
and speculate about the changing landscape of American adoption more
broadly.

This book began with disappearance; it ends there as well. How do we
study closure as an outcome of institutional precarity? How do we write
institutional atrophy and dissolution? The blank space left when things, people, places, go missing or cease to be? Things, people, places, simultaneously
here, but also elsewhere? Nowhere? How do we write foreclosure? And not
only foreclosure in terms of the mortgage crisis and Recession, to which this
story is intimately stitched, but also foreclosure in the sense of preclusion and
exclusion. When the field and the future rupture, and we can no longer do
the work we once set out to do? When once concerned with openness, we

find ourselves confronted with myriad forms of closure? Specifically, what can the quiet death of a small adoption agency reveal about how the temporal, affective, visual, and economic dynamics of intimate speculation cohere in the United States in the decade after the Recession?

This chapter knits together the stories I was told about the closure. It is a journey of my interlocutors' attempts to make meaning in the wake of loss. It is a final form of intimate speculation. Close your eyes. Closing in. To come to a close. Sorry, we're closed. Closed cases. Closed files. Closed adoption. Open. When one door closes, another opens. Adoption is a practice often carried out with arms open and eyes closed. How do we open up closure? In the wake of a massive unraveling, the process of tying up loose ends is also, inevitably, a sort of beginning. The stories I was told cohere around three dimensions of closure: financial foreclosure, enclosures of mothers and motherlands, and closure as the affective remains of loss. In closing, the multifaceted notion of closure, I suggest, illustrates how the splintering economic, visual, and temporal elements of intimate speculation collapsed back into one another in the agency's implosion.

"GRADUAL AND THEN SUDDEN"

On a sunny July afternoon in 2016, I sat in an office in a large glass and steel high-rise in a downtown Chicago law firm. The office belonged to Richard, one of First Steps' board members and also an adoptive father. When asked about the closing, he recounted,

> I would say it was—to quote a Hemingway character—it was gradual and then sudden, because the agency was sort of operating on thin ice, more or less. We periodically would have discussions about, you know, "What would we need to do if we had to wind up? We're not ready to make that decision." So those occurred through several years, and we were never ready to do it. And it was always, you know, more adoptions in the pipeline. And, but we went through 2013 into 2014 [which] were pretty rough, and then a quarter of 2014 looked pretty good, and then everything just sort of dried up again.

Flows were stemmed. The agency's closure was precipitated by a combination of social and economic factors that led to a great deal of volatility and precarity in the final years of its existence. Despite the passage of time, the last weeks of the agency's life were present in the minds of the former staff and board members I encountered upon my return to Chicago in 2016. As Tammy, a contract social worker, put it, "It was just highs and lows. It was just such a roller coaster." Barbara recalled, "Now, there had been discussion, because she [Stella] had said to me, 'I don't think we're going to be able to survive.' And I encouraged her. I said, 'I don't think so either. I don't know how you're going to dig yourself out of this, I really don't.' "

.   .   .

end, n. The limit of duration, or close, of a period of time; the termination, conclusion, of an action, process, continuous state, or course of events; the terminal point of a series.[1]

.   .   .

Given all the potential for disruption inherent to the adoption process, the bureaucratic closing of the agency proved to be a relatively smooth undertaking. When it finally became clear that the work of the agency could not continue, the decision to close was arrived at rather quickly by Stella and an executive committee assembled by the board. Transfer plans were put into place for families in process. In addition to being transferred to other agencies, prospective adoptive parents were reimbursed between $2,000 and $3,000, a portion of what they had paid in fees. Holly and Stella called over one hundred in-process applicants to relay the news. The phone calls were followed up with letters and information about transferring to other agencies. Holly explained, "And that was, I think, our saving grace, because I didn't call people and say, 'We're closing.' I called people and said, 'We're closing, but here's a chance for a plan. Your adoption will not be halted.' " Her words called to mind Rosalind's use of *will*. The child *will* find its way to you. The closing of the agency created a wave of redirections, but allowed for applicants to continue their adoption processes elsewhere. The closure was a permanent institutional end, but it did not—for the most part—result in fallen-through adoptions. Holly insisted, "The people who saved us were those agencies who took our files . . . If they would have said no, these adoptions would have fell through . . . I don't think we put as much stock into that—that that was going to be our saving grace—but that's what saved me." Here, Holly easily tacks back and forth between individual and institutional rescue: the other adoption agencies saved her, personally, but also saved the agency, in a sense, through the continuation of First Steps applicants' adoptions. "I don't think any family was delayed," she added.

The board, assisted by Stella and Jenny, got to work figuring out how to divide up the small amount of money that was left. As Jonathan, the board president, recounted:

> It was basically a process of sitting down and then kind of doing the math and just saying, you know, we have this much money, we can allocate it to these things, and then working with families to—and then the other part of it, which is what DCFS kind of requires before you actually close, is you have to at least transfer all your families somewhere. You can't just leave people hanging.

Familial futures hung in the balance as First Steps staff scrambled to transfer cases. Tammy, who was responsible for the transfer of several families to another agency, described her clients' reactions: "'We're sad it's closing, but thankful that there's—' I think they were thankful there was already a plan. Like, they weren't stuck in the middle of their adoption having to go start over and search for an agency." We were sitting on Tammy's front porch. It was summer in Chicago and her street was being resurfaced. Our conversation was punctuated by the whir of heavy machinery, and colossal clouds of dust floated down the street, coating her patio furniture. She continued, raising her voice above the bulldozer down the block, "I know so many [agencies], like, AAI out west, just closed, no, didn't tell a single person. Not even an e-mail, nothing. They just suddenly were closed on families." Another cloud of dust blew toward us as she finished, referring back to First Steps:

> It wasn't really fair to take any more families, because they knew it was just going to keep being a struggle. And that it was probably inevitable, and so why keep taking in more families? So that's why, yeah, like, they got to a point where they had fulfilled their mission over the years that they were open, and then they probably couldn't, in the way they should.

Jonathan, the former board president, spoke similarly, echoing Stella's language of the bumpy road:

> We just didn't feel that we could in good faith, given our financial situation, continue to accept new applicants into our programs not knowing that we had the financial wherewithal to see those people through to the conclusion of their adoption. It just—everything told us that there just wasn't a real good road here.

At the time of the closing, the wait for a domestic adoption was as long as two and a half years. It was becoming increasingly difficult to predict whether or not the agency would still exist at the culmination of those adoptions. A temporal horizon was receding.

Although operationally the process appeared seamless, the closure proved disruptive for both staff and families. Corinne's perspective differed from Tammy's in terms of the closing's impact on waiting adoptive families. When I asked her if anything in particular stuck out to her about the closing, she pointed to "the lack of preparation for workers and families." She sighed, "I think that was the hardest part for me and for a lot of the families. Like, 'Oh my gosh. You're telling us this and now you're closing.' I mean, I don't even— it was less than a month that everybody knew . . . like, everybody was a little blindsided." Corinne also noted the ripples felt by families in the midst of the closure as a form of disruption: "So I think for the families who were, like, kind of right at the cusp of doing—of a major part of their process, that was the hardest. Kind of, like, 'Oh my gosh. This isn't going to be a smooth, fluid thing. You're messing everything up and we're scared.'" The adoption process was choppy to begin with, but the closure represented a change in course scaled up to the institutional level. Small as the agency was, this was a fall-through of immense proportions.

Many accounts of the closing revealed a tension between predictability and shock, the simultaneously measured and abrupt character of the closure, its un / predictability. Tammy too, despite her comments about family transitions, expressed surprise when she initially heard the news of the closure:

> I remember being surprised. Like, being pretty surprised. Like, all along I feel like I was listening to, like, "Oh, we might have to close. Maybe we'll merge. Maybe we'll this. Things aren't going well." You know, and then all of a sudden it seemed like there was no talk of anything, and then we're closing. And I was, like, wait, what? . . . I was at the same time, like, "Whoa, okay. Pretty shocking." So I think it was. Yes, that was pretty sudden. And I think right off the bat when I heard, I of course went, I think I called Stella—you know, I was like, "Wait, what?"

Like Richard, Tammy expressed an experience of the closure as both gradual and sudden. Her repeated reactionary "Wait, what?" reenacted and encapsulated a sort of staccato disruption to a temporality previously perceived as smooth. The epitome of an *unexpectation,* a future drastically shifted. For the most part, individual adoptions did not fall through as a result of the closure, but something else did.

The agency as a physical and spatial entity disappeared. The office was dismantled by the staff. All files kept on-site were organized chronologically and alphabetically, picked up by a DCFS truck, and relocated to Springfield. Holly remembered, "Oh, it was mad. I mean, we spent, like, four Saturdays or, three or four, just filing and putting into boxes and filing, and then DCFS actually came with a moving truck." When I spoke to Stella in the midst of the move, she told me about a former intern who had volunteered to label and alphabetize approximately 1,700 files and sell all of the office furniture on Craigslist. Stella somberly admitted, echoing Holly's language of the saving grace, "If she hadn't walked in, I swear to God, that's where, you know, I think the universe and my fate lead. If she hadn't come in when she came in, I'd be dead today."

Thus were the nuts and bolts of closing up shop. But what prompted the closing itself? In moving from the how to the why, another board member, Jeremy, offered some insights into the internal and external factors that precipitated First Steps' hectic final months and eventual closing:

> You know, if I had to take a top-line view of it and say sort of, there were a couple of sort of macro-trends and maybe a couple things inside the agency that led towards its closure, and it was all sort of moving in that direction anyway now, you know, in hindsight it's easier to see it that way.

A peculiar confluence of social and economic factors occurred in the years following the Recession that made it impossible for First Steps to continue its operation. The most pressing of these was simply running out of money, due in part to crippling debt.

FORECLOSURE

"First Steps probably never should have continued after that Illinois law passed that you had to be a nonprofit," Jenny, the agency's business manager, admitted, looking down into her coffee as she sat talking with me in a small bakery no more than two blocks from the recently foreclosed building First Steps had once occupied. It was June of 2016, and the agency had been closed a little over a year. Echoing Richard's sentiment of gradual suddenness, Jenny said,

I just kept saying, "We don't have any money. [If] we're going forward like this, we're not going to be able to cover our debt and this is coming due and this is coming due and it just—I'm no longer advertising, so how can we do this?" And then we got to this point where I just said, "Okay, I'm going to slow down on paying the bills." And it actually was very sudden.

The most straightforward reason for the closure was that the agency could no longer afford to keep the lights on and pay its employees. As Stella confessed on the eve of the closing, "We're like a month and a half behind on the rent." A year later, Dotty recalled, "We weren't paying our bills, and if we were, just small amounts." She continued, sadly, "Jenny was there watching it all die, and having to deal with creditors and all of that." Jenny told me, "We were having a cash emergency, because we hadn't placed in months." Cash flow was tied directly to the flow of babies. She went on, "Everything requires capital and money and I just don't think there was the—just didn't quite have the—ugh." She cut herself off in frustration. A year after the agency closed, Jenny was still fielding calls from creditors on her personal cell phone. Toward the end of our conversation, in which she disclosed to me that she had worked without pay in order help with the wind-down, Jenny offered, "I actually think that it's great that we didn't really keep going into more debt just to keep going, because then it becomes not about the mission. It becomes about the money." Mission and money, it turns out, were never mutually exclusive.

The little nonprofit looked a lot like a failing business, or a bad mortgage. To understand an ending, it is often necessary to go back to the beginning: in this case, First Steps' rebirth in 2006 as a nonprofit organization after a previous life as a for-profit enterprise. After the transition to nonprofit status, it became a struggle to keep the doors open, and the agency experienced several periods of financial precarity (the "roller coaster" referred to by Tammy). As Dotty recalled after the closing, employing the first of many sinking-ship analogies, "We always laugh about, the boat's now off the bottom of the ocean. We're now floating again. And so, we had those bursts of infusions of money, but for the most part it was a slowly sinking ship." I think this comparison to a sinking ship is important for historical reasons to which I will return. As Jenny mentioned, the agency's struggles first began with this peculiar switch to nonprofit. Indeed, the very structure and philosophy of "nonprofit" was at odds with the neoliberal capitalist logics undergirding the formerly for-profit enterprise, and so much of the socioeconomic milieu in which it was embedded.

First Steps transitioned from for-profit to nonprofit after the passing of Illinois's Adoption Reform Act (HB 3628) in 2005, which mandated that all adoption agencies in the state carry a 501(c)(3) not-for-profit designation.[2] The act also introduced new requirements concerning disclosure of fees and policies, created a Bill of Rights for both birth and adoptive parents, and raised licensing standards for organizations offering adoption services. A press release announcing the new legislation quoted then-governor Rod Blagojevich: "With these reforms, we're making sure that adoptions are about building families—not making a profit. I'm proud to sign into law this bill that sets Illinois up to be a model for the rest of the country regarding adoptions" (quoted in Illinois.gov 2005). State representative Sarah Feigenholtz echoed, "This legislation aligns Illinois with the best standards to improve adoption practices. It protects children and birth parents, helps to create and sustain nurturing adoptive families, and will ensure adoptions are done in a charitable manner." Richard, who was on the executive committee that oversaw the closure, noted:

> So the irony of it is, although the state requires you to be, not just a not-for-profit, but a 501(c)3 not-for-profit under Federal rules, that means that the IRS then looks at you for not-for-profit purposes as a charity, but of course the adoption part of the business is not a charity. It's fee-for-service.

This shift from profit to charity was complicated for a "fee-for-service" entity initiated as a business.

The Adoption Reform Act was designed to extinguish predatory adoption practices. A far-reaching side effect of the reform is that it recalibrated the economics of adoption in a way that disproportionately affected small agencies lacking endowments, large donor bases, and the staffing and expertise to market their services and apply for external funding. First Steps was one such agency, and in its case, the switch from for-profit to nonprofit required a buyout of the original business that economically crippled the agency in the decade that followed. As a private enterprise, even after the shift to nonprofit, First Steps did not receive any public financial support, and continued its operations much as before.

For First Steps, this recalibration, which was meant to further distance adoption from a capitalist profit-driven enterprise, actually produced an economic situation that was eerily similar to the lending crises that had sparked the Recession. Dotty's comparison of the agency to a sinking ship was instructive. In some ways, First Steps was like a subprime-mortgaged house. In the final years, it was deep under water. "We essentially bought the agency from Dotty," Jonathan explained. Dotty, the founder and the creditor. To facilitate the transition to nonprofit, First Steps had merged with its partner organization, a small nonprofit specializing in adoption and advocacy for HIV+ children. The boards of both organizations were recombined and reconstituted, and the newly merged nonprofit paid / owed Dotty for the value of the original business. That value was then taken on as a debt obligation that First Steps paid in installments through the end of the life of the agency. By the time I spoke with board members, no one could remember the exact original valuation, but it was estimated to fall between $200,000 and $300,000, hovering near the median price for a home in Chicago. One board member referred to the debt as "this added weight that other agencies aren't dealing with."

Richard told me, "The economics of the not-for-profit were always kind of precarious. Some years were better than others, but it was just the nature of the business." Richard had a habit of referring often to "business" and "markets" when discussing the nuances of First Steps' operation, highlighting private adoption's function as a "marketplace" (Raleigh 2017). The transition to nonprofit had failed to erase or transcend capitalist economic logics, begging the question: How does a nonprofit entity survive under the conditions of capitalism? Richard shared with me his perspective on the changes that followed the Adoption Reform Act, which disproportionately affected small agencies like First Steps:

> The other agencies were consolidating. The change in the law was actually ran through, primarily, sort of on the theory that it was going to push lesser skilled then perhaps even, you know, negligent or criminal factors in the adoption area out of business. Get rid of a lot of the intermediaries that were working in the business. And be ultimately safer and better for adoption and adopted children in the long run. So that was the theory, but we all know, it was also pushed through by the large agencies because they saw this as a way to consolidate the business in what was going to be a shrinking business. Adoption was already shrinking at that point.

The purpose of the act, according to Richard, was to purge bad brokers; a side effect was the elimination of "good little agencies" too. He continued, "And, that's in fact what happened, it became harder and harder, as a small not-for-profit, to make money, to fundraise, competition with the larger ones and so on. And to find a niche that worked." The act amplified capitalist competition and the potential for monopolies within the newly nonprofit field.

Adoption was beginning to decline, which meant that First Steps' income was also declining. The buyout was unaffordable, but there was no other way to keep the agency running.

As Richard suggests, some agencies were just too big to fail. Several staff and board members made a point to mention First Steps' relatively small size in comparison to larger competitor agencies. Dotty insisted, "We were one of the last little agencies in the area to close." She laughed, adding: "Jonathan always called us the 'Little Agency That Could' and I'm proud of the fact that we were so highly regarded and respected and that we had every certification known to man, at great expense to us." Indeed, the small size of the agency was a reason adoptive parents often cited for choosing First Steps to build their families. "We liked that it was small," noted one adoptive mother; "It felt comfortable. And we liked that it was local, and it just felt like a good fit for us."

"And, you know, agencies are closing like mad," Holly told me in 2016; "Places are just closing." She was right; the closure was not unique, and larger agencies were closing too. The same year First Steps shuttered, Baker Victory Services in Buffalo, New York, phased out its private adoption program, shifting its focus to foster care and other social services. A news article noted that in the year before the closure, "the agency performed just seven adoptions, including three domestically and four international adoptions, down from 33 in 2008–2009" (Drury 2015). Two years later, California-based agency Independent Adoption Center (IAC) closed its doors and declared bankruptcy, spawning headlines like "Concord Adoption Agency Closes, Leaving Parents in the Dark" and "Adoption Agency's Sudden Closure Leaves Prospective Parents Hanging" (Brinkley 2017; Villareal 2017). IAC's president cited the changing landscape of adoption, including a decline in the number of potential birth parents seeking services. In early 2018, Colorado agency Adoptions by Heart was suspended and ultimately shut down by the Department of Human Services after several complaints. According to a spokesperson, this occurred when the agency did not have the financial means to appeal the initial suspension (Morfitt 2018). In 2017, *Consumerist*, an online news site produced by Consumer Reports, published an article entitled "What Can You Do When Your Adoption Agency Goes Bankrupt?" suggesting that these closures constitute an emerging trend (Quirk 2017).

Holly lamented, "It's just, the small were just getting so small . . . a lot of people aren't willing to take that risk when it comes to $30,000 and family planning." First Steps' small size was attractive to potential clients because of the offer of intimacy, but its size also increased the riskiness of the adoption process. Barbara echoed, "So you don't have the personal feel there [at bigger agencies] that some people really kind of want, so I could see why they'd choose to work with us." One board member who had adopted from First Steps offered, "And, you know, Stella answered the phone in the middle of the night, which created a sort of relationship with her that drew us closer to the agency." He continued, noting the disproportionate impact of the buyout due to the agency's size: "So as a result [of the buyout], you know, this little agency had a sort of financial obligation that an agency its size couldn't—wouldn't—have, in that we were retiring this installment note to Dotty." The existence of the agency itself relied on this promissory relationship: "credit / debt can be seen as a method devised for a debtor to borrow speculative resources from his / her own future and transform them into concrete resources to be used in the present" (Peebles 2010: 227). As Harney and Moten (2013: 64) contend, "If you want to do something, forget this debt, and remember it later."

One of the financial difficulties that the agency had long battled was a lack of a strong donor base, which became necessary after the transition to nonprofit, as the agency relied solely on adoption fees and donations for income. As Jenny observed, "We just don't have the depth of people to support us." I sat in Dotty's dining room as she told me, "The other factor in the closing, really, Kate, was we were tapped out in terms of approaching our donors. We had some donors—we had some big donors—but, you know, they can only give for so long." She went on, "It wasn't a very sexy thing to give money for an agency, just to us, but it was the only way we could be put in a position to keep helping kids." This child-centered statement reveals how the brokerage function of the agency (unsexy as it is) gets obscured by the ends of adoption. Corinne observed, "We really weren't bringing in nearly enough money from the fundraising events." Dotty mentioned that in the later years, even in the case of an influx of donations, "Nothing would jump-start us anymore. We would just go through that in a month, paying back all the money we owed to people." Living, in a sense, paycheck to paycheck, it became impossible for the agency's shrinking assets to keep pace with its liabilities. As Jonathan observed:

> First Steps, being a small agency, always operated on a very thin margin. We never had a lot of money. We never had, you know, a lot of facilities. We didn't have an endowment, you know, all that. So, you know, it was always a challenge to balance our income against our ongoing expenses, right?

An endowment is a gift that keeps on giving, a way to secure the future. Donations only provided temporary relief. Fundraising was a constant stressor. In the end, Jonathan said, "I don't miss the financial struggle at all, and the constant need to raise money." Stella asked the question, "Can we sustain?" The answer was no.

In the later years, First Steps had raised adoption fees in an effort to offset the discrepancy between assets and liabilities. Michael, the board treasurer, explained:

> You know, we were the small one but we were also charging some of the lowest fees, and so we made a decision to raise those fees and even when we raised the fees, we were still at the low end of the rate for adoption agencies. We felt like we needed to in order to continue on as an organization, but we still didn't want to raise them too much to price people out of our services. Because that was something that was important to Dotty and Stella and the staff at First Steps.

Corinne moved to another agency after the closure, and noted, "Fees are a lot higher at [the other agency] and I think Stella had made a comment one time: 'Well, that's probably why they're in business and we're not.' So it's like that. The pricing was nice for First Steps families, but it's also not cutting it for the agency." As a fee-for-service organization, First Steps charged approximately $13,000 per domestic placement during my first few years of fieldwork; toward the end, the fees were almost doubled in an effort to keep pace with other agencies, to offset the dwindling numbers, and to keep the agency afloat. It was too little, too late.

In the months before the closing, the board had considered trying to merge with another agency in the region, but it proved impossible to find a partner willing to take on the debt left over from the buyout. As Jonathan noted, "We couldn't operate the agency and support the debt obligation. And we went out to look for major partners, you can imagine that. Nobody wanted to take on that debt." Melissa, another contract social worker, told me about another small agency nearby that had recently merged with a much larger national agency. The smaller agency "had a huge endowment, makes it very enticing," she said, "while First Steps had a huge debt." The debt foreclosed survival in more ways than one.

Returning to the discourse of the small agency, Jonathan argued, "The economics of adoption are such now that I think agencies have to be big." He finished, "There's no other way to say it—it's really unfortunate. I mean a lot of life lessons there, I guess, but at the end of the day, they don't have money. Without a lot of money, it's very difficult to adopt, to run an adoption agency. They really just don't have the resources." In one sentence Jonathan drew attention to the imbalances that make adoption possible, and the structural alignment between adopters and the agency. Capital is required to adopt *and* to run an adoption agency. Michael made a similar connection between a decrease in donations and a decrease in adoptions: "There were certainly times where [we] would see, you know, large drop-offs in the number of adoptions, and then also, you know, in donations as well." He explained that during and after the Recession,

> I think we saw, especially on the donation side—probably also on the domestic adoptions—where there was a decrease in the adoptions that we handled and also on the donations, and I don't think we ever saw it, you know, tick back up. When things started to recover, it just kind of stayed down at that lower level.

As a nonprofit fee-for-service organization, First Steps depended on its ability to place children in order to collect fees. But in the final years, those placements grew fewer and farther between. First Steps' size, nonprofit status, and overwhelming debt obligations were all deeply intertwined with changes occurring in adoption more broadly. The sinking of the debt-saddled agency-as-ship was highly contingent on supply.

ENCLOSURES

The financial contours of the closure hinged upon dual forms of enclosure in the broader adoption landscape: domestic "keeps" and closed sending countries, the precarity of mothers and motherlands, respectively. "So do you think that the debt was one of the primary things that caused the closure for First Steps?" I asked Tammy that dusty July afternoon on her front porch. "I don't think that's what caused it," she said, "I think that's what caused them not being able to merge. I feel like it's the—it was all of it. Like, the downturn in domestic, which had been happening for a long time." Money was a problem, but the financial consequences of the agency's shift to nonprofit status were exacerbated by a marked drop-off in placements over the last several years of the agency's operation—Corinne had referred to this in one of our conversations as "a lack of birth parent activity."

Tying supply-side challenges to the burden of the buyout debt, Jeremy noted, "So we sort of had this kind of financial commitment that other agencies our size didn't have, and then, you know, we were suffering from what a lot of other agencies were suffering from: decreasing volume." He frowned, before continuing, "And eventually those two lines were going to intersect somewhere down the road." A common theme in my post-closure discussions with staff and board members was what Jeremy referred to as "the demise of domestic adoption." Various news outlets have commented upon this trend, in tandem with a parallel waning in international adoption, referring to a "critical adoption shortage" and "steady decline" (Koch 2013; Kingsbury 2013). According to the National Council for Adoption's 2017 edition of *Adoption by the Numbers,* domestic private agency adoptions in the United States declined from 20,254 in 2007 to 16,312 in 2014 (Jones and Placek 2017: 4). Jeremy explained, "You know, the phone doesn't ring. You know, the hospitals don't call." The debt to Dotty was problematic in terms of money going out, but there was also less money coming in. Jeremy continued:

> When the volume of adoption sort of tailed off, the point where we got to—if there was fewer than, like, one placement a month—if there weren't as many as twelve placements in a year, you know, it became obvious that that was our sort of breaking point. If we couldn't do that, we weren't going to be able to meet all our financial obligations.

Dotty explained how this final "tailing off" was unlike those she had experienced previously:

> It was a gradual thing, and then there'd be some spikes every first of the year; we would always get all these babies. Like, January, February, March, a few in April and May, and then by summer it was a desert again, and in the fall it was horrible. A few at the end of the year, but it was—I did that little informal study and it was always the same. But that last year we were in existence, it wasn't. We didn't even get the rush, ever.

Here, Dotty explains the chronic highs and lows referenced by Tammy in the beginning of this chapter. But why so few placements?

The agency's outreach efforts, while not wholly ineffective, were not sufficient to bring the domestic numbers up. In the intervening years, the number of expectant / birth mothers and babies ebbed, and flowed, and then ebbed, and ebbed, and ebbed. There was only one domestic expectant mother in process at the time the agency closed. Certain staff and board members noted a troubling lack of marketing by First Steps, in contrast to other more successful agencies. Corinne noticed that she was much busier at the agency she had moved to after the closure, and when asked why, she suggested that the other agency "has the money to do more marketing stuff." She continued, "They have a marketing person, and so, I don't know, just getting the name out there. I think just having more resources, probably." In an earlier conversation, Stella had mentioned First Steps' inability to pay for advertising: "And then you add on the paid advertising, Google, national agencies, profiles online that we couldn't afford, and I really believe we sat down and thought, what if we did get fifty thousand dollars? Could we sustain? I don't think so." "There isn't room for the mom-pop thing anymore," she lamented. "Even the birth mothers know that. They know the Cradle [a very large agency in the region] brand and they know to go online to look for profiles." This recurring language of "activity," "volume," "marketing," "advertising," and "brand" illustrated the neoliberalization of the intimate work of adoption.

Marketing alone may not have been the problem though. There was possibly something deeper, demographic. Tammy, who had moved to the same agency as Corinne, noted:

> [They] hired an out[reach person]—someone—a marketer, like, a marketing person. So, where Stella was trying to do marketing, they have an actual trained marketing person running that. So, and again, it's not like it's brought in thousands of birth moms. They're just not there.

The notion of the disappearing "birth mother" resurfaces.

Where were the expectant mothers? This is a difficult question to answer, because it is challenging to count and track women who might consider adoption, but then decide against it. How do you account for perceived absence? It is difficult to calculate many factors related to adoption, as the federal government does not keep national adoption statistics.[3] However, First Steps' former staff and board members offered their perspectives on the changing landscape of domestic adoption from the front lines. For Stella, there was a cultural "shift" that had much to do with openness. She observed, "The shift in the culture about placing babies, now I think it's more open. People are willing to consider keeping them. The family usually knows. Before it was a secret. Now they're looking at it differently." Jenny said similarly, "We don't really have a horrifying stigma against single parenting." And when I asked Tammy what she felt had spurred the drop-off in domestic numbers, she responded, "I feel like it could be—is it a whole mix? Are there less unwanted pregnancies? I don't know if abortions are up. I don't know if more people are keeping their babies. You know, if it's probably—in the reality, it's probably a whole mix of all these things."

Empirically, there *was* a steep decline in numbers of unplanned pregnancies in the United States between 2008 and 2011, which was accompanied by a decrease in the number of abortions as well (Guttmacher Institute 2016). Although mechanisms linking this data to trends in adoption is lacking, there is a notable exception. The National Council for Adoption's trademarked Adoption Option Index—which combines survey data and vital statistics data with abortion statistics from the Guttmacher Institute—calculates "the relative frequency of infant adoptions per 1,000 abortions and births to unmarried women" (Jones and Placek 2017: 6).[4] Between 1996 and 2014, for the nation as a whole, this index fell from 9.5 to 6.9, so about seven adoptions per 1,000 abortions and nonmarital births. In the state of Illinois, the 2014 index was 4.8; only thirteen states were lower (2017: 35). While this source is singular and has certain limitations, these numbers would support social workers' and board members' perceptions of domestic adoption's decline.

Dotty, who had at one point tried to start an embryo adoption program to bolster First Steps' dwindling domestic numbers, spoke with me about broader trends in reproduction, finally attributing the closing of the agency to a problem of supply-and-demand:

> More and more mothers here in the U.S. are keeping their children, because there's not the stigma ... So there's that, there's certainly the morning-after pill. There's much more education now, sex education. So there are fewer— I mean, the number of teenage mothers who are pregnant has drastically dropped. So everyone is sort of scrambling now for—people who genuinely want to provide a home to kids and can afford it can't find kids, and that's why I think embryo adoption—this is a little off the subject, but that was something I was really hoping we could have gotten started—is part of the new way that egg donors, sperm donors, of course, IVF, all those assisted reproductive techniques are now quite in demand. So I think it's all that combination, you know, for all those reasons, we always had plenty of families. We always had a long list of families from the day we opened until the day we closed, so that wasn't the issue, the issue is the children.

Embryo adoption is an option available to biological parents who have embryos remaining after fertility treatment.[5] If they choose not to place their embryos for adoption, the embryos must be stored indefinitely or destroyed, as Dotty mentioned: "Or, they just want to indefinitely keep paying the fee that—the biological parents—to keep those, just in case. You just hold onto what's yours, you know, whether it's the very first moment of life or, or an actual baby."

Her insistence that we hold onto what's ours is profound. In her opinion, which aligned with many of the staff and board members with whom I spoke, as well as my observations of fall-throughs in the preceding years, more and more mothers were holding onto what was theirs. Dotty continued, "And I just think it takes an awful lot for any mother or couple to give up any part of themselves . . . So the whole landscape is just so vastly changed."

I want to return now to the comparison of the failing agency to a sinking ship, because I think it becomes more meaningful when considered within the context of this shrinking supply of mothers and babies. Dotty was not the only person to make this maritime analogy. When asked how the other board members processed the closure, Jeremy told me, "A lot of people thought, like, 'I don't want to be the one at the helm when this ship goes down, because I don't want it to be me that killed this great little agency that had been doing this great work.'" Within the context of transracial adoption, this metaphor of the agency-as-ship and the shipped—"the fleshly wreckage that capital wrought" to use Christina Sharpe's language (2016: 26)—is historically anchored in the transatlantic slave trade. This mooring is inextricably entwined with the notion of bad debt and its condition of possibility: credit. As Taylor C. Nelms (2012: 239) argues, "It was credit then—the transformation of future expectations, hopes, risks, and uncertainties into present value via speculation, and the imagination of future gains that made such speculation possible—that funded both the slave trade and the Financial Revolution," and in more recent memory, sparked the Recession.

In *How All Politics Became Reproductive Politics,* historian Laura Briggs (2017: 192) argues that "the foreclosure crisis was (and still is) disproportionately felt by single mothers and children," often women of color.[6] She contends:

> The Moynihan Report narrative that had animated the welfare reform smears of the 1990s—that the moral failings of Black single mothers were the cause of all the poverty in the Black community, as well as much of what ailed the nation—was more than a way to blame the vulnerable rather than the lenders for the recession. It was, substantially, the cause of the recession. (194)

Fred Moten (2013) notes, "the subprime debtor [is] clothed in and tainted by the sin / garment of pathological black maternity" (243), referring to blackness as "the collective being that is more precisely understood as being-in-collection insofar as the latter term denotes a debt that is not only incalculable but also subprime" (239). In pointing out this parallel, I am not suggesting that the Chicago women approaching First Steps for adoption services and the women Briggs and Moten are describing as subprime debtors are the same women. The expectant mothers approaching First Steps were primarily renters—often unstably housed—and experienced a level of economic vulnerability that did not allow them to purchase homes, even on suspect credit. But I want to highlight the slotting of black motherhood into these dual ascribed roles: on the one hand, fodder for the foreclosure crisis, and on the other, origin point of both First Steps' existence and its annihilation. Both failed to produce the capital and commodities needed to keep the ship afloat—both positions are secured by legacies of dispossession and economic abandonment. The ship becomes a handy rhetorical device for illustrating these historical echoes.

If the agency was a sinking ship, then the expectant mother constituted what Christina Sharpe (2016) theorizes as a hold: "The *hold* is the slave ship hold; is the hold of the so-called migrant ship; is the prison; is the womb that produces blackness" (27). She holds onto what is hers. Sharpe contends:

> Reading together the Middle Passage, the coffle, and, I add to the argument, the birth canal, we can see how each has functioned separately and collectively over time to dis / figure Black maternity, to turn the womb into a factory producing blackness as abjection much like the slave ship's hold and the prison, and turning the birth canal into another domestic Middle Passage with Black mothers, after the end of legal hypodescent, still ushering their children into their condition; their non / status, their non / being-ness . . . The birth canal of Black women or women who birth blackness, then, is another kind of domestic Middle Passage; the birth canal, that passageway from the womb through which a fetus passes during birth. *The belly of the ship births blackness; the birth canal remains in, and as, the hold.* (74)

Chattel slavery, specifically the system of *partus sequitur ventrem*—"that which is brought forth follows the womb" (Sharpe 2016: 79; Spillers 1987: 79)—is perhaps the original form of American intimate speculation. The child is an unpayable debt, a future, an image, an affect. After centuries of dispossession, you just hold onto what's yours. These final moments of the agency-as-ship were characterized by a kind of sinkhronicity: a condition of being chronically sinking, of living in a "sunken place" (Peele 2017). A seafaring ship and the -ship in kinship derive from different linguistic roots, but they both mean to cut.[7] The black child, cut via adoption from an originary maternal context, "determines the prospect of capital accumulation within this niche market."[8] Is it a coincidence when David Harvey (2014: 9) likens capitalist societies to cruise ships? He writes, "In the bowels of this ship there is an economic engine that pounds away day and night supplying energy to it and powering it across the ocean. Everything that happens on this ship is contingent on this engine continuing to function. If it breaks down or blows up, then the ship is dysfunctional." In transracial adoption, black bodies—mothers, infants—are the engine, the capital. And the womb is the hold. Everything is contingent upon it. As Harney and Moten (2013: 91) contend, "Uncertainty surrounds the holding of things."

A hold is one kind of space, not wholly unrelated to a keep. The noun form of "keep" refers to an innermost sanctum, walled off, protected from the open outside, a refuge. According to several First Steps staff and board members, mothers seemed to be "keeping" their children. The use of the word "keep" is instructive when used to describe an outcome in opposition to adoption, and also within the context of closure. Positive Adoption Language advocates actually insist on using the verb "to parent" rather than "to keep." According to *Parents Magazine,* a publication espousing "positive adoption language," to use the word "keep" in discussing a mother's decision to parent her child suggests that "the child is a possession" (Positive Adoption Language). The corollary to this is that adoption is a form of dispossession. To *keep* something—to *hold* onto what's yours—implies a form of closure, the opposite of exchange. To keep or to hold is to close off, to enclose, to foreclose. Keeping describes the way the decision to parent is perceived by those whose future is foreclosed by the fall-through. But the closure was not simply a result of more women "keeping" their babies. There were simply fewer babies overall.

According to Stella, the need for adoption services was decreasing as contraception use increased: "You don't need it as much, that's right. That's right, and I think people are definitely more tuned into that [contraception] now than they were before. Before it was to tying tubes." The Guttmacher Institute (2015) reports that between 2007 and 2012, the use of highly effective contraceptives, such as the intrauterine device (IUD), more than tripled. It is plausible that the decrease in pregnancies led to a corresponding decrease in babies available for adoption. Stella continued, referencing a perceived cyclical nature of adoption trends, "So, you know, I just hope it works out for those people who do make that choice [to keep / parent their babies], I really do. And the pendulum may swing again. But, for right now it seems to have swung the opposite way." The pendulum of adoption time, swinging, ticking, cycling, stalled.

Jonathan noted, with a poor prognosis for the practice of domestic adoption, echoing Stella's notion of the pendulum "going the other way":

> I don't think domestic adoption is going to economically recover. I really don't. I just don't think that—I don't see why it would. I think things are going the other way and they're going to continue going the other way. I think, Plan B, you remember that. The morning-after pill has just changed the world in that regard. You know, hard to feel bad about that, right? I don't think, you know, if people don't want or aren't ready or for whatever reason, better to do it as soon as possible. And, I just don't see, absent some degree of horrific, you know, like some virus that wipes out mass numbers of adults and leaves kids alive, I just don't see any reason why that's going to change.

It would take the equivalent of an apocalyptic pandemic, in other words, to reignite domestic adoption, according to Jonathan. He went on, echoing the language of keeping:

> Also, the other phenomenon there is, for whatever reason, it just seems like young women who have unplanned pregnancies just seem more likely to keep the babies than they used to, and I don't know if—I don't understand what drives that . . . And maybe it's because they can. Where it's like, you know, we used to be in a world where if you got pregnant at 16, 17, 18, you had to give the baby up for adoption. And now you don't have to do that.

First Steps' birth mothers were often older, in their twenties and sometimes thirties, but during the years following the Recession, the rate of unplanned pregnancies (and the birthrate overall) declined across the board, not only for teens. Fall-throughs, as illustrated in the preceding chapters, constituted another form of keep.

Among staff and board members, there was a sense that of the few expectant mothers who remained, many were going to competitor agencies or placing their children privately. Richard argued, "And the domestic market had gone to the bigger agencies. To the extent there was a domestic market." I asked if he had any sense of why that was, and he answered quickly and matter-of-factly, "People aren't putting their babies up for adoption." Richard continued, echoing others with whom I had spoken:

It's less of a stigma, in a lot of communities, to have a baby and to keep it within the family, whether it's within the immediate family or just part of the community. So I think that there's just fewer babies for adoption in the United States, plus lower birth rates, generally. Probably that as much as anything. And also, I think, just to the extent there are domestic markets, a lot of people still handle domestic adoptions through private transactions. Where that's legal. And to the extent it's not legal, the larger agencies have basically swooped in, and they have a better infrastructure for everything from a pipeline of knowledge to finding birth mothers to taking them all the way through the process. Stella admitted that over time her connections at the various hospitals, you know, got weaker.

The brokerage was breaking down. Holly added:

It's just the small are getting smaller and the big are getting bigger, and there was a couple organizations in the suburbs that were closing. I mean, it just—it wasn't a defeat. It was just the nature, and everyone was telling us, same thing. You know, domestic was pulling us through and it's not anymore. And we believe in our international work, but it doesn't pay the bills.

First Steps' size, which fostered the intimate and personal environment and treatment clients often lauded, turned into a weakness that could not be overcome. When First Steps was founded, it carried out domestic adoption exclusively. During the last decade or so of its institutional existence, international adoption was included among its services. But even with international adoption's increasing popularity, the numbers were not enough to keep the agency afloat. Closure was occurring on a global scale (see Raleigh 2017).

Many of First Steps' staff and board members lamented a perceived decrease in international adoption over the past few years that mirrored the downturn in domestic adoption. Dotty noted, "We, as a small agency, were dependent on the trends that were going on, and not only in America but in foreign countries." The addition of First Steps international programs in the Caribbean and Africa housed multiple forms of racialized black vulnerability under the same adoption umbrella, and reproduced this vulnerability through the process of adoption. In carrying out my research, I was always more interested in domestic adoption as a particular U.S.-located reconfiguration of kinship—one that I felt had been relatively neglected by the recent wave of ethnographic work on adoption—but while in the field, I was constantly facing the encroachment of international adoption upon my carefully staked-out conceptual and ethnographic territory, despite the fact that I found myself in an agency whose founding mission was primarily domestic.

This encroachment itself is indeed an ethnographic fact. The closure involved an important eclipsing of domestic adoption by international adoption, a covering over of the here of Chicago with the elsewhere of Africa and the Caribbean, exacerbating existing domestic erasures. My interlocutors located broken hopes and dreams in struggling international programs, which despite drawing interest, could not sustain the agency without parallel increases in the domestic program.

The implementation of the Hague Convention on the Protection of Children and Co-operation in Respect of Intercountry Adoption (commonly referred to as "the Hague" or "the Hague Convention") was broadly considered one of the primary factors in the decrease in international numbers. Dotty opined that families would have to turn to foster care because there simply were not children available via private adoption—domestic or international:

> I think, you know, the obvious reasons [for the closure] are just not that many kids left—the kind of children that many white middle-to-upper-class people are looking for—they're the ones with money and adoption costs money. Because there is no lack of children in the DCFS system to adopt, and I think more people are starting to turn to DCFS, apparently because there's just so few free kids available, and also because all the foreign programs that were so substantial have closed to Americans, because the State Department, our State Department, is very, very, concerned about child-buying and all the stuff that the Hague prohibits.

She continued, employing the language of opening and closing to describe sending countries:

> And nothing in sight in terms of opening. As you know, Guatemala's been closed a long time, and those kids are just overflowing in the agencies, they're in the orphanages. And so many of those children were, you know, given up legally, but they, none of them came out of that. I'm trying to think of other big kind of—Russia, you know that story—because several children were murdered, and sent back; a single mom put that kid on the airplane and sent them back, and, so that. Again, it's the same dynamic, you know, what happens is true. But it ruined it for everybody. There's very few countries left. There are a few African countries, but they too have been shut down quite a lot. Ethiopia has slowed to a trickle.

Flows were stemmed. Closed. Shut. Shuttered. Between 2009 and 2015, First Steps attempted to get several international programs off the ground—

including efforts in China, Uganda, Russia, Colombia, and Ethiopia—but all were fleeting. While trends in domestic adoption are difficult to track with certainty, scholars do agree that over the past several years, international adoption has declined markedly, and State Department data support this conclusion.[9] At the time of the closing, First Steps' efforts were focused most strongly on Haiti and Liberia.

When I started at First Steps in 2009, a new program in Haiti was gaining steam. Throughout my fieldwork, Haiti was First Steps' primary international program. However, shortly before the closure, Haiti began the process to implement the Hague Convention, which drastically limited the number of children First Steps could place in the United States. Dotty explained:

> So that was the other main thing, we should put that down: that Haiti, which was our biggest source of income, really, for a while—it joined the Hague, which was admirable, and then that was the downfall. I think people pretty much stopped adopting from there. It was too hard. And too long, and too much money. So those factors all converged.

Haiti and her children became a source of revenue, keeping the agency-as-ship afloat. Richard echoed, likening sending countries to economic markets, and gesturing toward the polysemy of what Sharpe (2016) refers to as the weather:

> It was just an econom—it was a perfect storm. So that, the shrinkage of the adoption industry, the agency's decisions to focus first on a couple of African continent markets that opened up and then dried up almost immediately, for one reason—political turmoil, lack of infrastructure, disease. And then Haiti, which was a very healthy market other than the fact that Haiti would suffer massive natural disasters every few years or so.[10]

A climate of precarity threatened the extraction of black children from volatile "markets" across the Atlantic. Richard continued, explaining the slow-down from Haiti:

> Basically, people stopped coming to us to adopt from Haiti for the most part, because [of how] it was perceived, with the changes, with Haiti adopting the Hague Convention. And basically, Haiti put a moratorium on bringing anybody home for a year to a year and a half, and people just moved on. People made other decisions. So, and that also stopped a pretty crucial part of our income. Because there were certain things that had to happen in the adoption pipeline, [to] keep it to certain thresholds. Then you would get more fees in.

Slowdowns and delays at the front end of placement could—and did—result in defaults and overdrafts on the operations side. Closed countries led to closed agencies. Richard went on, relating the international fluctuations back to Dotty's attempts to diversify the agency's offerings, "And I think Dotty was always hopeful we'd stay alive long enough to really bloom the—keep the Haiti market alive and move into other markets, but over time, all those other markets closed." The agency's attempts to "bloom"—like a flower, to open up—were troublingly out of sync with larger trends of closure in the adoption landscape, far beyond Dotty's, Stella's, and the board's control. Indeed, the more First Steps tried to open up, the more it closed down.

This lack of access to children abroad was compounded again by First Steps' small size and limited resources. Dotty insisted, "You know, we were always like—in terms of starting an international program—a few steps behind what happened. And part of that was because we were so small." Holly concurred that the bigger agencies had an advantage by virtue of being able to offer more options to apprehensive and impatient prospective parents:

> The burden to get there [Haiti] is pretty high and just made adoption too difficult for families. I think what was a big issue is we didn't—we didn't have enough programs to sustain the risk. So families were very much aware that any country could shut down in a second, and where does your money go? You know? I mean, granted, you're going to lose a lot of money, but, you know, at least you can switch to another program, or—and we didn't have that. And I think families were getting very savvy about that, and so then the bigger organizations get bigger and the smaller ones go away. To mitigate the risk.

Jeremy also used the language of risk in describing the difficulty in keeping international programs afloat, and the futility of relying upon international adoption as a lifeline in lean times. He draws, again, on the metaphor of sinking, of drowning:

> I think international adoption is fraught with so much risk. It's hard not to grasp for that when you're sinking, right? If you grasp for something [and] your hand comes on an anvil, you know you're going to take your hand away pretty quickly. And that's sort of how we felt. You'd be like, "Well, maybe if we can get this country going, or this country going, or this other country going, then that would save the agency," and it really was about that. It was, we were going to save the agency. And we reached out and essentially what we found were things that could torpedo the agency had it been healthy.

All of a sudden, within the context of international and transracial adoption—in which white savior narratives are often prominent—there is a great deal of confusion over who needs saving. Many doors—both literal and proverbial—were closing, but new ones were not opening, putting the future of the agency at risk. The ship was sinking, and staff and board members looked abroad for lifelines.

One survival strategy staff deployed was the visualization of racialized vulnerability. On November 1, the first day of National Adoption Month 2014—mere months before First Steps' collapse—an emergency fundraiser was held at the home of a wealthy agency supporter. Staff, board members, adoptive parents, and other friends of the agency mingled, nibbled on cookies and hors d'oeuvres, and enjoyed sangria. Agency staff circulated soliciting donations. The "marketing flyer" for the event featured a large image of a very young black child. It appeared to be a candid photograph taken from above and in front, a close-up of the child's head and shoulders. The child looked down, not directly into the lens, as if captivated by some object just outside the frame. In large, bold, capitalized letters below the photo were the words "HE NEEDS YOUR HELP." Below, there was a brief statement about the agency and its "mission that extends far beyond adoption services." In a sidebar on the right-hand side of the page was a list of First Steps' accomplishments in the areas of humanitarian aid and adoption. The humanitarian aid—"raising funds to support Liberia" during the current Ebola crisis, and the evacuation of thirty-five orphans from Haiti after the 2010 earthquake— was foregrounded. Near the center of the sidebar, text read, "A baby with no arms or legs was placed in 2 hours." Disaster seemed to be a necessary condition of possibility for the agency's existence. In lettering that matched the plea below the photograph of the child, the flyer read, "WE NEED YOUR HELP." The agency had become vulnerable, like the child pictured. Both were in need of rescue. Both had uncertain futures. Both were at risk. The grammatical parallelism, by equating the agency with the child, effectively erased the tremendous racial and socioeconomic power and privilege that was condensed into First Steps' institutional existence.

The fundraiser attendees gathered in the living room of the large house to listen to the evening's program. Stella spoke very briefly, thanking the guests for their presence and providing an outline of the invited speakers. Although the fundraiser was held to cover operating costs, the entire focus of the program was on international adoption and humanitarian aid. Tammy made some remarks about Haiti before showing a video that was made shortly after the Haitian earthquake in 2010. In the video, agency staff arrive in Haiti by private plane, gathering children whose adoptions were in process at the time of the earthquake, and bringing them to the United States. Footage of (predominantly white) waiting adoptive parents being united with their Haitian children was set to Christina Aguilera's moving ballad "Lift Me Up," which the singer / songwriter premiered at the Hope for Haiti Now telethon on January 22, 2010. At the First Steps fundraiser, guests listened to Aguilera's haunting voice accompanied by the weeping tones of violins, as they watched parents and staff members literally lift up vulnerable children. In the video, new parents laughed, wept, embraced their children, raised them above their heads, kissed them, stroked their faces. Intimacy, affect, kinship, and vulnerability were all captured on the screen. A social worker landed in Port au Prince nine days after the earthquake, and her voice could be heard over Aguilera's. "I was just, oh, so thankful that we found each other," she said of her experience encountering the busload of children waiting to be airlifted to the United States. Rosalind's prognosis rings true—the child will find its way to you. The video ended with powerful footage of the children who remained in the Haitian orphanage. The camera panned over cribs, gesturing to the alternative future that supportive viewers could offer. Adoption became spectacle in the service of raising funds.

Two guests had come from Liberia to discuss the plight of children orphaned by Ebola. Chester was born in Liberia but came to the United States to attend college and remained for many years until he met Susan, an old friend of Dotty's, born in the Congo, the daughter of white American missionaries. They worked together at an orphanage in Monrovia, and First Steps was piloting a new international adoption program with them. There was one waiting prospective adoptive family—a test case. The program was on hold because of the 2014 Ebola outbreak. Chester spoke poignantly, with just a hint of an accent, about the history of Liberia as a nation established for former American slaves. Susan told the story of adopting her child through First Steps, and described her current work during the Ebola crisis. She compared the "war" against Ebola to the civil wars that had gripped the country between the late 1980s and early 2000s. She handed out small metal silhouettes of Africa, imprinted with the word "Peace." The orphanage children had carved them from bullet casings. This scene prompts one to ponder the sociohistorical conditions that would lead white Americans to adopt black children from an African nation established for freed American slaves. And the ethical and political implications of the use of these children, and children suffering in Haiti—the first postcolonial free black republic—as the fundraising face of an agency founded with the mission of finding families for African American and biracial children in the United States.[11] Indeed, "never being on the right side of the Atlantic is an unsettled feeling" (Harney and Moten 2013: 97).[12]

The last time I saw Stella, we met for lunch. It was 2015 and the agency was in the process of closing. She told me about a lawyer she had talked to who was "looking for an Illinois presence" and was possibly interested in merging with an adoption agency. Stella went on, explaining how the lawyer turned down First Steps' offer of a merger: "She said, 'You know, I get a call every week from agencies that are in debt, baby boomers with founders.'" "Baby boomers with founders?" I repeated, confused. Stella responded, "Founder issues and founder debt. I said, 'What can I tell you?' So they never called back. We weren't, we were in a position—people liked us, would maybe have liked to take on—but not with the debt thing which was there." She continued, "That was an issue. So, you know, what do you do, Kate? I don't know. Better minds than I, than mine. I think maybe I didn't figure it out either, so I don't know. And it was just . . ." "It's really hard," I agreed. She sighed, "I think had Liberia taken off . . . If Liberia had worked out, I think we could have pigeoned along." The shipped become buoys, but the weight is too great.

CLOSURE IN THE CLOSURE

Thus far, this book has told a story about adoption as process in both nominal and verbal terms: processes and processing. To speak of the closure of First Steps was to articulate a finality conditioned by a complex range of emotional factors; the temporal logics of the (fore)closure were affective, as well as specular and economic. It was a march to the end that took place over almost a decade. As in the discourse of adoption as process, the language of a journey was common in my final conversations with the staff of First Steps, although this time they were relating the death of the agency rather than the birth of a baby.[13] "And so, it was the end, and I really—we had run out of road. It was a good run, it really was, all those years. Twenty-one or two years we were," Dotty recalled forlornly, her quick replacement of the pronoun "I" with "we" further underscoring what others had relayed about her central role in the life of the agency. Arman (2014: 23) notes, "Closures are different to many other forms of organizational change because they involve the definite 'ending' of an organizational entity." Unlike a fall-through, there was no chance to start over. This was the end, singular. Dotty often compared (c)losing the agency to a kind of death: "It just died. I mean, we couldn't go any further. We were reflective of the times."[14] She recalled, "I remember the last board meeting. It was just a blur. I don't re—I remember being there; I don't remember a lot of it. It was so sad. It was like a funeral. Like a death, you know?" The loss implied by the closure clung to her, over a year later: "It's still inescapable that the thing is over." Referencing the linear, processual, and perpetual unfolding of time, and sounding more than a bit like Stella, she concluded, "There's an end—a beginning and an end to everything, right?" In the wake of First Steps' closing, I asked those I had come to know over the past several years to relate to me what that ending felt like.

"I must have checked out mentally," Jenny—who had adopted both her children through First Steps—admitted that afternoon in the bakery. She continued,

> I have to say that it was both sad and a relief. I was kind of relieved, because we really weren't a viable organization. While we worked really hard and we really stayed true to our mission, I think that as the board realized that we really didn't have the resources to continue, we shut it down. And that was the right thing to do. So emotionally I would say it was more a relief. Also a little sad because, you know, I feel very fortunate because I was an insider, so I copied my kids' records and I have them. But, I think it was time. Just, you know, a little bit of regret that we couldn't make it work or we couldn't turn it into something else, which we tried, but we just didn't have it, the will, really, so. Anyway.

Jenny's use of the term "viable" at once calls to mind feasibility, biological notions of survival, and a fetus's ability to live outside the womb. Her mention of the will is reminiscent of Stella's and Rosalind's future-oriented philosophy, combining a sense of willpower and ontological future tense. "It was time," she says. Here, the lack of will prevented a new start. The will dissolved, taking the future along with it.

Holly had referenced a feeling of uncertainty and impending collapse: "the feeling of how this is going to last, you know?" She recounted, "Everyone was just sad, like, sorry it had—but they knew that it was [closing]. I don't think it shocked anybody." She referenced a sadness she had felt at the ending of relationships with her colleagues after she moved away from Chicago to start a new job: "I think it's just because I moved away and I don't see anybody and I don't—when it was done, we were done. Like . . . like done, you know?

Well, we spent every day together, you know?" Holly's comments emphasize the finitude of being done, and done in.

Corinne—as a contract social worker who was not as involved in the day-to-day workings of the agency—did feel a sense of surprise: "But, yeah, that was kind of interesting to get the information through e-mail and kind of be shocked." Like Holly, Corinne also referenced her own personal lack of emotional closure, stemming from a similar inability to connect with her colleagues in the aftermath:

> I can't recall any type of, like, closing meeting or anything they did. Like, after the agency closed, they did get together for a social gathering—I wasn't able to make it to that—for the staff. So, yeah, there wasn't really a ton of closure, I guess, for me. And I'm sure I probably would have gotten more of that had I been able to go to that social gathering.

Pauline Boss (2012), who has written extensively on the concept of ambiguous loss, notes that within "a culture that craves certainty" (456), it is difficult to grasp the fact that closure—like preparation, as Dotty noted—is "a mythical, unobtainable goal" (457).[15] "Closure never really happens," Boss insists (457). The ambiguity of loss creates an open end, is open-ended. This open-endedness structured a link between the affective experience of the closure and notions of the future. For Tammy, the closure rendered moot a series of questions that had arisen for her over the past year, in a sense eliminating a number of uncertainties about the future:

> I would say that one part of me felt some relief for everybody involved, especially Stella. Part of me felt a lot of relief for her, like she needed this. And kind of for myself. Kind of thinking, what's the future? Like, Stella needs to leave soon; who's going to take over? Should I think about stepping up and doing that? But, like, wow, that's a huge job. Like, is Holly interested? She just had another baby. How is she going to do it? Kind of being, like, what's next? Like, how is this going to go on? So kind of feeling, a sense of, oh, that solves all that, like, how to do, like, oh no, what do we do?

That solves all that. A closure can be a form of clarification, a resolution in which all questions are answered.

Relief came up again and again in my final conversations with staff and board members. In addition to carrying out home studies, Barbara had been responsible for the agency's licensing accreditation with DCFS. When asked if she missed working at First Steps, she responded,

I have to tell you that I was kind of at the end. I mean, the fun days are over, and all that. The DCFS stuff—every time that rep would come, I would go into a nervous wreck, because I was sure they were going to find something that was my fault and they were going to close the agency . . . Well, we weren't a bad agency. We were never trying to pull wool over their eyes. We were pretty honest with them, and they work with a lot of different agencies, and big agencies, and files that were really crap files, so the files weren't that bad, but I always freaked out. And I don't miss that piece of it. I don't miss all the paperwork, keeping up with every month, monitors going out to do, you know, you went on those monitoring visits.

One of the cases for which I had accompanied Barbara on monitoring visits was Annette's. When I returned to Chicago, I was unable to get in touch with Annette, but Barbara told me that after the closure, she had not wanted her license transferred to a new agency. "Wasn't going to do it," Barbara said. "We went to all the families and said, 'Here are your options.' And after a long thinking, thought about it and everything, she said, 'You know, I don't know if this is for me.'" Annette's adoption journey ended with First Steps' closing. I had also observed Barbara's home study work with Tim and Erin, who became pregnant before they received a match. Since they had a newborn at the time of the agency's closure, they were not allowed to transfer their license, but encouraged to reapply with a new agency once the baby was one year old.

Prospective parents, understandably, struggled with the news. That the closure came as a surprise to some highlights the critical importance of maintaining a façade in the face of inner chaos and institutional breakdown for the success of brokerage. Stella told me about the difficulty of conveying the news to the prospective adoptive couple who was enrolled in the Liberia program:

So that was very stressful. They came in, after we told them we were closed, they thought, "Now what's going to happen to us?" And they felt betrayed and they were just beside them[selves]—so they came and sat in my office one day for forty-five minutes with me. Twenty of it was in silence. It was terrible. It was terrible. He was twitching, to keep from crying, and she was crying, and I was almost crying.

The agency's closure represented the foreclosure of certain possibilities for future kinship for prospective parents in the middle of the process, but also for those who had already completed their adoptions. When I asked a mother who had recently adopted domestically if she remembered how she felt when she heard that the agency was closing, she became noticeably distraught. "I cried," she said, continuing,

> Barbara told me in person. She came out for a visit. And I just burst into tears. I just was sad, for us, and I was sad for my son, because it's his only connection to his birth family. And I was sad because I felt like they did a service, a good service, in an adoption world where that doesn't always happen. I just felt like their motives were pure, and they really provided a good service, and I was sad that that wasn't there anymore.

Here she constructs the agency as innocent, "pure," doing "good" work. A year after the closing, as we sat talking quietly in a suburban Starbucks, she looked at the ceiling in an attempt to stem the tears. She added, "I really came to feel like they were—I mean, those were the people who watched us become a family, so I think we were just personally sad." Another adoptive mother I spoke to after the closing also lamented the loss of connection and community, saying, "I'm going to miss them, because we went to the picnics every year and it was a nice little community, and we were all connected by First Steps, and now that connection is no more." The labor of connection entailed by brokerage continues beyond the finalization of the adoption. Various forms of kinship and future connection were curtailed by the agency's closure.

There was a common refrain of concern about future contact between birth parents and adopted children. Holly told me,

> I mean, I think a lot of birth moms are going to lose touch with their children and vice versa. Because the physical closing of the agency—it was just, you know—we packed the boxes. I sent those to DCFS so they could properly file them, but you know darn well that the birth moms, host families, and the kids are not going to be savvy enough, will not—you know what I mean? It was hard for *me* to figure out and this is what I do. I was reading over that policy and talking to all kinds of—I'm like, "what?" You know? It was not clear, and especially birth moms who are transient . . . those birth moms find a number written. They find in a folder, and—"Oh, this is the agency"—and it's all they remember, you know? Or they know where—we've had birth moms knock on the door, because they remember where we're at.

Disappearance reverberates into the future, as the work of connection breaks down. Holly continued,

> I mean either way, they would go through the registry and that type of thing, but again, that takes sav—you know, that takes savvy that they just—and just help. Lots of [adoptive] families call us with teenagers and talk to the

same person who placed that child. And so that was hard. That's where we actually had some of the most frustrated families, was "Where the hell is my file going?" You know, like, "I need this, and I need that, and make sure you give us this post-placement report," and they just kind of assumed we would always be there.

Perpetuity was never a given. Certain futures were contingent on the continued existence of the agency. Another adoptive mother relayed the following when asked how she felt about the closing, referencing death and the future:

Oh my gosh, so sad, I mean, a lot of memories. And I also thought that if the birth mothers didn't remember anything else, they would remember where they went and they could get in touch with us through First Steps if they needed to be. So it was sort of like, you know, a family member passing away. It was like a link to our children's past is just gone, you know what I mean?[16]

Temporality gets cut off in both directions as links are severed. She followed up, "It was very, very heartbreaking." The mother who had begun crying when I asked about the closure echoed the language of lost links. Her son's birth mother had closed the adoption after a period of openness. She related to me,

I think especially for my son, that was the biggest thing. I felt like, gosh, like it would have been so easy for her to get a hold of us if she ever changed her mind. Or his birth father. And that was sad to me, but it was also sad that, you know, I'm sad that Stella isn't there to tell him the story of what she remembers. So that was—I think it was both. So part of me is pragmatic, and it's like, well, by the time he's eleven he can—he has his paperwork—he'll be able to find her very easily. But I'm sad that she—that it might be harder for her, even though she—I think for some people it's harder than others. She has an education and I think she can easily navigate the system through DCFS and find us. Where maybe my girls' birth family, that might be more complicated for them. But yeah, I did feel like it's such a tangible link and it isn't there. Yeah, and that's important.[17]

The closure of the agency cemented the closure of this closed adoption, foreclosing the possibility of future openness and future kinship.

Members of the board experienced a mix of anxiety, loss, and relief. Jeremy recounted to me: "I think that, you know, despite having had many, many conversations about it, and what we thought was sort of a growing consensus about it, I think at the very end when the potato was put on the fork, I think a lot of people got nervous." He admitted, "I had all those feelings, but I felt like, you know, my job as a board member is not to feel any kind of way. My job was to get it done." He finished, "Oh, there was all kinds of grief, yeah, yeah. You know, for Jonathan, for Richard. For Stella." For Dotty too: "So I think it was certainly a lot of grief. I still feel it," the founder told me. "It was, you know, an identity for me, really, and a purpose," she said. But there was relief too. "I never want to work that hard again," she added.

Richard, who like Jeremy, was also an adoptive father, noted, referencing hope and uncertainty,

> For those of us who'd been there the longest, I think the feeling was acceptance. I mean, we knew this was coming. We didn't know how long; we kept hoping for a miracle, and every year it was, "Okay, we're trying a new market, and it could be a miracle," but it never happened.

We knew this was coming; we just didn't know when. Michael echoed this sentiment of acceptance: "I think we'd all resigned ourselves that that's what needed to happen. I don't think, you know, anyone was happy about it, because of the good work that we were able to do."

"So, yeah. It's been difficult," Stella explained, telling me about the reactions she had received from prospective adopters when sharing news of the closing:

> The people have been nice—98 percent. I mean, I'm calling up, crying, thanking me even though they're unhappy and it has disrupted their journey. Thanking me, telling me why they chose us to begin with. So yeah. It's been a lot of stress, trying to get this all done. How do you figure it out? When is the last day? What does that mean if it's the last day? Where does this go, where does that go? How do we—what about this day, oh, we have to get this closed—and it's still, kind of a few things are up in the air.

What *does* it mean if it's the last day? How do we close processes, institutions, chapters of lives and books? The closing of the agency provided an opportunity for Stella to reflect on her own journey. When I asked her if she would continue to work in adoption, she said, "I'm kind of—not burned out, I don't feel burned out, but I'm, like, I need some downtime, and I'm not twenty. So—and I don't want to risk the rest of my future based on this." She then went on to say that she would like to do part-time or as-needed hospice work. "I just don't want anything to do with adoption anymore," she said. She went on, "To be part of this triangle, this group, I have felt pain, and I'm done. I'm done. I gotta take care of my kids. But I am totally done. It is a painful, tender journey." The affective contours of the closure further underscored the speculative and contingent nature of adoption and the structures that enabled it.

CONCLUSION: BEGIN AGAIN

A final brief exchange between Stella and me highlights similarities in how projects of all kinds come to a close. The last time I saw Stella, we met over a buffet lunch at an Indian restaurant near the agency. Rising from the table with her plate, she asked me if I wanted anything more to eat. Having finished one full plate, I said facetiously, "I think I'm good for now. It's how I keep this figure." "Mm-hmm," Stella laughed. I looked at her, and in a moment of openness, I shared, "I think it's the dissertation, like, I just haven't been eating." I was a week out from my defense. Stella said, "Well that is a lot of pressure, you know?" And I responded, "Yeah, I feel like once it's over, next week, I will just, like, *eat*." Stella nodded. "Like, I'll gain, like, fifteen pounds," I finished. Stella looked at me wistfully from across the table and said, "Well, that's how I feel about this," meaning the closing of the agency, "I feel once it's over, my life can re-begin." Even this ending, which at times felt so absolute, proved also to be a beginning.

Foreclosures, enclosures, and closure. Debt, holdings, and endings. The various facets of intimate speculation—temporal, affective, visual, economic—collapsed into the closure of the agency. The complex entanglements of institutional failure help to shed light on what may be next for adoption in America. Early on in my fieldwork, Stella had impressed upon me the importance of "going with the flow" throughout the adoption process, which was often unpredictable. In our last conversation, she told me, "Things go on, and they evolve, and the trick is to adapt with them, right? And, incorporate and grow and not stagnate and sit in the puddle." *Stay open to change* was the message. Perhaps the closure, then, was not a failure to adapt, but a form of evolution in and of itself, or at the very least, a harbinger of changes to come in the way Americans invest in building not only new kin relations, but a whole host of social formations. At the same time that the closure revealed changes in the landscape of adoption, it also exposed the historic and enduring relationships between capital, intimacy, and inequality that continue to structure disparate access to particular kinds of futures. Transracial adoption itself is an "afterlife" of these histories, to use Saidiya Hartman's (2007: 6) terminology, and this story of closure is one afterlife of adoption.

Conclusion

INTIMACY'S INTRICACIES

WHO CAN HAVE A FUTURE, and who cannot? The story of First Steps doubles this question through the frames of the highly contingent imagined child and the institutionally unstable adoption agency. Intimate speculation points toward an answer. The child-to-be both embodies and receives a particular future through the labor of expectant parents, prospective adoptive parents, and social workers. The agency ensures its future by continuing to connect children-to-be to prospective adopters, but that future comes undone when social workers are unable to produce adoptive kinship. Uncertain futurity multiplies possible ends, and indeed, there is no single ending to this story. A (happy) family is an end. A fall-through is an end. The closure was an end. A conclusion is an end. And these are all beginnings too. Sometimes we have to start over. The adoption process troubles, doubles, and triples linear conceptions of time by design. Its flows, fits, and starts complicate any neat trajectory from beginning to end(s). As a "processing process," it is deeply structured by contingency and speculative logics. At First Steps, an ending could feel like a mission accomplished.

After the closure, there was a recurring feeling among staff and board members that the agency had accomplished its founding mission, which was to find homes for children of color.[1] Stella said sadly in 2015, "And so there comes a time—we fulfilled our mission. Everybody's now doing that [transracial adoption]. What was unique to us is no longer unique to us across the board, so we say thank you, and we wish you the best." Holly added, "I think we were all holding onto Dotty's original mission. And, I think something was said about, you know, whether we were the only ones—originally we were the only ones doing this work, but we weren't in the end. Lots of other organizations had taken on our mission." She finished, "And so yeah, not that we gave up our mission, but it had worked, and it's great … You know, we filled a need that other places wouldn't." Board members felt similarly. Jeremy said,

> I think in part it fulfilled its mission because it did something at a time when other people wouldn't do it, right, at a time when other people wouldn't do African American adoptions, at a time when other people weren't doing LGBT adoptions. They fulfilled that need, and in fulfilling that need, they helped other people in other organizations get over that hurdle, and you know, start to view African American children differently, African American children and adoptions, you know, as children in adoptions, right?

In the United States, the status of black children as "children" is often contested (Bernstein 2011; Sharpe 2016). As this book has shown, transracial adoption provides a striking example of how black children are variously constructed as gifts, commodities, and imagined futures. Through these imagined children, both blackness and future kinship could be brokered.

Richard's comments were especially instructive. He offered, "First Steps' niche was no longer exclusive." He continued, "I think the mission ran its course … So, sometimes, as in a lot of businesses, it's often the case that the people who get in first aren't the people who last the longest. Because they take all the risk." First Steps had speculated on transracial adoption itself. The building of families across racial lines was a risky proposition. Richard went on, "I mean, you know, crossing that race line in adoption was a big deal for people, and so, you know, First Steps became the specialists at it." But eventually, he said, "Other people figured out how to do it well, or to do it well enough, and people stopped freaking out about it." This transition from transgressive kinship practice to social norm risks masking adoption's internal contradictions, and the structures of inequality that make it (im)possible. Richard finished with a big question:

> You know, turn on *20–20* and there's some family in Omaha who's adopted twelve Ethiopian kids and it's the most beautiful thing that anybody's ever seen. And eventually, it sort of broke the barriers down a little—enough that suddenly it wasn't that hard a thing to do … So as those things started to move more away from the agency, there's somewhat of a question there: Does the world really need First Steps as it's currently constituted? Right? And I don't think you need to answer that question, right? It's: Can you survive?

Does the world really need First Steps? The world needs adoption, right? Harvard law professor Randall Kennedy (2004: 478) paints a rosy picture of transracial adoption, in Richard's phrasing, "the most beautiful thing that anybody's ever seen":

> The emergence of "rainbow families" formed by adoptions is a fascinating, poignant, encouraging landmark in the maturation of American race relations. It is the story of adults of all backgrounds who have decided to share their lives with vulnerable children. It is the story of adults willing to do so even at the cost of having to cross racial lines that all too many still perceive as impassable frontiers. It is the story of progressive reform.[2]

In the same vein, literary historian Peter Conn (2013: 20) has argued that adoption presents a positive symbol of humanity's potential: "Adoptive families should be understood not as second-best deviations from some order of nature but instead as positive metaphors, emblems of an increasingly interconnected, global, hybridized, and mobile humanity." But what if adoption is also a negative metaphor? I join critical adoption scholars in suggesting that adoption is also a symptom of something deeply broken in our world.

On November 4, 2014, in honor (and critique) of National Adoption Month, a white adoptive mother and blogger published an informal interview with her adopted seven-year-old Ethiopian daughter. When asked about the month's celebrations—defined for the child by the mother as "a time of the year when there is a lot of stuff on the internet, TV, radio about adoption"—the child replied,

> I don't think it's right for people who adopted children to talk on the TV and I think that because the children who are adopted have more to say than moms and they know exactly how it feels but the parents don't know exactly how it feels. I think having a special time to talk about adoption is okay because it is interesting but if it's just like a big party and people only talk about the happy stuff then it feels sad to me because adoption is sad because bad stuff has to happen to make adoption happen. (Ethioanonymama 2014)

This is a radical departure from the rosy picture painted by Kennedy and Conn. "Bad stuff has to happen to make adoption happen"; adoption is literally contingent upon "bad stuff." Those immediately involved in the adoption process are keenly aware of this tenuous balance. On my first day at First Steps, Stella told me, "This work is equal parts joy and heartbreak." Kimberly said similarly, "I had said to literally hundreds of people who tell me about how adoption and adoption law must be so wonderful and happy. I always say, 'Well, that's true if you think babies come from storks.' "[3] She continued, "If you know the reality, no, there's a huge amount of pain and grief, and suspicion, and discomfort, and pain." Her doubling of "pain" here drives the point home. An adoption plan is a kind of contingency plan. The joy depends on heartbreak—is inextricable from it. The contradictions of adoption resonate with tensions undergirding the so-called American Dream.

Adoptive belonging has been crafted alongside American national belonging, in a context that allowed for the imagination of the United States "as a metaphorical adoption narrative in which all citizens were adoptees" (Herman 2008:8). As the quotes from Kennedy and Conn illustrate, adoption—particularly transracial adoption—is often portrayed as a progressive, utopian, colorblind solution to the racism, classism, patriarchy, and heterosexism that have long afflicted American society. A symbol of American equality blooming from the most foundational of social arrangements: the family. However, as an American social practice, adoption is deeply rooted in long histories of race, class, and gender oppression and economic abandonment. Various forms of disaster are its conditions of possibility. It is a profoundly individual solution to a set of deeply structural problems. In a nation founded on values of equality, this form of family-building is premised on disparity and unequal access to power and resources. Transracial adoption is, in a sense, quintessentially American, in that it contains at its heart a tension long identified by scholars to be the foundation of American identity: the contradiction between the competing ideals of diversity and equality (Mitchell 2002; Spiro 2008; Urcuioli 1998). I do not mean to suggest that adoption—as we understand it in the contemporary United States—should be abolished. But I wonder if perhaps we are using it the wrong way. Is it too radical to imagine a world in which parents do not relinquish their children solely due to lack of resources? Indeed, when a "choice" feels like the only choice, is it really a choice? That adoption becomes an individual salve for deep and widespread structural inequities is a matter of reproductive justice. It is important to ask if and why an adoptive future is truly a "better" future.

It is clearly not enough to interpret adoption as a beautiful gift that is "the best of a bad situation" or a "win-win." Nor is it sufficient, however, to condemn the practice as rooted in well-oiled and coherent hegemonic political and economic systems (though that critique is important). For example, what are we to make of the complicated reality that at First Steps transracial adoption entailed white care for black children in an antiblack world, a transracial intimacy premised on the deep structural inequities that made these children available for adoption in the first place? Stevie Larson (2016: 11–12) has argued, in the case of transnational adoption at least, that *messiness* is actually the proper object of analysis. As this book has shown, when we imagine adoptive families only as the logical, progressive, utopian outcome of adoption (or, alternatively, critique them only as evidence of a violent structure of racial and socioeconomic domination), adoptive kinship's very conditions of possibility, its inherent messiness—namely temporal distortions, individual and institutional precarity, relative perceptions of powerlessness and lack of control, and the taxing social work of reengineering family formations—is erased.

But I want to further characterize this messiness with a term borrowed from Donna Haraway: noninnocence. Haraway uses the concept at various points in her *Staying with the Trouble: Making Kin in the Chthulucene* (2016), as well as earlier texts, notably "A Cyborg Manifesto" and "Situated Knowledges." In "A Cyborg Manifesto," she argues, " 'we' cannot claim innocence from practicing such dominations [of 'race,' 'gender,' 'sexuality,' and 'class']" (1991: 157). In "Situated Knowledges," she continues, "The standpoints of the subjugated are not 'innocent' positions" (191). In *Staying with the Trouble*, the notion of noninnocence often emerges embedded within anxieties about the human impact on the planet in the age variously referred to as the Anthropocene, Capitalocene, or Plantationocene. Here, Haraway is acutely concerned with the world's growing population, insisting on the slogan: "Make Kin, Not Babies" (which prompts various speculative fabulations for how we might think about future iterations of the place of adoption, and reproduction more broadly, in U.S. society). Noninnocence is helpful, I think, for capturing the space between two dominant narratives of adoption: that it is either wholly utopian or dystopian. The messiness of adoption points to its noninnocence.[4] Staying with the noninnocent trouble of adoption—illuminating the deeply speculative and contingent nature of adoptive kinship formation—illustrates its sometimes redemptive motivations and often troubled conditions of possibility, as well as its multiple and fragile outcomes. When the child becomes an imagined future, the question reverberates: *Who can have a future, and who cannot?* The ethnography of adoption through the lens of intimate speculation can help us think about the ways in which anthropology, and the anthropologist, are noninnocent too. On the snowy car ride with Dawn and Stella that opened this book, I was made painfully aware of my own noninnocence.

In addition to revealing the minutiae of the everyday practices and structures of private agency adoption—the application process, interactions between social workers and parents, the on-the-ground implications of adoption policy, and so on—the preceding chapters have demonstrated that adoption is a useful lens through which to examine a wide range of issues salient to the study of kinship, race, class, and speculation in contemporary American society. In contrast to many studies of adoption that have focused on the adoptive family as the eventual outcome of the adoption process, by shifting the temporal frame to the months leading up to the birth of the child, I have highlighted practices of preparation for a future that is far from certain or logical, one produced by and within neoliberal regimes of precarity.

Let us return to the tripartite definition of speculation:

> The conjectural anticipation of something.
>
> The exercise of the faculty of sight; the action, or an act, of seeing, viewing, or looking on or at; examination or observation.
>
> Engagement in any business enterprise or transaction of a venturesome or risky nature, but offering the chance of great or unusual gain.[5]

Working within intersecting logics of anticipation, visualization, and investment, social workers and others involved in adoption speculate intimately in an attempt to transform subjects—(imagined) children, adults, and the relationships between them—from becomings (the elements of emergent, speculative, and contingent kinship) into fixed categories of exchange and relationality. This fixity is an end. The narratives of First Steps' accomplished mission suggest that agency staff imagined they were no longer needed because they had, in a way, fixed what they saw as the problem—children of color in need of adoptive families. The position of the social worker as broker is essential to understanding the intricacies and intimacies of this process of creating future kinship. The concept of intimate speculation allows us to see how speculative logics tie together affective, temporal, visual, and economic mechanisms and experiences at the scale of family-building. In this way we can see not only the reverberations of neoliberalism in everyday life, but also a prime example of the limits of working only at the scale of states and economies (Briggs 2017). Intimate speculation shows how political economic concerns shape and are shaped by time, connection, and interpersonal encounters across a range of smaller scales (Bear et al. 2015).

As a mode of engaging with the future in the present, intimate speculation attends to both the micro-practices of everyday life and the larger sociocultural structures that both shape and are shaped by those practices. As a theoretical concept and social practice, intimate speculation reverberates beyond the bounds of adoption, as a mode of building futures within a broader cultural context that has become increasingly and unstably anxious, visual and surveilled, and capital-oriented.[6] Its theoretical applicability can be extended to other social and political practices in which affect, sight, and economy converge at the intersection of future-making, speculative visions, structural violence, and social transformation. It might help us think about immigration through the terrors and contingency felt by families severed at the southern border of the United States. It might illuminate marriage and childrearing in new ways through the possibilities and contestations posed by millennial demographic trends and queer and trans* intimacies. It might expand our understanding of housing by elucidating the long-term aftermath of the foreclosure crisis and the disparate accumulation of assets across populations. It might allow us to approach environmental crisis through the persistent desire to profit from indigenous resources within a context of increasing disposability. And it might alter our understanding of the pursuit of higher education through futures increasingly constrained by unpayable debt and the casualization of labor in the neoliberal university.[7] Race, class, and gender shape all of these things, the very contingency of so many American Dreams and Nightmares. These are but a few examples of how intimate speculation has theoretical and practical implications for helping us comprehend relationality and inequality within, but also beyond, the way the state and the economy produce and manage them for us. This is because, at its most fundamental, intimate speculation is a mode through which we already make sense of the expansive and manifold costs of living and being together.

To speculate intimately, through the imagined child as a future—one in whom complicated temporal, affective, *and* economic investments are made by a range of actors—lays bare the complex stakes of adoption as a mode of making families in the contemporary United States. Adoption, therefore, can teach us a great deal not just about kinship, but also about brokerage, value, social inequality, visibility, hopes, dreams, anxieties, and loss. An end in itself, it can also be a means to an analytical end, something good to think with. Armed with the insights it affords, we may be able to imagine other, better futures. This is an end, but it is not *the* end.

· · ·

end, n. The latter or concluding part (of a period, action, etc.).[8]

· · ·

NOTES

PROLOGUE

1. As Behar (1996: 6) notes, this is an instance where I could have worked methodologically to overcome the resulting discomfort:

> Even saying, "I am an anthropologist, this is fieldwork," is a classic form of the use of method to drain anxiety from situations in which we feel complicitous with structures of power, or helpless to release another from suffering, or at a loss as to whether to act or observe.

2. "In line with animal vultures, social scientists of the urban poor could be accused of a morbid attraction to the wounded, sick, and dead," Knight argues (2015: 214). She continues, "Vultures don't just clean up the dead. By ingesting the dead, the dead become part of them. Is this an example of the defining characteristic of the anthropological encounter as colonial? . . . The anthropologist is a narrative-stealing informant, an intimate, a feeder, and even, a friend. But she does go home at the end of the day" (215–17).

3. Ethnographic countertransference, put simply, is the affective response we have to our research and research subjects—how our research *moves* us. In the case of qualitative research, ethnographic countertransference "can affect all choices made regarding the research project, such as who to study, what to ask, what to record, and how to record" (Halbrook and Ginsburg 1997). Halbrook and Ginsberg (1997) argue, "In the qualitative tradition, where human beings interact with other human beings for prolonged periods of time, ethnographic countertransference has the potential to destroy the validity of many otherwise solid studies." However, in the context of cultural anthropology—this "most bizarre form of witnessing" (Behar 1996: 165)—and other humanistic forms of inquiry, ethnographic countertransference may present as equal parts blessing and curse, plunging us more deeply into the social immersion we seek, but also conditioning our objects of study in protracted ways of which we must be aware. We, as anthropologists in the field, are often evidence too. This countertransference infiltrates every thought, action, and

interaction in the field—it is a product of individual sensibility conditioned simultaneously by a range of larger social and structural factors. It is unavoidable. Avery Gordon (2008: 22) has a perhaps more elegant theorization of the same process—a form of haunting: "To be haunted and to write from that location, to take on the condition of what you study, is not a methodology or a consciousness you can simply adopt or adapt as a set of rules or an identity; it produces its own insights and blindnesses." In psychoanalysis,

> The transference-countertransference is a chaotic field of energy in which, by virtue of the compelling force of that field, memories are remembered and forgotten, desires are forged and reforged, and a story is the affective consequence of the dynamics of speaking and listening within a dyadic relation. (42–43)

I am inclined to think that these drives, hauntings, relations, and chaotic fields of energy matter a great deal. For anthropologists, "the field" itself is chaotic and energy-laden.

4. I had never been more in need of an ethnographic alter ego, a la John Jackson's caped and charismatic Anthroman©®™. Jackson (2005: 25–26) developed the character as way to confront his own "ethnographobia":

> Anthroman was a way for me to envision stepping outside myself, to be fearless about social research by visualizing myself protected from harm by my own superhuman powers of observation and analysis. It somehow felt safer than just being some inconsequential graduate student asking black nationalists, or drug dealers, or architects, or grandmothers, or street vendors, or anyone else intrusive questions about their everyday lives and loves. I used Anthroman as a psychological and methodological conceit that helped me to watch myself protectively from above, allaying some of my anxieties in (and of) the field.

5. Sara Ahmed (2017: 32) explores a similar tension between "turning away from" and "turning toward" suffering.

6. *Oxford English Dictionary* 2014b.

INTRODUCTION

The title of my introduction borrows its grammatical construction from artist Theaster Gates ("To Speculate Darkly"), who employs it in response to writer Leonard Todd, who wrote about a potter named Dave Drake (Gates 2010). "I imagine . . ." Todd speculated, over and over, about the life of Dave, who was a slave in South Carolina. Gates's artistic exhibition centered on Dave the Potter in an attempt to reimagine "what history does" and to combat racialized erasure. Imagination, whether directed toward the past or toward the future, is deeply political.

1. See Bear et al. (2015) for a critique of capitalism as a logic.

2. Both Sara Dorow (2006) and Signe Howell (2006) have produced ethnographic accounts that are more focused on process, institution, and bureaucracy

within the context of transnational adoption. Elizabeth Raleigh (2017) also offers an account of bureaucratic process through the lens of private adoption (both domestic and transnational) as a market.

3. Arjun Appadurai (2013: 298) has argued that "we need to reopen the many meanings of the idea of 'speculation,' all of which have strong linguistic, religious, and vernacular inflections, so that we can gain a better picture of the way in which the sciences of anticipation today interact with the quotidian strategies and practices of future-making." In the edited volume *Anthropologies and Futures,* Sarah Pink and Juan Francisco Salazar (2017: 5) argue for "an engaged futures-oriented anthropology," noting that "ethnography has been to date a neglected method for studying futures." In order to explore the complicated relationship between processes, roles, and affect surrounding adoption, my analysis builds upon theories of futures trading, notions of the child as future, and the affective connections among futurity, hope, risk, anxiety, and uncertainty, offering a theorization of speculation that includes temporal and affective forms of investment. Caitlin Zaloom's (2006) ethnographic work on futures trading provides an apt analogy to the private adoption process in which an agreement is made for the delivery of a future child. However, there are other equally useful noneconomic ways of thinking about the child as future, such as Lauren Berlant's (1997) notion of the infantile citizen, Lee Edelman's (2004) conception of reproductive futurism, and Liisa Malkki's (2000, 2010) explorations of children as the representation of utopic or dystopic futures. Ann Anagnost (2008: 50) has observed "an anxiety about national futures in relation to children," and Claudia Castañeda (2002: 1) has interrogated notions of "the child as a potentiality rather than an actuality, a becoming rather than a being: an entity in the making." The present analysis is an attempt "to make futures ethnographically thinkable" (Pink and Salazar 2017: 5).

4. *Oxford English Dictionary* 2014d.

5. Contingency is one of those troublingly expansive concepts that at times seems to describe everything, and I join a number of scholars in my attempt to anchor it in some meaningful way to the realities of social life. Contingency, argues Andreas Schedler (2007: 54), "is an elusive abstraction commonly defined by other elusive abstractions, like chance, uncertainty, freedom, and unpredictability, whose boundaries and internal relations are rather opaque." Contingency, though, "is at the core of understanding how futures play out" (Pink and Salazar 2017: 16).

6. According to Laura Bear, Ritu Birla, and Stine Simonsen Puri (2015: 387–88), speculation, defined as "the making present and materializing of uncertain futures," "always exists alongside the formal knowledge practices of modernity—risk, evidence, and calculation." Like speculation, contingency—"the fundamentally unpredictable quality of experience" (Malaby 2002: 285)—is based in uncertainty, and also tied to anticipation: "Coping with contingent events means coping with the future . . . The future is the motherland of uncertainty" (Schedler 2007: 66).

7. See Luhmann 1996. This notion of risk is also central to intimacy, as Viviana Zelizer (2010: 269) contends:

Intimate social relations thus defined depend on various degrees of trust. Positively, trust means that the parties willingly share such knowledge and attention in the face of risky situations and their possible outcomes. Negatively, trust gives one person knowledge of, or attention to, the other, which if made widely available would damage the second person's social standing.

8. See Cox (2015) for a critical discussion of the social construction of black girls as "at risk."

9. Social historian Ellen Herman (2008) has also described risk as a central element of American adoption.

10. My approach to adoption builds upon a strong foundation established by studies of nonnormative kinship, such as gay and lesbian kinship (Hayden 1995; Weston 1997) and assisted reproduction (Franklin 1995; Ragone 1994, 1999, 2004; Strathern 1992; Thompson 2005). This book, with its attention to relative powerlessness and dissolution, as well as an intersectional focus on race, gender, and class inequalities, is situated squarely within the new kinship studies. However, it departs from existing literature on adoption in a number of ways.

Traditionally, adoption's interest to anthropologists lay in its ability to unsettle prominent notions of kinship by descent, and as a way into debates about nature versus nurture (Howell 2009). Although many book-length accounts of transracial adoption in the United States exist outside the discipline of anthropology (Fogg-Davis 2002; Patton 2000; Quiroz 2007; Raleigh 2017; Rothman 2006; Simon and Roorda 2000), recent anthropological interest in *transnational* adoption as a "distinct subfield" (Kim 2010: 10) has interrogated international adoption through the lenses of race, culture, national belonging, and globalization (cf. Dorow 2006; Howell 2006; Jacobson 2008; Yngvesson 2010). The present analysis shifts the focus from global forms of movement to an exploration of temporal unfolding as an equally important analytic shaping actors' experiences. Yngvesson and Coutin (2006) have explored the temporal dimensions of international adoption and migration through the lens of documentation. Domestic adoption in particular presents a case in which time perhaps figures more prominently than space in the exchange of children, but in which similar logics of stratification and belonging are at play. An analysis of adoption as an engagement with contingency highlights interconnections between multiple strands of kinship studies, and tracks crucial ways in which notions of kinship are ever evolving. Herein I strive to augment theories of adoption as a form of circulation, whether cultural (Jacobson 2008), gift (Modell 1999), or market (Goodwin 2010); a rethinking of classic notions of kinship (Weismantel 1995); or a lens on identity formation and belonging (Kim 2010; Yngvesson 2010), imagining adoption as a complex form of future-craft, thereby bringing adoption studies into conversation with broader interdisciplinary literatures on exchange and futurity.

11. As Jessaca Leinaweaver (2018) has argued, "all kinship is adoptive."

12. See U. S. Census Bureau n.d.

13. See Economic Policy Institute n.d.

14. This number does not include individuals who identified as mixed race on the 2010 Census form.

15. See CensusScope 2010.

16. Chicago Public Schools (CPS) publishes demographic data annually.

17. "Low income" is defined by eligibility for free and reduced lunches. See Chicago Public Schools n.d. and National Center for Education Statistics 2011.

18. River Glen is a pseudonym.

19. When I started my fieldwork in 2009, the majority of expectant mothers resided in some of the poorest Chicago neighborhoods. By 2015, most local expectant mothers still lived in Chicago, with an occasional mother located in the suburbs, but there were also an increasing number of expectant mothers living out-of-state (they had located the agency on the internet, or had already been linked with an Illinois family).

20. In their 1972 statement, the members of the NABSW (1972: 1) contended:

> The National Association of Black Social Workers has taken a vehement stand against the placement of Black children in white homes for any reason. We affirm the inviolable position of Black children in Black families where they belong physically, psychologically, and culturally in order that they receive the total sense of themselves and develop a sound projection of their future.

In the interest of family preservation, the association cited difficulties, both in racial identity development and learning necessary coping mechanisms, as impediments to the parenting of black children by white parents, noting that black parents were much better suited for preparing and socializing black children for life in a racist society. The statement included a call to child welfare agencies to work harder to find black adoptive families for black children, critiquing the ways in which black families were often excluded from the pool of potential adopters, unable, for structural reasons, to "maneuver the obstacle course of the traditional adoption process" (3).

21. Years into my fieldwork, a well-known adoption agency in the Chicago area featured a special "grant program" that "subsidized" the adoption of African American children. Upon my investigation in 2013, in this program, the "Program Fee" and "Placement Fee" to adopt an African American child were $3,200 and $6,700, respectively, as opposed to $8,700 and $17,200 for a nonblack domestic child. According to the agency's website, these fees were "subsidized by the agency and other charitable organizations." The website went on to explain, "We have a reduced fee structure for our African American Adoption Center because of the need we have for adoptive parents wanting to adopt African American children." While the conscientious subsidization of adoption was ostensibly an effort to counteract the economic disparity that results in African American families earning less and having fewer assets on average than white families, this practice simultaneously appeared to place differential valuation on the children based on race. The United States has a long history of agencies varying adoption fees based on the race of the child, but not as a corrective strategy for making same-race placements possible in the African American community. Charging differential fees has long been a simple reflection of the racist notion that black children are the least desirable and most difficult to place and so, therefore, should cost less (see Quiroz 2007).

22. Although social workers generally approved families to adopt children from zero to six months, most babies went home with their adoptive parents within days of being born.

23. Although there is a troubling lack of comprehensive national adoption statistics—a fact lamented by many scholars of adoption—2010 Census data reveals that 2.4 percent of American children under 18 are adopted, and half of those adopted children are Hispanic and / or nonwhite (Kreider and Lofquist 2014). That resulting 1.2 percent are not all transracially adopted, so it is safe to assume that the percentage of transracially adopted children is even smaller. The present analysis primarily concerns domestic adoption because of the unique forms of investment it requires in a pregnancy rather than a living, breathing child, but I have included ethnographic examples from international adoption where the processes are similar (such as the wait for a match / referral, pre-adoption training, and the home study process), since, due to the nature of the agency's work, domestic and international logics often overlapped.

24. Following sociologist Avery Gordon (2008), various adoption scholars have explored the notion of haunting (see Dorow 2006: 26). On the question of one's personal connection to the research, Ruth Behar (1996: 6–7) adds:

> How can you write subjectivity into ethnography in such a way that you can continue to call what you are doing ethnography? Should we be worried that a smoke alarm will blare in our ears when the ethnography grows perilously hot and "too personal"?

25. Anthropologists have grappled with the complexities of ethnographic counter / transference through the concept of native anthropology. Sonia Ryang (2005: 154) writes of "the hierarchy that allows some to talk about themselves comfortably with self-importance, while making others quietly delete themselves from their text." Kirin Narayan (1993: 671) argues for a more nuanced and complex definition of what it means to be native: "those who are anthropologists in the usual sense of the word are thought to study Others whose alien cultural worlds they must painstakingly come to know . . . I argue against the fixity of a distinction between 'native' and 'non-native' anthropologists." Therefore, *native* and *non-native* are flexible categories that are never mutually exclusive.

26. Technically, I was always first and foremost a researcher at First Steps. I completed my formal social work practica elsewhere, and none of the work I did at the agency counted toward my graduate degree.

27. There are three legally recognized ways to adopt in the United States: adoption from foster care, private agency adoption, and independent adoption. Adoption from foster care involves the permanent adoption of a child from the public foster care system. Since the primary goal of foster care is family reunification, not all foster children are available, or "legally free," for permanent adoption. Foster children become available for adoption only after parental rights have been terminated, usually involuntarily. Unlike private forms of adoption, adoption from foster care is very inexpensive, and often free. Independent adoption—also referred to by members of the adoption community as "private adoption" or "private private adoption"

to distinguish it from agency adoption—occurs when a prospective adoptive parent or couple collaborates with a lawyer, rather than an adoption agency, to locate and work with potential birth parents. It unfolds similarly to private agency adoption, but the lawyer fulfills the mediating role of the agency, so the fees are often less, as the process does not include a social worker to fulfill tasks such as counseling and expectant mother support. Informal adoption within and between kin networks is also practiced, particularly within communities of color, but it is not formally recognized by the state.

28. A very small number of adoption professionals asked me to use their real names. However, I have followed anthropological convention and given all respondents pseudonyms, both to protect sensitive information and to enable the most honest account possible on my part.

29. See Amnesty International 2014.

30. According to the Education Commission of the States (2014):

> Today, the average black or Hispanic high school student currently achieves at about the same level as the average white student in the lowest quartile of white achievement. Black and Hispanic students are much more likely than white students to fall behind in school and drop out, and much less likely to graduate from high school, acquire a college or advanced degree, or earn a middle-class living.

Harvard University's Achievement Gap Initiative (2014) concurs:

> Compared to whites, significant gaps for African-American and Hispanic students are evident in virtually every measure of achievement: NAEP math and reading test scores, high school completion rates, college enrollment and college completion rates. In addition, there is wide variability across states in educational investment and outcomes.

31. http://invest.uncf.org/impact (accessed October 21, 2014).

32. In 2015, the *Chicago Tribune* produced a chart based on abandonment and relinquishment data since the Safe Haven law was passed in Illinois in 2001. Between 2001 and 2015, 75 babies were abandoned (38 subsequently died) and 110 were relinquished legally through Save Havens (Brinson 2015).

33. For an in-depth analysis of Safe Haven laws through the lens of reproductive justice, see Oaks 2015.

34. It is difficult to ignore the neoliberal appeal to consumption here.

35. This emphasis on black men and boys often comes at the expense of black women and girls (Cox 2015; AAPF n.d.).

36. A similar photo also "went viral," capturing a black boy offering water to a group of police officers in riot gear during the unrest that followed the death of Freddie Gray in Baltimore.

37. The image was a striking example of the power of the public traffic in positive affect. "Likes" and "shares" abounded, as did critiques of the individualizing nature of the photograph's erasure, as evidenced by the following quote from Jonathan Jones (2014), writing for the *Guardian*:

Liking this picture as a definitive image of America's race crisis is the equivalent of locking yourself in and turning up the volume to weep at *Frozen* [Disney's latest animated princess feature] while the streets are burning outside. Which is exactly what white Americans apparently want to do. Truth is a flimsy thing. It can be destroyed by a hug.

Salon contributor Anoosh Jorjorian (2014), in an effort to reconcile the image of Devonte and the officer with recently released footage of the killing of Tamir Rice, argued similarly:

> But the larger story it [the photo] seems to tell *is* a lie. We wish that this heartwarming connection would signal a transformation, a break with a long history of white police officers harassing, stop-and-frisking, detaining, beating and killing African-American boys and men. Yet it's unclear how much of a transformation the hug might have engendered in the Portland P.D., which has its own history of shooting an unarmed black man, or even in Sgt. Barnum himself. In the wake of the grand jury verdict in the death of Michael Brown, some Portland police officers had changed their Facebook profile pictures to badges wrapped in bracelets that read, "I am Darren Wilson." Barnum and 30 other officers had "liked" one of the photos. (The police chief ordered the photos to be taken down and an investigation is in progress.) Barnum's CNN interview is a carefully crafted piece of P.R. for police, during which he downplays race ("just as a person to a person") and refers to it only in code ("at-risk youth"). His defense of policing as-is coupled with a refusal to engage with race head-on hardly indicates a new leaf in law enforcement.

38. Bullock played Leigh Anne Tuohy in the film *The Blind Side,* which was based on a true adoption story. Tuohy, a white woman, along with her white husband, Sean, adopted African American offensive lineman Michael Oher as a teen. Oher, a former foster child, went on to play professional football.

39. This prompts us to imagine the kinds of radical structures that might produce white cops who love black and brown people (or whether this is actually structurally impossible, given the nature and history of policing in the United States).

40. By drawing attention to the uncertainty and precarity that characterize adoption, I do not mean to suggest that so-called "traditional" biological reproduction is a "sure thing." It most certainly is not (cf. Ford 2017; Knight 2015; Rothman [1986] 1993). Adoption simply adds additional layers, increasing the number of possible things that could go wrong. In this way, adoption is akin to surrogacy in the way that it separates the social parent from the gestational parent, but without even the partial biological link often present in surrogate arrangements, prospective adopters' claims to kinship are yet more tenuous.

41. The private agency process is built around the gestational clock—preliminary paperwork is rarely done before the fourth or fifth month of pregnancy ("proof of pregnancy" is required), while matching adoptive parents with an expectant mother rarely takes place before the sixth month. Thus, the semicircle could also be seen to represent the swell of an expectant mother's belly or even a divided egg. Kelly Ray Knight (2015) employs a similar typology of time to discuss the experiences of poor,

pregnant, addicted women in San Francisco, who variously operate on hotel time, addict time, jail time, biomedical time, treatment time, etc.

42. In early 2014, as I was concluding my doctoral fieldwork, Stella—having taken over as agency director when Dotty retired—found herself carrying out an impossible load of both administrative and clinical duties as the agency searched for a new director of domestic adoptions. During this time, Stella not only handled all expectant / birth mother work as the interim director of domestic adoptions, but also frequently met with prospective adoptive parents as the agency's executive director. In my time at the agency, however, Stella's work never included prospective adoptive parent home studies.

43. This particular analogy is intentional rather than coincidental—adoption and divorce both involve the dissolution of existing legal kinship.

44. In examining the ways in which prospective adopters are often elevated above others in the adoption process, sociologist Elizabeth Raleigh (2017: 5) draws attention to the often "customer-centric approach" of social workers within this fee-for-service domain.

45. **end,** n. *Archery.* *(a)* The place at which the mark is set up. *(b)* The number of arrows shot from one end of the range (*Oxford English Dictionary* 2014b).

46. As early as the 1980s, Paul Sachdev (1989) suggested an "adoption rectangle" that also included the adoption agency and its personnel, and more recently Linda Seligmann (2013: 43) has pointed out "the power adoption agencies and brokers can exercise in structuring family formation." "Adoption constellations" (cf. Grand 2011) and "adoption mosaics" have also been referred to by adoption professionals as alternatives, but the notion of a triad has remained dominant in adoption discourse.

47. Kathleen Stewart (2012: 524) describes this emergent quality of precarious processes: "the tactility and significance of something coming into form through an assemblage of affects, routes, conditions, sensibilities, and habits."

48. Amy Speier (2016), in her ethnography of fertility tourism in the Czech Republic, identifies the individuals who connect lower-middle-class IVF consumers to fertility clinics abroad as brokers performing intimate labor: those who "sell care" within a context of "so much stress and hope." These brokers, she argues, "embody the intersection of intimate labor and a heightened commodification of intimacy" (61). In Speier's ethnography, the rise of DIY approaches among seekers of IVF treatment led to the decline of fertility brokerage services. Elizabeth Raleigh's insightful *Selling Transracial Adoption* (2017) is one of the only existing studies of adoption to focus explicitly on adoption providers. I join her in shifting the analytic focus from outcomes to process, although my study differs from hers in several ways, including my attention to the temporal dimensions of the adoption process and my methodological approach.

49. Drawing on Boris and Parreñas's (2010: 7) notion of intimate labor—"work that involves embodied and affective interactions in the service of social reproduction"—Mankekar and Gupta (2016: 18) suggest that "theories of affective labor enable us to rethink the relationship between intimate labor and capitalism in the contemporary moment." As Boris and Parreñas (2010) contend, "the daily praxis

of intimacy . . . is increasingly commodified in late capitalism" (8), and intimate labor is "a key lens for examining the impact of macrostructural forces of economic globalization and the neoliberal state" (10). Intimate, reproductive, and affective labor are thus deeply imbricated. Adoption is an ideal site to explore these entanglements and their relationship to neoliberal formations.

50. Referring to brokerage as "a sort of glue of social life" (2014: 38), Faist notes, "By studying brokerage as a social mechanism we contribute substantially to the understanding of the (re)production of (in)equalities in social life. After all, brokerage may significantly affect the social position and life chances of those agents involved" (41).

51. This conceptual frame is not without critique. Rockefeller (2011: 557) notably cautions that the concept of flow can overemphasize a "managerial perspective" at the expense of attention to individual agency and "small-scale organizational phenomena."

52. See Dusky 2011.

53. Here I distinguish between "birth mother" with a space, and "birthmother" without a space. The former was used at First Steps, and the latter is a term popularized by Lee Campbell, founder of Concerned United Birthparents (CUB), specifically to emphasize its similarity to kin terms like "grandmother" or "stepmother."

54. In the postwar years, premarital sex was increasingly common as access to birth control lagged: "for women born after 1949, the odds were that they would have sex before they reached age twenty" (Fessler 2006: 7). The result, according to Ann Fessler, was "an explosion in premarital pregnancy and in the numbers of babies surrendered for adoption" (8). Many of these pregnant women—particularly those of middle-class backgrounds—were sent to maternity homes at the behest of their families, and relinquished their babies before returning home. Due to the prevalent use of coercive methods forcing young unwed women to part with their new infants, many in the adoption community have referred to this period as the "Baby Scoop Era."

55. There are indeed women who are proud to call themselves birth mothers, even before the birth. My argument is about the violence of ascribing this label prematurely and without any input from the woman in question. It raises the temporal stakes of the adoption process in significant ways.

1. SUSPECT AND SPECTRAL (M)OTHERS

1. Madeleine Reeves (2013: 512) notes in her work on restitution documents in postsocialist Moscow, "Suspicion itself becomes the dominant mode of governing uncertainty."

2. For example, evil Ursula's snarky and conniving sidekicks in Disney's *The Little Mermaid,* or the scene in the film *Love Actually* when Aurelia cautions Jamie not to disturb the eels at the bottom of the pond.

3. Anthropologist E. Summerson Carr (2010: 12) describes the linguistic practices of women in drug treatment as "formally replicating prescribed ways of

speaking about themselves and their problems without investing in the *content* of those scripts."

4. Scholars of adoption have long made a discursive association between adoption and the figure of the stranger. Judith Modell's (1994) ethnography is *Kinship with Strangers,* and Barbara Melosh's (2002) more recent social history of adoption is *Strangers and Kin.*

5. Nicole Fleetwood (2011: 111) refers to hypervisibility as encompassing "both historic and contemporary conceptualizations of blackness as simultaneously invisible and always visible, as underexposed and always exposed."

6. Although First Steps was founded specifically to serve African American and biracial children, domestic adoption in the United States is also haunted by a troubling history of the removal of Native American children from their communities through adoption and boarding schools. While this must be acknowledged as part of a larger racial history of adoption in the United States, a detailed account of the adoption of Native children is beyond the scope of this particular study. This history has been addressed in depth by scholars elsewhere (cf. Harness 2014), and due to the passage of the Indian Child Welfare Act in 1978, which places the adoption of Native children under the authority of tribal governments, the only ethnographic reflection I can offer on this type of adoption exists in a form that First Steps' expectant mothers had to sign disavowing any Native ancestry. Based on Stella's accounts and my own observations, it seemed that First Steps' expectant mothers very rarely claimed Native American ancestry, and in cases in which they did, there was often a lack of documentary proof of tribal affiliation.

7. According to Melosh (2002: 255), "In the 1950s and 1960s, 80 percent of white children born out of wedlock were relinquished for adoption; by 1980, fewer than 4 percent of unwed mothers made that decision." Ann Fessler (2006: 108), who has recounted these women's stories in depth, cites one study reporting that between 1952 and 1972, white mothers relinquished children to adoption at a rate ten times that of African American mothers.

8. In 1986, the White House Working Group on the Family (WHWGF) furnished a report to President Reagan entitled *The Family: Preserving America's Future.* The report outlines what the working group, based on seven months of research, took to be the state of the American family, and provides guidelines for the development of pro-family policy. The report located the "root of child poverty" in illegitimacy:

> This—not economic trends, not lack of compassion, not official unfairness—this is the root of child poverty in America: the formation of households without a bread-winner, usually through illegitimacy, often through desertion. This is the brutal fact: only one-fifth of children are in single parent families, but they make up over one-half of all children in poverty. (23)

Drawing on the work of Charles Murray, the writers of the report went on to insist that welfare only increased child poverty, by enabling poor mothers to bear father-less children. The report pointed to adoption as a viable route for pregnant teens, children themselves whose futures were at risk: "For the pregnant adolescent, adoption can be an option which builds futures and builds families" (33). According to Solinger (2001: 198), "throughout the Reagan-Bush era, adoption was promoted as a cure for child poverty and a way to reduce welfare costs."

9. As Brighenti (2010: 2) observes, "women and minority groups" are often the object of the gaze, but rarely its subject. "While minority group members are often forbidden to look back," argues Brighenti, "they are not so much stared at as rendered invisible" (29).

10. *Oxford English Dictionary* 2014b.

11. In the case of South Korean birth mothers, Hosu Kim (2016) draws on Lisa M. Cacho's notion of social death as a combination of rightlessness and misrecognition. Kim also identifies the surrender of parental rights as a form of legal erasure (8). Christine Ward Gailey (2000) and Jodi Kim (2009) have also described the phenomenon of social death within the context of transnational adoption.

12. The term "ghost" is commonly used in American English slang as a verb. An Urban Dictionary user defines it as "to avoid someone until they get the picture and stop contacting you" (miggelzworth 2010).

13. "To give the benefit of the doubt" is bound up with notions of guilt and innocence: "to give a verdict of Not Guilty where the evidence is conflicting; to assume his [*sic*] innocence rather than guilt; hence in wider use, to incline to the more favourable or kindly decision, estimate, or the like" (*Oxford English Dictionary* 2014a).

14. Knight (2015: 157) observes a similar phenomenon she calls the "seeable child," which affords poor addicted women in San Francisco access to various resources: "The 'seeable child' justified the interventions of care and coercion, access and loss."

15. See Casper 1998; Duden 1993a, 1993b; Sandelowski 1994: 240; Stabile 1998; Wendland 2007: 226.

16. Incredibly, social workers were much less interested in the medical diagnostic value of the ultrasound as a mode of detecting abnormalities in the fetus, perhaps because the agency's embrace of so-called "special needs" adoption rendered such a fetus equally adoptable, at least ideologically.

17. Scholars writing on the use of ultrasound in particular have long observed the link between this technology of seeing and the production of knowledge about mother and fetus. In the case of adoption, sonograms also allow the social workers to "know" the expectant mother. Sandelowski (1994: 234) observes that through ultrasound, "The prenatal and professional knowers of the fetus are spectators, engaged in acts of looking." Social workers, as an example of these "professional knowers of the fetus," use a range of ocular technologies—Palmer (2009: 186) calls these "visual ways of knowing about foetal development"—in an attempt both to know the expectant mother and to predict the future outcome of the adoption process. These technologies of surveillance and visualization confer upon social workers a form of "epistemological privilege" (Sandelowski 1994: 239) over the expectant mother. "In the case of fetal ultrasonography, reading a fetal sonogram is an 'analogue' of getting

to know the fetus," argues Sandelowski (241). In providing evidence, proof, "'the truth' about prenatal existence" (Palmer 2009: 176), visual technologies provide social workers with a sense of certainty in an otherwise highly contingent process. But this sense of certainty is just that—merely a sense—and is constructed through larger national discourses that conflate seeing with knowing and further "an association between vision and objectivity, as well as between ultrasound and scientific objectivity" (177).

In the contemporary United States, the visualization of pregnant women's bodies, particularly through ultrasound, as a way to produce knowledge and affect particular pregnancy outcomes, is profoundly political, as evidenced by conservatives' use of fetal imagery and transvaginal ultrasound in anti-abortion legislation and discourse. As Petchesky (1997: 140) contends, "the impulse to 'see inside' [has] come to dominate ways of knowing about pregnancy and fetuses." This is particularly evident in the Women's Ultrasound Right to Know Act, proposed by Americans United for Life, which attempted to require physicians to perform ultrasound on women seeking abortion (Rodriguez 2014). These kinds of policies function on the assumption that seeing the fetus creates a deeper connection, one that would override the desire to terminate the pregnancy.

In adoption, the power of sight is evident both before and after the birth. Stella and Barbara would often warn prospective parents that simply seeing the new baby could be enough to convince a new mother that adoption was not the correct path. As Selene texted Stella shortly after the birth of her daughter (referenced in the Introduction), "One look at her and I just culdn't [*sic*] bring myself to giving her away." The ultrasound visually separates mother from child, at a moment (pregnancy) when they are as intimately united as two human bodies can be. In adoption, the ultrasound is the first step in a long process of separating mother and child—indeed, "punching" an image out of its context (Beck 2011).

18. See Beck 2011; Jusionyte 2015.

19. Recognizing the expansive potential of their products, FakeABaby's creators add the following disclaimer:

CAUTION: This item has the potential to be used irresponsibly. By completing and submitting the form below, you agree not to use this product for purposes which may be illegal, immoral, fraudulent or hurtful to others. Like almost any item in existence, this product may be used for fun or for evil, depending solely on the intentions of the user. It is designed as a novelty / gag device. Be sure your "mark" has a sense of humor before unleashing this product upon them! We again urge CAUTION when using gags which have the potential of causing emotional harm (as almost any gag or practical joke does). KNOW YOUR VICTIM. Many people will not find this issue humorous in the slightest. Be sure your "mark" has an "evolved" sense of humor. All Products Sold or Distributed by Acme Novelties LLC, FakeABaby.com, TrixiePixGraphics.com, FakeNewspapers.com are not real. They are Fake Gag Products. We do not produce or reproduce any real documents or products. Medical or otherwise. All products are our original works of Art made for the sole purpose of entertainment. All of our products, including but not limited to our Fake Personalized Ultrasounds, Fake Personalized Sonograms, and Fake Personalized Pregnancy Papers are intended for Gag and Joke purposes only. We do not sell products with real doctors' names or use signatures of any kind. All products are stamped FOR ENTERTAINMENT ONLY.

FakeABaby.com Product Disclaimer, www.fakeababy.com/2d-fake-ultrasound-sonogram-personalized/(accessed February 12, 2015).

20. As many feminist scholars have argued, through the ultrasound, the mother is skinned and erased (see Casper 1998; Duden 1993a, 1993b; Stabile 1998; Wendland 2007).

21. The term "poster child" originated in the 1930s to describe the use of images of children—often sick or otherwise suffering—in fundraising efforts by charitable organizations. This legacy continues today, often within the context of humanitarianism.

22. Frantz Fanon, of course, would have a great deal to say about this dual hailing. It is also worth noting that my own racial heritage is ambiguous—even to me, due to the nature of my adoption—but I was often categorized as black or biracial by others, especially in Chicago. In Northern California where I attended college, I was much more likely to be asked the infamous "What are you?" or be spoken to in Spanish.

23. When I think back on these experiences, I am reminded of Ruth Behar's (1996: 177) words: "anthropology that doesn't break your heart just isn't worth doing anymore." The affective intensity of adoption often overflows the legal and bureaucratic structures of the process. It often overflows ethnography.

24. This is at least true in heteronormative and cisgender contexts.

25. Illinois Putative Father Registry, www.putativefather.org/faq.aspx (accessed December 2, 2014).

26. See Seligmann 2013.

27. The Latin comes from Proto-Indo-European *spek-,* to observe (Harper 2018).

28. Not that this information always has predictive power.

2. PROTECTIVE INSPECTIONS

1. HIPAA, the Health Insurance Portability and Accountability Act, governs the circulation of certain forms of personal health information. Adoption agencies are not subject to the act, which applies primarily to healthcare providers.

2. Michael Power (1997) takes care to differentiate audit from inspection. One primary difference, he argues, is that forms of inspection can escalate (from a scheduled visit to a raid, for example). However, the home study had no potential for escalation. Applicants had one shot, essentially; they either passed or they failed. The scheduled nature of the home study made it appear more like an audit and less like an inspection. There is also a difference in target: auditing, Power contends, "increasingly takes the management system as its primary object," while inspection

"focuses more on the substantive conduct of the inspectee" (130). In this respect, the home study resembles an inspection. As Power notes, "Some forms of inspection produce certificates in the form of licenses whose message is fairly clear: the organization, individual, or other object is 'fit' for a defined purpose and has met certain minimum standards" (124). This sounds a lot like a home study, though technically the home study did not directly produce the license. Rather, it produced a thorough written account on which the decision to license was based.

3. Based on ethnographic fieldwork on adoption in Spain, Susan Frekko, Jessaca Leinaweaver, and Diana Marre (2015: 714) contend, "On one level, the screening process ensures that prospective parents are suited to be parents. But on another level, it *produces* suitable parents." Drawing on Carr's (2010) notion of "flipping the script," the authors explore the ways in which adoptive kinship in Spain is forged through language via "communicative vigilance": "careful speech and careful silence that exclude certain topics from talk" (704). In encounters with social workers, "speech (and avoidance of speech) produces kinship" (707). In the case of the home study, the burden rests on prospective parents not only to speak in a particular way, but to *look* like fit adoptive parents (Mariner 2018).

4. Indeed, there is an important class reversal here. The professionalization of social work began with the tradition of "friendly visitors," who visited homes to check up on the poor "and to teach them, largely by moral precept, the 'right' ways of living" (Ehrenreich 1985: 55). As Ehrenreich notes, the rejection of class-based authority in the 1920s led to the development of social work expertise as a special category of authoritative knowledge. It should also be noted here that the sense of invasion experienced by the prospective adopters I encountered was also likely a largely heterosexual experience, as LGBTQ+ individuals must often enlist outside resources and expertise in becoming parents whether through adoption or other forms of assisted reproduction, and are often the targets of added scrutiny and discrimination. That is, the surveillance of the home study might feel less out-of-the-ordinary to certain already-targeted populations.

5. Prospective adoptive parents are thus targets of a specific form of subjectification (Foucault [1977] 1995) via the intensive monitoring and evaluation of the adoption process.

6. As Power (1997: 129) notes, "audit and surveillance emerge from different programmatic ideals." The aim of audit is evaluation, whereas the aim of surveillance is control. Monitoring perhaps rests somewhere in the middle.

7. Power (1997: 12) refers to auditing as "a collection of pragmatic and humble routines which may add to confidence about the veracity of statements made by the auditee but not in a way that can be easily quantified. Verification emerges as a more negotiated and interactive practice than is commonly imagined." This verification is required because, as Power notes, audit and other forms of "checking up" arise "in situations of doubt, conflict, mistrust, and danger" (1). See also Douglas (1992) and Shore and Wright (2000: 77). In transracial adoption, these dynamics of trust are racialized, with guilt mapped onto blackness, and innocence mapped onto whiteness (Bernstein 2011; Cacho 2012; Wanzo 2008).

8. The social workers perform too. As Power (2007: 6) notes, "organizations must be seen to act *as if* the management of risk is possible."

9. *Oxford English Dictionary* (2014b).

10. Historical accounts estimate that Brace's program moved between 200,000 and 250,000 children during its 76-year run (Holt 1994; Herman 2008); one scholar has reported that the program moved 150,000 children from New York City alone (Cook 1995). Brace's was a Protestant project, but "baby trains" also moved children within the Catholic community (Creagh 2012).

11. Brace was inspired by the notion that children were bearers of positive and negative potential, and that early intervention in the form of removal and "placing out" could alter their future trajectories. The *Annual Report* (1876) writes: "These little waifs of society were destined to become the fathers and mothers of this Republic. If they were neglected the permanent interest of the Republic would be neglected" (quoted in Nelson 1984: 9). Thus the protection of children was, and continues to be, portrayed as an investment in a safe and secure national future.

12. "In America, belief in a protected childhood was the product of three forces—natural rights ideology, commitment to civic education, and the increasing number of bourgeois families . . . Childhood was no longer seen only as the time to form a moral adult, but also the time to forge a separate citizen of the republic" (Nelson 1984: 6).

13. Ticktin (2017: 578) argues:

In the contemporary era, we are embroiled in a search for a space of purity, a space outside corruption and contamination, a space emptied of power that can ground both tolerance and action; innocence provides us with such a conceptual space. Yet, because innocence is both mythical and ephemeral, we are constantly displacing politics to the limit of innocence in a never-ending quest, and in the process the structural and historical causes of inequality get rendered invisible.

The very concept of innocence, Ticktin argues, creates a savior subject (583).

14. Shore and Wright (2000: 62) describe four main roles of new specialists and experts created by audit culture:

First, they develop a new expert knowledge and a discourse which create the classifications for a new framework or template of norms, a normative grid for the measurement and regulation of individual and organizational performance. Second, their grid and expertise are used for the design of institutional procedures for setting targets and assessing achievements. Third, certain of these experts staff and manage the new regulatory mechanisms and systems, and judge levels of compliance and deviance. Fourth, they have a therapeutic and redeeming role: they tutor individuals in the art of self-improvement and steer them towards desired norms.

This speaks to the various kinds of labor social workers perform as brokers and auditors, particularly the fourth item, which highlights their role in the production of fit parental subjects.

15. Amazon.com product page, www.amazon.com/Homestudy-Boot-Camp-Step-By-Step-Preparing/dp/061583017X (accessed September 2, 2014).

16. This statement is additionally racialized within the context of American transracial adoption, given the long and violent history of comparing black people to animals.

17. "Do the animals seem relaxed around all family members, or do they seem to avoid or appear anxious around one or two particular family members?" "How much time does the pet spend interacting with family members?" "If the child [nieces and nephews Tim and Erin had mentioned earlier] is near the pet, how is he or she supervised?" "How does the presence of the animals affect the family's interactions?"

18. The Hague Convention on the Protection of Children and Co-operation in Respect of Intercountry Adoption was concluded in 1993 and governs international adoption with the goal of preventing international child trafficking. Agencies in the United States that perform international adoptions must be certified in compliance with Hague guidelines by the federal Council on Accreditation. When First Steps achieved accreditation, the agency extended Hague standards to their domestic practice as well. Audit functions at multiple scales.

19. The home visit in particular offers an opportunity to rethink transparency through the frame of interiority, openness, and the public / private distinction as they shape the intersection of spatial and visual practices. Many anthropologists have investigated transparency as a political and legal technology, but in much of this analysis, the visual notion of seeing through has become entirely metaphorical, or at best, muted. However, this existing anthropological literature on transparency captures a great deal of terminological slippage among a broad range of binaries that unite concerns over knowledge, visibility, and space: transparent / opaque, known / unknown, true / false, visible / invisible, present / absent, open / closed, public / private, exposed / concealed, surface / depths, light / shadow, clear / obscure, disclosed / enclosed, accessible / restricted. These slippages reflect conceptual fluidity rather than analytic confusion, and an ethnographic reality that overflows the bounds of the language used to describe it. Indeed, the project of much of this literature is to trouble these categories (see Bear 2013; Beck 2011; Birchall 2011; Phillips 2011; Teurlings and Stauff 2014).

In thinking through transparency both in terms of access to information and targeted visual practice, I scale down from a focus on the state and global structures of power as commonly interrogated sites of transparency, to the "street level" (Lipsky 2010) encounters between social workers and their clients. The contributors to an edited volume on transparency and conspiracy address seeing through the surface of power itself, located in a range of diverse but traditional sites of control, including the state, police, financial institutions, and the media (West and Sanders 2003: 11). I focus instead on potential adopters as the targets of transparency efforts. Rather than illustrating how state power erases itself (cf. Sharma 2013), the visual-spatial politics of the adoption process reveal how individual subjects are in / effectively seen through in an effort to gain particular forms of predictive knowledge, which aid in social workers' placement of clients into new categories of parenthood.

20. As recently as 2010, incarcerated women in California were being forcibly sterilized (Schwarz 2014). In 1976, the Hyde Amendment pulled federal funding for abortion from Medicaid coverage, except in cases of rape, incest, or a threat to the mother's life (Herold 2013). Studies have shown that black children are removed from homes by Child Protective Services at a disproportionately high rate (Rivaux et al. 2008).

21. This was an issue that made conducting this ethnography *during* the adoption process, rather than retrospectively, particularly complicated.

22. Like "innocent," terms such as "nice" and "clean" are culturally linked to whiteness in the United States (Low 2009; Zimring 2016).

23. This in sharp contrast to practices like stop-and-frisk, which disproportionately affect people of color (Gelman, Fagan, and Kiss 2007).

24. In terms of both space and state, within the context of adoption, public and private are "co-constitutive cultural categories" (Gal 2002: 80).

25. This form of surveillance is one of the ways that audit functions as a central tool of neoliberal governance (Pels 2000; Shore and Wright 2000; Strathern 2000).

26. Comfort for the social workers, who work to reduce risk. The experience of being audited, as this chapter has shown, is markedly uncomfortable.

27. Shore and Wright (2000: 62) continue, "Audit thus becomes a political technology of the self: a means through which individuals actively and freely regulate their own conduct and thereby contribute to the government's model of social order."

28. To draw on Bernstein's theorization of "scriptive things," the home study—along with its requisite checklists—is a practice that scripts behavior in certain ways. Bernstein (2011: 71) notes, "a script is a dynamic substance that deeply influences but does not entirely determine live performances, which vary according to agential individuals' visions, impulses, resistances, revisions, and management of unexpected disruptions." A prompt, then, reveals a script rather than a specific behavior. Power (1997) explores how the audit itself creates the auditee.

29. Although Barbara mentions the monitoring visits that occur during the six months between placement of the child and finalization of the adoption, all of Annette's visits were routine follow-ups during her wait for a match. She did not successfully adopt before First Steps closed in 2015.

30. "Good" clients even drink "good" wine.

31. It is entirely possible that my presence prompted the confession, since I had been in Annette's house previously when the wine was visible. Perhaps, like Jeanine, Annette worried I might disclose this fact to Barbara, and it seemed less risky to simply confess than to be found in violation of duty of candor.

32. DCFS website, www.illinois.gov/dcfs/Pages/default.aspx (accessed February 20, 2014).

33. Larson (2018) terms this "whiteness behaving badly."

34. As Elizabeth Bartholet (1999: 84) notes, "Parental screening has enormous costs from the perspective of those screened and categorized by the system. A dec-

laration that a person is unfit, or marginally fit, to parent another human being is a serious condemnation. A denial of the opportunity to parent constitutes for many people a denial of what is most meaningful in life."

35. See Haraway (1997).

3. TEMPORAL UNCERTAINTIES

1. Lynn allowed me to sit in on her training, but I was not allowed to speak to the parents in attendance as part of my research.

2. This also helps to highlight how adoption anxiety is both linked to and distinct from pregnancy anxiety.

3. Openness can also connote the emergence of adoptive status into the realm of socially acceptable identity traits, no longer to be kept secret from the child or others.

4. This is a term Stella often used to loosely describe the beginning stage of the adoption process. Even the beginning was an end of sorts.

5. In introducing the edited volume *Modes of Uncertainty,* Limor Samimian-Daresh and Paul Rabinow (2015: 2) state, "rather than investigating how cultures cope with risk, these studies demonstrate how they attempt to create *certainty*." "Uncertainty as a concept," they argue, "reflects a way of observing the future" (7).

6. Sara Ahmed (2014b: 8) notes, "We tend to will what is not present, in the sense of here as well as now. It is the futurity and distance of will that seems to render will faulty. We go wrong when we try to gather what is not within reach."

7. Linda J. Seligmann (2013: 82) noticed a similar emphasis on fate in her study of transracial and international adoption in the United States, which she traces to a particular manifestation of popular religiosity: "That an adoption was 'meant to be' was a powerful response to the ambivalence adoptive parents experienced from family members and the general public." Sara Dorow (2006: 67) has observed similarly, in the case of international adoption from China, that "stories of destiny and magic help facilitate the production of unique children and parents, meant for each other."

8. I walked into the office one day in November of 2014 and Jenny and Holly were talking about the weight prospective adopters often gain during the adoption process. Holly attributed this to the stress and anxiety that prospective parents experience while waiting, and mentioned one mother who had gained twenty-five pounds.

9. Here, I borrow a formulation from Timmermans and Buchbinder (2010). In their analysis of newborn genetic screening, infants whose test results come back abnormal but do not fit a specific diagnosis exist in a liminal space. Timmermans and Buchbinder refer to these infants as "patients-in-waiting," a term that references the anticipation and disrupted temporality built into life in these liminal zones. It is also a term that implies an inability to produce a prognosis. The analysis explores how parents and clinicians manage diagnostic and prognostic uncertainty, noting how "the initial positive results of newborn screening come as a shock to almost all

parents" (413), entailing a collapsing of dual temporalities: the genetic past from whence the abnormality originated, and the prognostic future that will unfold as a result. Subsequent testing entails more waiting, and all of its attendant affective experiences: "the weeks or occasionally months of suspense can be an intensely anxious period" (414). "The socio-medical phenomenology of patients-in-waiting," they add, "is thus defined by uncertainty, a rollercoaster ride between alarm and hope" (418). Prospective adoptive parents who have experienced a fall-through (or several) are frequent fliers on this roller coaster.

10. It is important to note that many prospective adoptive parents seek adoption for reasons other than infertility, and many have biological children in addition to adopted children.

11. Internationally, each country has its own age restrictions.

12. Social workers variously attributed this perceived scarcity to increasingly effective contraceptive technologies (and their wider use and acceptance), as well as the increasing social acceptability of single motherhood and increasing competition as new adoption agencies were established, and more prospective parents turned to internet-based independent adoptions as a cost-cutting measure. The lack of revenue from dwindling adoptions was ultimately what forced the agency to close in early 2015.

13. The dominant affective aspect of waiting is anticipation, a temporal orientation that unites a range of emotional experiences including hope, uncertainty, and anxiety. Adams et al. (2009: 247) refer to anticipation as "an excited forward-looking subjective condition" characterized by "nervous anxiety." It brings the speculative future into the present, and involves a "telescoping of temporal possibilities" (249), and in this way allows a kind of "temporal folding" in which different temporalities are brought together (Cole and Durham 2008). Adams et al. (2009) analyze regimes of anticipation on a massive scale, interrogating notions of collective fear and hope. A careful examination of the practice of waiting helps scale this notion to the intimate and individual social practice of American adoption, in which anticipation can be considered a semi-permanent state of being. Anticipation laces temporality and affect around a sense of uncertainty and expectation, implicating an "array of affective states . . . not only anticipation and preparation (tied to hope), but also surprise, uncertainty, anxiety, and unpreparedness (tied to fear)" (Adams et al. 2009: 249).

14. Culturally, hope is tied to a specific form of American "can-do" optimism and individualism. Amy Speier (2016) has examined the relationship between hope and persistence among American fertility travelers to the Czech Republic.

15. Lauren Berlant (2010: 94) theorizes a similar experience of cruel optimism: "the condition of maintaining an attachment to a problematic object *in advance of* its loss."

16. Hochschild (2012) has examined the emotional labor performed by flight attendants.

17. Although physicians agree that it remains unknown whether or not there is any truly "safe" amount of alcohol to be consumed during pregnancy, studies show that it is the peak blood alcohol level (BAC) that affects a fetus most negatively. Fre-

quent, heavy drinking is required for the presence of fetal alcohol spectrum disorder (FASD) (May and Gossage 2011).

18. *Oxford English Dictionary* 2014b.

19. It is important here to acknowledge that fall-throughs did not only happen for adoptive families; though less common, expectant / birth mothers experienced fall-throughs as well. One afternoon I was sitting at McDonald's with Stella and a new expectant mother, Marie. Marie had come to First Steps late in her pregnancy because she had been working with another agency originally, but had found out that the family she was matched with had also been working with another expectant mother. This adoptive family had subsequently dropped Marie when the other mother went into labor. Upon hearing this, Stella stressed that when working with adoptive parents at the beginning of the process, it was First Steps' policy to strictly forbid working with more than one potential birth mother at a time. First Steps' prospective adoptive families were welcome to work with more than one agency at the beginning of the process, but once a match was made with a First Steps expectant mother, the adoptive family had to make a commitment to follow the adoption through to the end, thus becoming ineligible for other matches. This was a strategy for managing expectant mother risk and adoptive family morality.

20. Barbara Katz Rothman ([1986] 1993) has explored how in the case of biological reproduction and kinship after amniocentesis—"tentative pregnancy"—the fetus-as-child is very real to parents-to-be.

21. Malaby (2002: 283) also employs this play on words ("odds and ends") in thinking through the link between risk and contingency.

22. Linda J. Seligmann's (2013) ethnography of adoption in the United States contains similar accounts of international adopters' desire to avoid domestic fall-throughs.

23. This cultural image persists in the face of millennial trends toward later marriage and a declining birth rate.

24. Kath Weston (1997) has explored the consequences of the socially constructed nonprocreative nature of gay and lesbian kinship.

25. Edelman (2004: 11) writes:

> We are no more able to conceive of a politics without a fantasy of the future than we are able to conceive of a future without the figure of the Child. That figural Child alone embodies the citizen as an ideal, entitled to claim full rights to its future share in the nation's good, though always at the cost of limiting the rights "real" citizens are allowed.

26. In stark contrast to this imagining, an adoptee-led movement critiquing adoption practices has recently arisen. Some of these adoptees self-identify as "angry adoptees." Others reject that term, but have been identified as "angry" by supporters of adoption. The attribution of anger to those who protest social injustice has often been a tactic used to discredit social critique of the status quo (for example, the common stereotype of the "angry black woman").

27. It is important to note the extreme affective heterogeneity among expectant mothers. Their experiences span a huge affective range encompassing happiness,

sadness, melancholy, shame, guilt, relief, anger, hurt, and more—with none of these states being mutually exclusive of the others. This is not to say that prospective adoptive parents' affective experiences are monolithic—in this book my goal is not to generalize, but to draw attention to a set of patterns I have observed during my fieldwork.

28. In much the same way that the young toddler's delight at seeing the train was catching in Rosalind's workshop, "anxiety," writes Ahmed (2010: 36), referring to its contagious quality, "is sticky: rather like Velcro, it tends to pick up whatever comes near." If happiness is intentional, then perhaps anxiety is often unintentional; it is true that we often cannot specify an originary object on which to pin our anxieties. Ahmed notes that this is also sometimes true of happiness; at times we are not sure quite why we are happy. Recognition of our happiness in these instances somehow diminishes it—or even turns it into anxiety (33)—whereas recognition of our anxiety often seems to make us more anxious. Frighteningly prolific, anxiety breeds more anxiety. Indeed, the very precarity of our happiness can be the source of our anxiety. Ahmed also notes how, when happiness does not accompany a hoped-for object, we may be stricken by an anxious sense of self-doubt (37).

29. The way that time unfolds within the film is worthy of reflection. When dreaming, time moves more quickly and speeds up as one "goes deeper" into dreams within dreams, such that Cobb and Mal were able to grow old together while lost several "levels" down into dreams, and then awaken as their young selves, mere hours having elapsed in the waking world.

4. KINSHIP'S COSTS

1. Loïc Wacquant (2008: 121–23) describes a similar nearby neighborhood from his own ethnographic research, an area he refers to as "the hyperghetto":

> It is an understatement to say that poverty is endemic in North Lawndale and that daily life there is harsh and insecure. It suffices to take a drive along its scraggy avenues lined with rubbish-strewn vacant lots and burnt-out or crumbled buildings to realize *de visu* the scale of disaster that has befallen this sector of the ghetto ... Commercial establishments are as scarce as abandoned buildings are plentiful. North Lawndale has but a single supermarket, a single bank and a single hospital, as against fifty-four lottery outlets and an equal number of "currency exchanges," those check-cashing and bill-paying counters that, for usurious commissions, provide the poor with the financial services they cannot otherwise access. And no fewer than one hundred liquor stores.

2. This binary has been critiqued by Bear et al. (2015): "The category of immaterial (affective) labor creates a false binary that attributes inherently different creative energies and communicative powers to forms of labor ordered in a hierarchy of value."

3. This slang definition is omitted from the *Oxford English Dictionary* (2014b), but the proverbial phrase "to make ends meet" is included.

4. Dorow (2006: 6) notes, "To put the commands of *political economy* (circuits of exchange and value) in conversation with the desires of *kinship* is a potent mixture." Elsewhere, she contends, "It is perhaps by now a given that most forms of kinship are intertwined with market exchanges of various kinds, without necessarily being reducible to them" (2010: 70).

5. See Dorow (2010: 72) for more on "the slippage between object and subject" peculiar to adoptees.

6. *Regulation of Private Domestic Adoption Expenses*, www.childwelfare.gov /systemwide/laws_policies/statutes/expensesall.pdf (accessed July 24, 2010).

7. As Kohler-Hausmann (2007: 337) notes, "the dominant discourse about fraud erased recipients' poverty."

8. *Oxford English Dictionary* 2014b.

9. *Oxford English Dictionary* 2014b.

10. Another way to think about this is through Anna Tsing's (2005: 75) concept of "spectacular accumulation," which "occurs when investors speculate on a product that may or may not exist," such as the fetus.

11. Approaching this issue in particular, Kopytoff (1986) and others have broached the subject of slavery in their analyses (cf. Ertman 2010; Rothman 2006). From Kopytoff's (1986: 65) perspective, "Slavery is seen not as a fixed and unitary status, but as a process of social transformation that involves a succession of phases and changes in status, some of which merge with other statuses (for example, that of adoptee) that we in the West consider far removed from slavery." In the case of First Steps, an agency originally founded with the mission of serving the needs of African American women and children, the underlying link to slavery was even sharper and more socially problematic.

12. Zaloom (2006: 19) adds, "The contracts were a way to trade large amounts of grain even when these grains were still seeds in the ground . . . Futures contracts enabled traders to set the value of grain months ahead of its reaping with only symbolic reference to the physical commodity."

13. Bear et al. (2015) argue further, "the processes of financialization are uneven, specific, and contingent."

14. See also A Precious Gift (2005), Buckley (2001), Firth (2006), Gift of Life Adoptions (2010), and Gift of Adoption Fund (2009), for examples of lay understandings of the adopted child as a gift.

15. The notion of the gift surfaced again in my fieldwork in a conversation with an adoptive mother who worked for a nonprofit that provided financial assistance to those hoping to adopt, another kind of gift:

> You know, I work for a charity called Gift of Adoption, and we—because there's so many children who need homes, there's plenty of Americans who would want to help parent them and can do a great job, but many people—they talk about forty percent, Dave Thomas Foundation quotes forty percent of Americans consider adoption and just two percent more forward and one percent get across the finish line, and so we give grants of up to seventy-five hundred . . . To qualify parents to make it happen, yeah. And our hope is to get—honestly, our hope is to create an industry

of giving—because so many people want to help children without parents but don't understand, if you're not adopting, that there's another way you can help. So we give grants to make adoptions happen, and hopefully we'll create this industry of giving so we'll have enough money to give away to the people who are not moving forward now responsibly will actually be able to move forward responsibly, knowing that we'll be able to help them.

Adoption is therefore, a kind of industry of giving—a multifaceted gift economy, in which "contracting parties conjoin their respective futures and pasts, materializing their temporal bond, as it were" (Peebles 2010: 227).

16. Melodie's example of California highlights the fact that legally allowable expenses are determined at the state level. For the first few years of my research, Illinois had no stated maximum for birth parent expenses, so caps were usually set at the agency level.

17. IRS (2016), www.irs.gov/taxtopics/tc607.html.

18. Before I began fieldwork, First Steps sometimes placed American children abroad, often in Europe and Canada. By the time I arrived, this practice was fairly rare.

19. The fact that this situation ended in a fall-through makes the question of reimbursement moot.

20. In my time at the agency, I only encountered three white expectant mothers, one of whom was expecting a biracial child.

21. Katherine Browne (2009: 32) contends, "Our economic lives are full of choices, and our choices are full of mysteries. Studying moral frameworks, however tentative, can help us see into the power, fear, and commitment woven into many of these choices."

22. Thinking through the conceptual frame of intimate speculation and its logics of anticipation, observation, and investment underscores the necessity of understanding adoption within the frame of late capitalism. Laura Briggs (2010: 58) suggests, "adoption is above all the neoliberalization of child welfare," arguing that neoliberalism is best glimpsed at the scale of the household (Briggs 2017: 14). It is not just a concern for states and economies, but "a story about families tied together by intimate labors" (Briggs 2010: 60). In their call for a feminist approach to the study of capitalism, anthropologists Laura Bear, Karen Ho, Anna Tsing, and Sylvia Yanagisako (2015) draw our attention to "the centrality of kinship to capital accumulation and class relations." Taking as a primary object of analysis "the unstable, contingent networks of capitalism that surround us," the authors emphasize "the diverse and wide-ranging practices of life and production that cross-cut social domains," rather than attending explicitly to markets and economic practices. Writing in the genre of manifesto and adopting a first-person plural, they insist: "We understand capitalism to be formed through the relational performance of productive powers that exceed formal economic models, practices, boundaries, and market devices . . . Our questions about instability and generativity return us to the contingent production of inequality and structural violence."

1. *Oxford English Dictionary* 2014b.

2. The Adoption Reform Act grew out of a response to the "Baby Tamia" case, which made national news, shedding light on predatory adoption practices. In 2004, Tamia's mother, Carmen McDonald, suffering from postpartum depression, surrendered her infant to a for-profit organization based in Utah called A Cherished Child. The agency flew Carmen and Tamia to Utah, where Carmen decided against placing her daughter. Workers at the agency allegedly threatened to leave the mother stranded in Utah if she did not follow through with the placement, so Carmen signed away her parental rights and returned to Chicago alone. After the agency had placed Tamia with a middle-aged couple who were later arrested on drug charges, Carmen's mother, Maria McDonald, successfully challenged the adoption in court, and Tamia was returned to Illinois to be cared for by biological relatives. The reverberations of this case were still being felt as I finished my time at First Steps. The act, then, was created in response to a very serious fall-through / disruption.

3. For national quantitative data on adoption, see National Center for State Courts (2016) and United Nations (2009). These reports are less useful for the present analysis because of the way private domestic adoption is combined with other categories of adoption, like tribal and independent adoption and adoption from foster care.

4. The authors argue that unmarried women are more likely to relinquish infants to adoption than married women.

5. Scholars have drawn attention to the role of new reproductive technologies, such as IVF and embryo adoption, in the preservation and perpetuation of whiteness in the United States (Roberts 2002: 172; Speier 2016).

6. See also Harvey 2010: 1.

7. Proto-Indo-European *-skei* and *-(s)kep*, respectively (Harper 2018).

8. Laurence Ralph, personal communication, 2017.

9. Comprehensive numerical data on international adoption to the United States can be found at https://travel.state.gov/content/adoptionsabroad/en/about-us/statistics.html.

10. "But we, in the wake," writes Sharpe (2016: 92), "must acknowledge the ship *as* the storm."

11. From a marketing standpoint, international adoption was usually a good choice because the children already existed, and so were more easily imaginable as targets for aid and support. In order to use the domestic program in this way, poor, pregnant women of color would serve as those targets. Since it is so often the child, rather than the mother, that is perceived as a vulnerable future in need of protection, it makes sense that a suffering child abroad would serve as a more effective poster-child than a black pregnant woman receiving public assistance. This privileging of children over mothers is not particularly surprising in a nation that has been slowly dismantling *Roe v. Wade* with legislation that systematically places the "rights" of unborn children over those of the women carrying them.

12. Here, Harney and Moten (2013: 92) draw on migration historian Robert F. Harney, who contended that "once you crossed the Atlantic, you were never on the right side again."

13. Sharpe (2016) theorizes the wake not only as the ripples left by the ship, but also a form of mourning.

14. Organizational death is a meaningful concept in the literature on business administration and organization. Arman (2014: 25) explains, "The meaning of the term organizational death is literal in the sense that the physical and social arrangements of (part of) an organization cease to exist."

15. Ambiguous loss is a social and psychological phenomenon in which a loved one or significant other is either physically absent but psychologically present, or physically present but psychologically absent. Examples include adoptees and birth parents in closed adoptions, missing persons, and friends and family members with dementia. It is characterized by a pervasive uncertainty and open-endedness—as opposed to definitive closure (Boss 2012).

16. These references to a sort of birth mother amnesia were recurring. I am not sure what to make of them, but I think they should be noticed. They likely reveal assumptions about attachment, organization, intelligence, access, and capability—in Holly's words "savvy." Adoption as a form of misplacement.

17. There is a marked difference here between this desire for birth mother contact and the fears expressed by prospective adopters during the adoption process that a future birth mother might show up uninvited.

CONCLUSION

1. Adoption in the United States continues to be characterized by a tension between finding families for children and finding children for families (Ducre 2015: 67). Again, who is the client?

2. Although Kennedy does not provide a citation for the quoted phrase "rainbow families," it likely derives from one of America's earliest examples of hypervisible transracial adoption: Josephine Baker's "Rainbow Tribe." The term has also been used to describe families formed by same-sex parents and children (Hocevar 2014) and the Rainbow Family of Living Light, a "utopian countercultural group" founded in Oregon in the 1970s (McKinzie and Bradley 2013).

3. The traditional euphemism of the stork erases the ideological messiness of both conception and birth (and the birth mother). The cabbage patch functions similarly, erasing racialized histories (Fogg-Davis 2002: 1–2).

4. Intimate speculation is a sort of noninnocent analytic, imperative for what Haraway (2016: 1) calls "staying with the trouble," which she argues does not require an engagement with future temporalities, but a commitment to being "truly present." However, as Rosalind showed us, the call to be mindfully present is indeed a response to an imagined future. The world's population *will* balloon to 11 billion by the end of the twenty-first century, Haraway repeatedly warns us. Indeed, despite

the call to be present, Haraway is obsessed with the future. The last chapter of the book is experimental science fiction that takes place between 2025 and 2425 and wildly reimagines the future of human and nonhuman kinship.

5. *Oxford English Dictionary* 2014d.

6. On anxiety and insecurity, see Adams et al. 2009; Bhabha 1998; Bourguignon 2003; Cooper 2006. On visual culture, see Chapman 2013; Kozlowski 2013; Self 2015. On late capitalism, see Comaroff and Comaroff 2001; Harvey 2010, 2014.

7. As Briggs (2017: 18) argues, "In the United States, all politics are reproductive politics."

8. *Oxford English Dictionary* 2014b.

REFERENCES

AAPF. n.d. "Say Her Name." African American Policy Forum. www.aapf.org /sayhername/. Accessed May 28, 2018.

A Precious Gift Adoption Resource Center, Inc. 2005. www.apreciousgiftarc.com. Accessed June 10, 2010.

Adams, Vincanne, Michelle Murphy, and Adele E. Clarke. 2009. "Anticipation: Technoscience, Life, Affect, Temporality." *Subjectivity: International Journal of Critical Psychology* 28(1): 246–65.

Ahmed, Sara. 2010. "Happy Objects." In *The Affect Theory Reader*, edited by Melissa Gregg and Gregory J. Seigworth, 29–51. Durham, NC: Duke University Press.

———. 2014a. "Making Strangers." *feminist killjoys*. https://feministkilljoys .com/2014/08/04/making-strangers/.

———. 2014b. *Willful Subjects.* Durham, NC: Duke University Press.

———. 2017. *Living a Feminist Life.* Durham, NC: Duke University Press.

Amnesty International. 2014. "Chicago and Illinois: Gun Violence." April 1. www .amnestyusa.org/research/reports/chicago-and-illinois-gun-violence. Accessed October 12, 2014.

Anagnost, Ann. 2000. "Scenes of Misrecognition: Maternal Citizenship in the Age of Transnational Adoption." *positions: east asia cultures critique* 8(2): 390–421.

———. 2008. "Imagining Global Futures in China: The Child as a Sign of Value." In *Figuring the Future: Globalization and the Temporalities of Children and Youth,* edited by Jennifer Cole and Deborah Durham, 49–72. Santa Fe: School for Advanced Research.

Anderson, Ben. 2010. "Preemption, Precaution, Preparedness: Anticipatory Action and Future Geographies." *Progress in Human Geography* 34(6): 777–98.

Appadurai, Arjun. 1986. "Introduction: Commodities and the Politics of Value." In *The Social Life of Things: Commodities in Cultural Perspective*, edited by Arjun Appadurai, 3–63. Cambridge: Cambridge University Press.

———. 2013. *The Future as Cultural Fact: Essays on the Global Condition.* New York: Verso Books.

Arman, Rebecka. 2014. "Death Metaphors and Factory Closure." *Culture and Organization* 20(1): 23–39.

Ayto, John. 2006. *Word Origins* (2nd ed.). London: A&C Black.

Barter Books. 2012. "The Story of Keep Calm and Carry On." YouTube video, 3:00, posted by "BarterBooksLtd," February 28. www.youtube.com/watch?v = FrHkKXFRbCI. Accessed April 2, 2013.

Bartholet, Elizabeth. 1999. *Family Bonds: Adoption, Infertility, and the New World of Child Production.* Boston: Beacon Press.

Bear, Laura. 2013. "The Antinomies of Audit: Opacity, Instability, and Charisma in the Economic Governance of a Hooghly Shipyard." *Economy and Society* 42: 375–97.

———, Karen Ho, Anna Tsing, and Sylvia Yanagisako. 2015. "Gens: A Feminist Manifesto for the Study of Capitalism." Theorizing the Contemporary, *Cultural Anthropology* website, March 30. https://culanth.org/fieldsights/652-gens-a-feminist-manifesto-for-the-study-of-capitalism.

Beck, John. 2011. "Signs of the Sky, Signs of the Times: Photography as Double Agent." *Theory, Culture & Society* 28: 123–39.

Beck, Ulrich. 1992. *Risk Society: Towards a New Modernity.* Translated by M. Ritter. London: SAGE.

Becker, Gay. 1997. *Disrupted Lives: How People Create Meaning in a Chaotic World.* Berkeley: University of California Press.

Behar, Ruth. 1996. *The Vulnerable Observer: Anthropology That Breaks Your Heart.* Boston: Beacon Press.

Berlant, Lauren. 1997. *The Queen of America Goes to Washington City: Essays on Sex and Citizenship.* Durham, NC: Duke University Press.

———. 2010. "Cruel Optimism." In *The Affect Theory Reader*, edited by Melissa Gregg and Gregory J. Seigworth, 93–117. Durham, NC: Duke University Press.

Bernstein, Robin. 2011. *Racial Innocence: Performing American Childhood from Slavery to Civil Rights.* New York: New York University Press.

Bhabha, Homi K. 1998. "Anxiety in the Midst of Difference." *Political and Legal Anthropology Review* 21(1): 123–37.

Birchall, Clare. 2011. "Introduction to 'Secrecy and Transparency': The Politics of Opacity and Openness." *Theory, Culture, & Society* 28: 7–25.

Boris, Eileen, and Rhacel Salazar Parreñas. 2010. "Introduction." In *Intimate Labors: Cultures, Technologies, and the Politics of Care*, edited by Eileen Boris and Rhacel Salazar Parreñas, 1–12. Stanford, CA: Stanford University Press.

Boss, Pauline. 2012. "The Myth of Closure." *Family Process* 51(4): 437–587.

Bourguignon, Erika. 2003. "Faith, Healing, and 'Ecstasy Deprivation': Secular Society in a New Age of Anxiety." *Anthropology of Consciousness* 14(1): 1–19.

Briggs, Laura. 2010. "Foreign and Domestic: Adoption, Immigration, and Privatization." In *Intimate Labors: Cultures, Technologies, and the Politics of Care*, edited by Eileen Boris and Rhacel Salazar Parrenas, 49–62. Stanford, CA: Stanford University Press.

———. 2012. *Somebody's Children: The Politics of Transracial and Transnational Adoption.* Durham, NC: Duke University Press.

———. 2017. *How All Politics Became Reproductive Politics: From Welfare Reform to Foreclosure to Trump.* Berkeley: University of California Press.

Brighenti, Andrea Mubi. 2010. *Visibility in Social Theory and Social Research.* New York: Palgrave McMillon.

Brinkley, Leslie. 2017. "Concord Adoption Agency Closes, Leaving Parents in the Dark." *ABC7 News*, January 31. http://abc7news.com/family/concord-adoption-agency-closes-leaving-parents-in-dark/1731119/. Accessed May 29, 2018.

Brinson, Jemal R. 2015. "Data: How Many Abandoned Babies Are Saved? Plus How Illinois' Law Works." *Chicago Tribune*, November 17. www.chicagotribune.com/ct-saving-abonded-babies-charts-20151116-htmlstory.html. Accessed February 12, 2017.

Brodwin, Paul. 2008. "The Coproduction of Moral Discourse in U.S. Community Psychiatry." *Medical Anthropology Quarterly* 22(2): 127–47.

Browne, Katherine E. 2009. "Economics and Morality: Introduction." In *Economics and Morality: Anthropological Approaches*, edited by Katherine E. Browne and B. Lynne Milgram, 1–40. Lanham, MD: Altamira Press.

Browne, Simone. 2015. *Dark Matters: On the Surveillance of Blackness.* Durham, NC: Duke University Press.

Buckley, Betsy. 2001. *The Greatest Gift: Reflections on International and Domestic Adoption.* Berkeley: Creative Arts.

Cacho, Lisa Marie. 2012. "White Entitlement and Other People's Crimes." In *Social Death: Racialized Rightlessness and the Criminalization of the Unprotected*, 35–60. New York: New York University Press.

Carp, E. Wayne. 1998. *Family Matters: Secrecy and Disclosure in the History of Adoption.* Cambridge, MA: Harvard University Press.

———. 2002. "Introduction: A Historical Overview of American Adoption." In *Adoption in America: Historical Perspectives*, edited by E. Wayne Carp, 1–26. Ann Arbor: University of Michigan Press.

Carr, E. Summerson. 2010. *Scripting Addiction: The Politics of Therapeutic Talk and American Sobriety.* Princeton, NJ: Princeton University Press.

Casper, Monica. 1998. *The Making of the Unborn Patient: A Social Anatomy of Fetal Surgery.* New Brunswick, NJ: Rutgers University Press.

——— and Lisa Jean Moore. 2009. *Missing Bodies: The Politics of Visibility.* New York: New York University Press.

Cassiman, Shawn A. 2008. "Resisting the Neo-liberal Poverty Discourse: On Constructing Deadbeat Dads and Welfare Queens." *Sociology Compass* 2(5): 1690–700.

Castañeda, Claudia. 2002. *Figurations: Child, Bodies, Worlds.* Durham, NC: Duke University Press.

CensusScope. 2010. "United States: Segregation: Dissimilarity Indices (2010)." www.censusscope.org/us/rank_ dissimilarity_white_black.html. Accessed January 6, 2011.

Certeau, Michel de. 1984. *The Practice of Everyday Life.* Berkeley: University of California Press.

Chakravartty, Paula, and Denise Ferreira da Silva. 2012. "Accumulation, Dispossession, and Debt: The Racial Logic of Global Capitalism—An Introduction." *American Quarterly* 64(3): 361–85.

Chapman, Sara. 2013. "The Rise of Visual Culture." *HuffPost United Kingdom Blog.* www.huffingtonpost.co.uk/sara-champan/the-rise-of-visual-culture_b_3635240 .html.

Chicago Public Schools. n.d. "CPS Stats and Facts." http://cps.edu/About_CPS /At-a-glance/Pages/Stats_and_facts.aspx. Accessed February 26, 2015.

Cole, Jennifer, and Deborah Durham. 2008. "Introduction: Globalization and the Temporality of Children and Youth." In *Figuring the Future: Globalization and the Temporalities of Children and Youth*, edited by Jennifer Cole and Deborah Durham, 3–23. Santa Fe: School for Advanced Research Press.

Collins, Patricia Hill. [1982] 1992. "Black Women and Motherhood." In *Rethinking the Family: Some Feminist Questions,* revised ed., edited by Barrie Thorne with Marilyn Yalom, 215–45. Boston: Northeastern.

———. 1991. *Black Feminist Thought: Knowledge, Consciousness, and the Politics of Empowerment.* New York: Routledge.

Comaroff, Jean, and John L. Comaroff. 2001. "Millennial Capitalism: First Thoughts on a Second Coming." In *Millennial Capitalism and the Culture of Neoliberalism*, edited by Jean Comaroff and John. L. Comaroff, 1–56. Durham, NC: Duke University Press.

Conn, Peter. 2013. *Adoption: A Brief Social and Cultural History.* New York: Palgrave Macmillan.

Cook, Jeanne F. 1995. "A History of Placing Out: The Orphan Trains." *Child Welfare* 74(1): 181–97.

Cooper, Melissa. 2006. "Pre-empting Emergence: The Biological Turn in the War on Terror." *Theory, Culture & Society* 23(4): 113–35.

Cox, Aimee Meredith. 2015. *Shapeshifters: Black Girls and the Choreography of Citizenship.* Durham, NC: Duke University Press.

Creagh, Diane. 2012. "The Baby Trains: Catholic Foster Care and Western Migration, 1873–1929." *Journal of Social History* 46(1): 197–218.

Cucchiara, Maia. 2013. " 'Are We Doing Damage?': Choosing an Urban Public School in an Era of Parental Anxiety." *Anthropology and Education Quarterly* 44(1): 75–93.

Dorow, Sara. 2006. *Transnational Adoption: A Cultural Economy of Race, Gender, and Kinship.* New York: New York University Press.

———. 2010. "Producing Kinship through the Marketplaces of International Adoption." In *Baby Markets: Money and the New Politics of Creating Families*, edited by Michele Bratcher Goodwin, 69–83. New York: Cambridge University Press.

Douglas, Mary. 1992. *Risk and Blame.* London: Routledge.

Drury, Tracey. 2015. "Baker Victory Expanding Dental, Foster Care Adoptions Services." *American City Business Journals,* December 14. www.bizjournals.com

/buffalo/news/2015/12/14/baker-victory-expanding-dental-foster-care.html. Accessed May 29, 2018.

Ducre, K. Animashaun. 2015. "Rac(e)ing to the Baby Market: The Political Economy of Overcoming Infertility." In *The Motherhood Business: Consumption, Communication, and Privilege*, edited by Anne Teresa Demo, Jennifer L. Borda, and Charlotte Kroløkke, 52–75. Tuscaloosa: University of Alabama Press.

Duden, Barbara. 1993a. *Disembodying Women: Perspectives on Pregnancy and the Unborn*. Cambridge, MA: Harvard University Press.

———. 1993b. "Visualizing 'Life.'" *Science as Culture* 3(4): 562–600.

Dusky, Lorraine. 2011. "Positive Adoption Language." *First Mother Forum*. www.firstmotherforum.com/p/positive-adoption-language.html. Accessed January 4, 2015.

Economic Policy Institute. n.d. "Poverty." http://stateofworkingamerica.org/factsheets/poverty/. Accessed October 26, 2014.

Edelman, Lee. 2004. *No Future: Queer Theory and the Death Drive*. Durham, NC: Duke University Press.

Edin, Kathryn J., and H. Luke Schaefer. 2015. *$2.00 a Day: Living on Almost Nothing in America*. Boston: Houghton Mifflin Harcourt.

Education Commission of the States. 2014. "Student Achievement: Closing the Achievement Gap." www.ecs.org/html/ issue.asp?issueid = 117&subissueID = 303. Accessed October 26, 2014.

Ehrenreich, John H. 1985. *The Altruistic Imagination: A History of Social Work and Social Policy in the United States*. Ithaca, NY: Cornell University Press.

Ertman, Martha. 2010. "The Upside of Baby Markets." In *Baby Markets: Money and the New Politics of Creating Families*, edited by Michele Bratcher Goodwin, 23–40. New York: Cambridge University Press.

Ethioanonymama. 2014. "A Seven-Year-Old Takes on National Adoption Month, Gotcha Day, and Generally Tells It Like It Is." November 4. https://ethioanonymama.wordpress.com/2014/11/04/a-seven-year-old-takes-on-national-adoption-month-gotcha-day-and-generally-tells-it-like-it-is/. Accessed February 17, 2015.

Faist, Thomas. 2014. "Brokerage in Cross-Border Mobility: Social Mechanisms and the (Re)Production of Social Inequalities." *Social Inclusion* 2(4): 38–52.

Fessler, Ann. 2006. *The Girls Who Went Away: The Hidden History of Women Who Surrendered Children for Adoption in the Decades before Roe v. Wade*. New York: Penguin Books.

Firth, Mary Durnin, dir. 2006. *The Giving*. CustomFlix Studio. Documentary.

Fleetwood, Nicole. 2011. *Troubling Vision: Performance, Visuality, and Blackness*. Chicago: University of Chicago Press.

Floersch, Jerry. 2002. *Meds, Money, and Manners: The Case Management of Severe Mental Illness*. New York: Columbia University Press.

Fogg-Davis, H. 2002. *The Ethics of Transracial Adoption*. Ithaca, NY: Cornell University Press.

Ford, Andrea. 2017. "Near Birth: Gendered Politics, Embodied Ecologies, and Ethical Futures in Californian Childbearing." PhD diss., University of Chicago.

Foucault, Michel. [1977] 1995. *Discipline & Punish: The Birth of the Prison.* Translated by Alan Sheridan. New York: Vintage Books.

———. [1963] 2003. *The Birth of the Clinic: An Archaeology of Medical Perception.* Translated by A. M. Sheridan. London: Routledge.

Franklin, Sarah. 1995. "Postmodern Procreation: A Cultural Account of Assisted Reproduction." In *Conceiving the New World Order: The Global Politics of Reproduction*, edited by Faye D. Ginsburg and Rayna Rapp, 323–45. Berkeley: University of California Press.

Frekko, Susan E., Jessaca B. Leinaweaver, and Diana Marre. 2015. "How (Not) to Talk about Adoption: On Communicative Vigilance in Spain." *American Ethnologist* 42: 703–19.

Gailey, Christine W. 2000. "Race, Class, and Gender in Intercountry Adoption in the USA." In *Intercountry Adoption: Developments, Trends, and Perspectives*, edited by Peter Selman, 295–314. London: Skyline House Press.

Gal, Susan. 2002. "A Semiotics of the Public / Private Distinction." *Differences: A Journal of Feminist Cultural Studies* 13: 77–94.

Gallagher, Mari. 2006. *Examining the Impact of Food Deserts on Public Health in Chicago.* Mari Gallagher Research and Consulting Group. www.marigallagher .com/wp-content/plugins/download-attachments/includes/download.php?id = 3777. Accessed May 17, 2018.

Gates, Theaster. 2010. "To Speculate Darkly." Opening Night Lecture, Milwaukee Art Museum, April 16. www.artbabble.org/video/chipstone/theaster-gates-opening-night-lecture-speculate-darkly. Accessed April 2, 2018.

Gelman, Andrew, Jeffrey Fagan, and Alex Kiss. 2007. "An Analysis of the New York City Police Department's 'Stop-and-Frisk' Policy in the Context of Claims of Racial Bias." *Journal of the American Statistical Association* 102(479): 813–23.

Georges, Eugenia. 1996. "Fetal Ultrasound Imaging and the Production of Authoritative Knowledge in Greece." *Medical Anthropology Quarterly* 10(2): 157–75.

Gift of Adoption Fund. 2009. "Mission and Vision." www.giftofadoption.org /aboutUs/missionVision.html. Accessed June 10, 2010.

Gift of Life Adoptions. 2010. www.giftoflifeadoptions.com. Accessed June 10, 2010.

Gilens, Martin. 2003. "How the Poor Became Black: The Racialization of Poverty in the Mass Media." In *Race and the Politics of Welfare Reform*, edited by Sanford F. Schram, Joe Soss, and Richard C. Fording, 101–30. Ann Arbor: University of Michigan Press.

Gill, Brian Paul. 2002. "Adoption Agency's and the Search for the Ideal Family, 1918–1965." In *Adoption in America: Historical Perspectives*, edited by E. Wayne Carp, 160–80. Ann Arbor: University of Michigan Press.

Gilliom, John. 2001. *Overseers of the Poor: Surveillance, Resistance, and the Limits of Privacy.* Chicago: University of Chicago Press.

Goodwin, Michele Bratcher. 2010. "Baby Markets." In *Baby Markets: Money and the New Politics of Creating Families,* edited by Michele Bratcher Goodwin, 2–22. New York: Cambridge University Press.

Gordon, Avery. 2008. *Ghostly Matters: Haunting and the Sociological Imagination.* Minneapolis: University of Minnesota Press.

Grand, Michael Phillip. 2011. *The Adoption Constellation: New Ways of Thinking About and Practicing Adoption.* CreateSpace Independent Publishing Platform.

Guttmacher Institute. 2015. "Use of Long-Acting Reversible Contraceptive Methods Continues to Increase in the United States." October 8. www.guttmacher .org/news-release/2015/use-long-acting-reversible-contraceptive-methods-continues-increase-united-states.

———. 2016. "Steep Drop in Unintended Pregnancy Is Behind the 2008–2011 U.S. Abortion Decline." March 2. www.guttmacher.org/news-release/2016/steep-drop-unintended-pregnancy-behind-2008–2011-us-abortion-decline.

Guyer, Jane. 2007. "Prophecy and the Near Future: Thoughts on Macroeconomic, Evangelical, and Punctuated Time." *American Ethnologist* 34(3): 409–21.

Habermas, Jürgen. [1962] 1991. *The Structural Transformation of the Public Sphere: An Inquiry into a Category of Bourgeois Society.* Translated by Thomas Burger. Boston: MIT Press.

Hacking, Ian. 1990. *The Taming of Chance.* Cambridge: Cambridge University Press.

Halbrook, Bernadette, and Rick Ginsberg. 1997. "Ethnographic Countertransference in Qualitative Research: Implications for Mental Health Counseling Research." *Journal of Mental Health Counseling* 19(1): 87–93.

Hancock, Ange-Marie. 2004. *The Politics of Disgust: The Public Identity of the Welfare Queen.* New York: New York University Press.

Haraway, Donna. 1991. *Simians, Cyborgs, and Women: The Reinvention of Nature.* London: Routledge.

———. 1997. *Modest_Witness@Second_Millennium.Female_Man_Meets_Onco-Mouse.* London: Routledge.

———. 2016. *Staying with the Trouble: Making Kin in the Chthulucene.* Durham, NC: Duke University Press.

Hardt, Michael, and Antonio Negri. 2000. *Empire.* Cambridge, MA: Harvard University Press.

Harness, Susan. 2014. "American Indian Transracial Adoption Bibliography." *Adoption & Culture* 4: 122–26.

Harney, Stefano, and Fred Moten. 2013. *The Undercommons: Fugitive Planning and Black Study.* Wivenhoe: Minor Compositions.

Harper, Douglas. 2018. *Online Etymology Dictionary.* www.etymonline.com.

Hartman, Saidiya. 2007. *Lose Your Mother: A Journey along the Atlantic Slave Route.* New York: Farrar, Straus, and Giroux.

Harvard Achievement Gap Initiative. 2014. *Facts on Achievement Gaps.* www .agi.harvard.edu/projects/FactsonAchievementGaps.pdf. Accessed October 12, 2014.

Harvey, David. 2010. *The Enigma of Capital and the Crises of Capitalism*. Oxford: Oxford University Press.

———. 2014. *Seventeen Contradictions and the End of Capitalism*. Oxford: Oxford University Press.

Hayden, Corinne P. 1995. "Gender, Genetics, Generation: Reformulating Biology in Lesbian Kinship." *Cultural Anthropology* 10(1): 41–63.

Herman, Ellen. 2008. *Kinship by Design: A History of Adoption in the Modern United States*. Chicago: University of Chicago Press.

Herold, Steph. 2013. "Medicaid Coverage for Abortion Care Elusive Even in States Where It Is Legal." *RH Reality Check*, February 26. http://rhrealitycheck.org /article/2013/02/26/medicaid-coverage-for-abortion-care-elusive-even-in-states-where-it-is-legal/. Accessed February 6, 2015.

Hocevar, Andreja. 2014. "Children in Rainbow Families." *Ljetopis Socijalnog Rada / Annual of Social Work* 21(1): 85–104.

Hochschild, Arlie Russell. 2012. *The Managed Heart: Commercialization of Human Feeling*. Berkeley: University of California Press.

Holt, Marilyn I. 1994. *The Orphan Trains: Placing Out in America*. Lincoln: University of Nebraska Press.

Homer, Aaron. 2014. "Devonte Hart: The Inspiring Story of the Boy in the Hug That Moved a Nation." *Inquisitr*, November 30. www.inquisitr.com/1644698 /devonte-hart-the-inspiring-story-of-the-boy-in-the-hug-that-moved-a-nation/. Accessed December 11, 2014.

Howell, Signe. 2006. *The Kinning of Foreigners: Transnational Adoption in a Global Perspective*. New York: Berghahn Books.

———. 2009. "Adoption of the Unrelated Child: Some Challenges to the Anthropological Study of Kinship." *Annual Review of Anthropology* 38: 149–66.

Illinois.gov. 2005. "Governor Blagojevich Signs Legislation Establishing Illinois as National Model for Adoption Reform." Office of the Governor, press release. www3.illinois.gov/PressReleases/ShowPressRelease.cfm?SubjectID = 3&RecNum = 4238. Accessed February 18, 2017.

Jackson, John L. 2005. *Real Black: Adventures in Racial Sincerity*. Chicago: University of Chicago Press.

Jacobson, Heather. 2008. *Culture Keeping: White Mothers, International Adoption, and the Negotiation of Family Difference*. Nashville: Rutgers University Press.

Jalongo, Mary Renck. 2010. "From Urban Homelessness to Rural Work: International Origins of the Orphan Trains." *Early Childhood Education Journal* 38: 165–70.

Johnson, Chloe. 2014. "Meet Devonte, the Little Boy with the Big Heart." *Paper Trail*, November 10. http://papertrail.co.nz/meet-devonte-little-boy-big-heart/. Accessed December 5, 2014.

Jones, Jo, and Paul Placek. 2017. *Adoption by the Numbers*. National Council for Adoption. https://indd.adobe.com/view/4ae7a823-4140-4f27-961a-cd9f16a5f362. Accessed May 29, 2018.

Jones, Jonathan. 2014. "The Touching Hug Photo from Ferguson Protests Is a Blatant Lie." *The Guardian,* December 2. www.theguardian.com/commentisfree/2014/dec/02/hug-photographs-ferguson-protests-lie. Accessed December 10, 2014.

Jones, Monica A. 2013. *Homestudy Boot Camp: A Step-by-Step Insider's Guide to Preparing for the Event Every Adoptive Applicant Must Pass before Adopting.* Simply Managed.

Jonsson, Lars-Eric. 2005. "Home, Women, and Children: Social Services Home Visits in Postwar Sweden." *Home Cultures* 2: 153–74.

Jonsson, Patrik. 2014. "Devonte Hart, Sgt. Bret Barnum, and the Hug Felt 'Round the World." *Christian Science Monitor,* November 29. www.csmonitor.com/USA/Society/2014/1129/Devonte-Hart-Sgt.-Bret-Barnum-and-the-hug-felt-round-the-world-video. Accessed December 5, 2014.

Jorjorian, Annoosh. 2014. "How Do We Reconcile Warring Images of a Boy Hugging a Cop and a Boy Shot Dead by a Cop?" *Salon,* December 10. www.salon.com/2014/12/11/how_do_we_reconcile_warring_images_of_a_boy_hugging_a_cop_and_a_boy_shot_dead_by_a_cop/. Accessed December 20, 2014.

Joyce, Kathryn. 2013. *The Child Catchers: Rescue, Trafficking, and the New Gospel of Adoption.* New York: Public Affairs.

Jusionyte, Ieva. 2015. "States of Camouflage." *Cultural Anthropology* 30(1): 113–38.

Kaufman, Sharon R. 2005. *. . . And a Time to Die: How American Hospitals Shape the End of Life.* New York: Scribner.

Kennedy, Randall. 2004. *Interracial Intimacies.* London: Vintage.

Kim, Eleana J. 2010. *Adopted Territory: Transnational Adoption, Korean Adoptees, and the Politics of Belonging.* Durham, NC: Duke University Press.

Kim, Hosu. 2016. *Birth Mothers and Transnational Adoption Practice in South Korea: Virtual Mothering.* New York: Palgrave Macmillan.

Kim, Jodi. 2009. "An 'Orphan' with Two Mothers: Transnational and Transracial Adoption, the Cold War, and Contemporary Asian American Cultural Politics." *American Quarterly* 61(4): 855–80.

Kingsbury, Kathleen. 2013. "Longer Wait Times, Higher Costs for U.S. Adoptions." *Reuters,* January 15. www.reuters.com/article/us-adoption-domestic-waits/longer-wait-times-higher-costs-for-u-s-adoptions-idUSBRE90E15Y20130115. Accessed May 29, 2018.

Knight, Kelly Ray. 2015. *addicted.pregnant.poor.* Durham, NC: Duke University Press.

Koch, Wendy. 2013. "USA Faces Critical Adoption Shortage." *USA Today,* January 10. http://usatoday30.usatoday.com/NEWS/usaedition/2013-01-11-Adoption-options-plummet-as-Russia-closes-its—doors_ST_U.htm. Accessed May 29, 2018.

Kohler-Hausmann, Julilly. 2007. " 'The Crime of Survival': Fraud Prosecutions, Community Surveillance, and the Original 'Welfare Queen.' " *Journal of Social History* 41(2): 329–54.

Kopytoff, Igor. 1986. "The Cultural Biography of Things." In *The Social Life of Things: Commodities in Cultural Perspective,* edited by Arjun Appadurai, 64–91. Cambridge: Cambridge University Press.

———. 2004. "Commoditizing Kinship in America." In *Consuming Motherhood*, edited by Janelle S. Taylor, Linda L. Layne, and Danielle Wozniak, 271–78. New Brunswick, NJ: Rutgers University Press.

Koster, Martijn. 2012. "Mediating and Getting 'Burnt' in the Gap: Politics and Brokerage in a Recife Slum, Brazil." *Critique of Anthropology* 32(4): 479–97.

———. 2014. "Brazilian Brokers, Boundaries, and Buildings: A Material Culture of Politics." *Journal of Material Culture* 19(2): 125–44.

Kozlowski, Lori. 2013. "Future of Content: Visual Culture and the Ephemeral." *Forbes*, July 17. www.forbes.com/sites/lorikozlowski/2013/07/17/future-of-content-visual-culture-and-the-ephemeral/#45d40a5d209d.

Kreider, Rose M., and Daphne A. Lofquist. 2014. "Adopted Children and Stepchildren: 2010." *Current Population Reports P20–572*. Washington, DC: U. S. Census Bureau. www.census.gov/prod/2014pubs/p20-572.pdf.

Lakoff, Andrew. 2007. "Preparing for the Next Emergency." *Public Culture* 19(2): 247–71.

Larson, Stevie. 2016. *The Fractured Values of Best Interests: Struggles and Spaces of Transnational Adoption*. ProQuest Dissertations.

———. 2018. "Whiteness Unsecured." Unpublished manuscript.

Layne, Linda L. 1999. "The Child as Gift: New Directions in the Study of Euro-American Gift Exchange." In *Transformative Motherhood: On Giving and Getting in a Consumer Culture*, edited by Linda L. Layne, 1–27. New York: New York University Press.

Leinaweaver, Jessaca. 2018. "Adoption." *Cambridge Encyclopedia of Anthropology*. www.anthroencyclopedia.com/entry/adoption. Accessed June 2, 2018.

Lipsky, Michael. 2010. *Street-level Bureaucracy: Dilemmas of the Individual in Public Services*. New York: Russell Sage Foundation.

Low, Setha. 2009. "Maintaining Whiteness: The Fear of Others and Niceness." *Transforming Anthropology* 17: 79–92.

Lubiano, Wahneema. 1992. "Black Ladies, Welfare Queens, and State Minstrels: Ideological War by Narrative Means." In *Race-ing Justice, En-gendering Power: Essays on Anita Hill, Clarence Thomas, and the Construction of Social Reality*, edited by Toni Morrison, 323–63. New York: Pantheon Books.

Luhmann, Niklas. 1996. "Modern Society Shocked by Its Risks." Social Sciences Research Centre in Association with the Dept. of Sociology, University of Hong Kong, Hong Kong. Occasional Paper 17.

Malaby, Thomas M. 2002. "Odds and Ends: Risk, Mortality, and the Politics of Contingency." *Culture, Medicine and Psychiatry* 26: 283–312.

Malkki, Liisa. 2000. "Figures of the Future: Dystopia and Subjectivity in the Social Imagination of the Future." In *History in Person: Enduring Struggles, Contentious Practice, Intimate Identities*, edited by Dorothy Holland and Jean Lave, 325–48. Santa Fe: School of American Research Press.

———. 2010. "Children, Humanity, and the Infantilization of Peace." In *In the Name of Humanity: The Government of Threat and Care*, edited by Illana Feldman and Miriam Ticktin, 58–85. Durham, NC: Duke University Press.

Manetti, Michelle. 2012. "10 Décor Trends (Yes, Including 'Keep Calm and Carry On') We're Done With for 2013." *Huffington Post,* December 14. www .huffingtonpost.com/ 2012/12/14/decor-trends-2013_n_2301245.html. Accessed February 3, 2013.

Mankekar, Purnima, and Akhil Gupta. 2016. "Intimate Encounters: Affective Labor in Call Centers." *Positions* 24(1): 17–43.

Maril, Robin S. 2013. "Regulating the Family: The Impact of Pro-Family Policymaking Assessments on Women and Nontraditional Families." *Texas Journal of Women and the Law* 23(1): 1–36.

Mariner, Kathryn A. 2018. "The Specular Un / Making of Kinship: American Adoption's Penetrating Gaze." *Ethnos* 83(5): 968–85. https://doi.org/10.1080/00 141844.2017.1377744.

Marx, Gary T. 1989. *Undercover: Police Surveillance in America.* Berkeley: University of California Press.

Mattingly, Cheryl. 2010. *The Paradox of Hope: Journeys through a Clinical Borderland.* Berkeley: University of California Press.

Mauss, Marcel. [1950] 1990. *The Gift: The Form and Reason for Exchange in Archaic Societies.* Translated by W. D. Halls. New York: W. W. Norton.

May, Philip A., and J. Phillip Gossage. 2011. "Maternal Risk Factors for Fetal Alcohol Spectrum Disorders: Not As Simple As It Might Seem." *Alcohol Research & Health* 34(1): 15–26.

McKinzie, Ashleigh E., and Mindy S. Bradley. 2013. "Deviance and Social Control in an Alternative Community: The Unique Case of the Rainbow Family of Living Light." *Deviant Behavior* 34: 599–617.

Melosh, Barbara. 2002. *Strangers and Kin: The American Way of Adoption.* Cambridge, MA: Harvard University Press.

miggelzworth. 2010. "Ghost." *Urban Dictionary.* www.urbandictionary.com/define .php?term = Ghost&defid = 5261671.

Mitchell, Harvey. 2002. *America after Tocqueville: Democracy against Difference.* New York: Cambridge University Press.

Miyazaki, Hirokazu, and Annelise Riles. 2005. "Failure as an Endpoint." In *Global Assemblages: Technology, Politics, and Ethics as Anthropological Problems,* edited by Aiwah Ong and Stephen J. Collier, 320–31. Malden, MA: Blackwell.

Modell, Judith. 1994. *Kinship with Strangers: Adoption and Interpretations of Kinship in American Culture.* Berkeley: University of California Press.

———. 1999. "Freely Given: Open Adoption and the Rhetoric of the Gift." In *Transformative Motherhood: On Giving and Getting in Consumer Culture,* edited by Linda L. Layne, 29–64. New York: New York University Press.

Morfitt, Karen. 2018. "Sudden Closure of Adoption Agency Leaves Dozens of Families in Limbo." *CBS News,* May 23. http://denver.cbslocal.com/2018/05/23 /adoption-agency-closure-limbo/. Accessed May 29, 2018.

Moten, Fred. 2013. "The Subprime and the Beautiful." *African Identities* 11(2): 237–45.

NABSW (National Association of Black Social Workers). 1972. *Position Statement on Transracial Adoptions.* http://c.ymcdn.com/sites/nabsw.org/resource/collection /E1582D77-E4CD-4104-996A-D42D08F9CA7D/NABSW_Trans-Racial_ Adoption_1972_Position_(b).pdf. Accessed July 22, 2014.

Narayan, Kirin. 1993. "How Native Is a 'Native' Anthropologist?" *American Anthropologist* 95(3): 671–82.

National Center for Education Statistics. 2011. *National Assessment of Education Progress (2011).* http://nces.ed.gov/nationsreportcard/pdf/main2011/2012457.pdf. Accessed February 20, 2015.

National Center for State Courts. 2016. "Trends in State Courts: Special Focus on Family Law and Court Communications." National Center for State Courts. Edited by Carol R. Flango, Deborah W. Smith, Charles F. Campbell, and Neal B. Kauder. www.ncsc.org/~/media/microsites/files/trends%202016/trends-2016-low.ashx. Accessed May 29, 2018.

Nelms, Taylor C. 2012. "The Zombie Bank and the Magic of Finance, Or: How to Write a History of Crisis." *Journal of Cultural Economy* 5(2): 232–46.

Nelson, Barbara. 1984. *Making an Issue of Child Abuse: Political Agenda Setting for Social Problems.* Chicago: University of Chicago Press.

Newman, Jonah. 2014. "Not Just Gary: Vacant Houses Plague Some Chicago Neighborhoods Too." *Chicago Reporter,* October 31. http://chicagoreporter.com/not-just-gary-vacant-houses-plague-some-chicago-neighborhoods-too/. Accessed July 3, 2017.

NICHD (National Institute of Child Health and Human Development). 2012. "What Is a High Risk Pregnancy?" National Institutes of Health. www.nichd .nih.gov/health/topics/pregnancy/conditioninfo/pages/high-risk.aspx. Accessed March 24, 2014.

Nolan, Christopher, dir. 2010. *Inception.* Legendary Pictures.

Oaks, Laury. 2015. *Giving Up Baby: Safe Haven Laws, Motherhood, and Reproductive Justice.* New York: New York University Press.

Oxford English Dictionary Online. 2014a. "doubt, n." Oxford University Press. www.oed.com.ezp.lib.rochester.edu/view/Entry/57076?rskey = 3PzSWI&result = 1. Accessed May 15, 2018.

———. 2014b. "end, n." Oxford University Press. www.oed.com.ezp.lib.rochester .edu/view/Entry/61863?isAdvanced = false&result = 1&rskey = dkOot3&. Accessed July 26, 2017.

———. 2014c. "performance, n." Oxford University Press. www.oed.com.ezp.lib .rochester.edu/view/Entry/140783?redirectedFrom = performance. Accessed May 3, 2018.

———. 2014d. "speculation, n." Oxford University Press. www.oed.com.proxy .uchicago.edu/view/Entry/186113?redirectedFrom = speculation. Accessed March 6, 2015.

Palmer, Julie. 2009. "Seeing and Knowing: Ultrasound Images in the Contemporary Abortion Debate." *Feminist Theory* 10(2): 173–89.

Patton, Sandra. 2000. *Birth Marks: Transracial Adoption in Contemporary America.* New York: New York University Press.

Peebles, Gustav. 2010. "The Anthropology of Credit and Debt." *Annual Review of Anthropology* 39: 225–40.

Peele, Jordan, dir. 2017. *Get Out*. Blumhouse Productions.

Pels, Peter. 2000. "The Trickster's Dilemma: Ethics and the Technologies of the Anthropological Self." In *Audit Cultures: Anthropological Studies in Accountability, Ethics, and the Academy*, edited by Marilyn Strathern, 135–72. London: Routledge.

Pertman, Adam. 2000. *Adoption Nation: How the Adoption Revolution Is Transforming America*. New York: Basic Books.

Petchesky, Rosalind P. 1997. "Fetal Images: The Power of Visual Culture in the Politics of Reproduction." In *The Gender Sexuality Reader: Culture, History, Political Economy*, edited by Roger N. Lancaster and Micaela di Leonardo, 134–50. New York: Routledge.

Phillips, J. W. P. 2011. "Secrecy and Transparency: An Interview with Samuel Weber." *Theory, Culture & Society* 28: 158–72.

Pink, Sarah, and Juan Francisco Salazar. 2017. "Anthropologies and Futures: Setting the Agenda." In *Anthropologies and Futures: Researching Emerging and Uncertain Worlds*, edited by Juan Francisco Salazar, Sarah Pink, Andrew Irving, and Johannes Sjöberg, 3–22. London: Bloomsbury Academic.

"Positive Adoption Language." *Parents Magazine*. www.parent.com/parenting /adoption/parenting/positive-adoption-language/. Accessed March 21, 2017.

Power, Michael. 1997. *The Audit Society*. Oxford: Oxford University Press.

———. 2007. *Organized Uncertainty: Designing a World of Risk Management*. Oxford: Oxford University Press.

Quirk, Mary Beth. 2017. "What Can You Do When Your Adoption Agency Goes Bankrupt?" *Consumerist,* May 9. https://consumerist.com/2017/03/07/what-can-you-do-when-your-adoption-agency-goes-bankrupt/index.html. Accessed May 29, 2018.

Quiroz, Pamela Anne. 2007. *Adoption in a Color-Blind Society*. New York: Rowman and Littlefield.

Ragone, Helena. 1994. *Surrogate Motherhood: Conception in the Heart*. Boulder, CO: Westview Press.

———. 1999. "The Gift of Life: Surrogate Motherhood, Gamete Donation, and Constructions of Altruism." In *Transformative Motherhood: On Giving and Getting in a Consumer Culture*, edited by Linda L. Layne, 65–88. New York: New York University Press.

———. 2004. "Surrogate Motherhood and American Kinship." In *Kinship and Family: An Anthropological Reader*, edited by Robert Parkin and Linda Stone, 342–61. Malden, MA: Blackwell.

Raleigh, Elizabeth. 2017. *Selling Transracial Adoption: Families, Markets, and the Color Line*. Philadelphia: Temple University Press.

Rapp, Rayna. 1999. "Forward." In *Transformative Motherhood: On Giving and Getting in a Consumer Culture*, edited by Linda L. Layne, xi–xix. New York: New York University Press.

————, with Deborah Heath and Karen-Sue Taussig. 2001. "Genealogical Dis-Ease: Where Hereditary Abnormality, Biomedical Explanation, and Family Responsibility Meet." In *Relative Values: Reconfiguring Kinship Studies*, edited by Sarah Franklin and Susan McKinnon, 384–409. Durham, NC: Duke University Press.

Reeves, Madeleine. 2013. "Clean Fake: Authenticating Documents and Persons in Migrant Moscow." *American Ethnologist* 40(3): 508–24.

Reich, Jennifer. 2005. *Fixing Families: Parents, Power, and the Child Welfare System*. New York: Routledge.

Rivaux, Stephanie L., Joyce Hames, Kim Wittenstrom, Donald Baumann, Janess Sheets, and Judith Henry. 2008. "The Intersection of Race, Poverty, and Risk: Understanding the Decision to Provide Services to Clients and to Remove Children." *Child Welfare* 87(2): 151–68.

Roberts, Dorothy. 1997. *Killing the Black Body: Race, Reproduction, and the Meaning of Liberty*. New York: Vintage Books.

————. 2002. *Shattered Bonds: The Color of Child Welfare*. New York: Basic Civitas Books.

Rockefeller, Stuart A. 2011. "Flow." *Current Anthropology* 52(4): 557–78.

Rodriguez, Sara. 2014. "A Woman's 'Right to Know'?: Forced Ultrasound Measures as an Intervention of Biopower." *International Journal of Feminist Approaches to Bioethics* 7(1): 51–73.

Rothman, Barbara Katz. [1986] 1993. *The Tentative Pregnancy: How Amniocentesis Changes the Experience of Motherhood*. New York: W. W. Norton.

————. 2006. *Weaving a Family: Untangling Race and Adoption*. Boston: Beacon Press.

Ryang, Sonia. 2005. "Dilemma of a Native: On Location, Authenticity, and Reflexivity." *Asia Pacific Journal of Anthropology* 6(2): 143–57.

Sachdev, Paul. 1989. *Unlocking the Adoption Files*. Lanham, MD: Lexington Books.

Samimian-Daresh, Limor, and Paul Rabinow. 2015. "Introduction." In *Modes of Uncertainty*, edited by Limor Samimian-Daresh and Paul Rabinow. Chicago: University of Chicago Press.

Sandelowski, Margarete. 1994. "Separate but Less Unequal: Fetal Ultrasonography and the Transformation of Expectant Mother / Fatherhood." *Gender and Society* 8(2): 230–42.

Saul, Heather. 2014. "Crying Boy's Hug with Police Officer Becomes One of the Most Shared Images of Ferguson Protests." *The Independent*, December 1. www.independent.co.uk/ news/world/americas/crying-boys-hug-with-police-officer-becomes-one-of-the-most-shared-images-of-ferguson-protests-9894878.html. Accessed December 10, 2014.

Schedler, Andreas. 2007. "Mapping Contingency." In *Political Contingency: Studying the Unexpected, the Accidental, and the Unforeseen*, edited by Ian Shapiro and Sonu Bedi, 54–78. New York: New York University Press.

Scherz, China. 2011. "Protecting Children, Preserving Families: Moral Conflict and Actuarial Science in a Problem of Contemporary Governance." *Political and Legal Anthropology Review* 34(1): 33–50.

Schneider, David M. [1968] 1980. *American Kinship: A Cultural Account*. Chicago: University of Chicago Press.

Schwarz, Hunter. 2014. "Following Reports of Forced Sterilization of Female Prison Inmates, California Passes Ban." *Washington Post,* September 26. www .washingtonpost.com/blogs/govbeat/wp/2014/09/26/following-reports-of-forced-sterilization-of-female-prison-inmates-california-passes-ban/. Accessed February 6, 2015.

Scott, James C. 1985. *Weapons of the Weak: Everyday Forms of Peasant Resistance*. New Haven, CT: Yale University Press.

———. 1990. *Domination and the Arts of Resistance: Hidden Transcripts*. New Haven, CT: Yale University Press.

———. 1998. *Seeing Like a State: How Certain Schemes to Improve the Human Condition Have Failed*. New Haven, CT: Yale University Press.

Self, Will. 2015. "A Point of View: Has the World Become Too Visual?" *BBC News Magazine*. www.bbc.com/news/magazine-31656672.

Seligmann, Linda J. 2013. *Broken Links, Enduring Ties: American Adoption across Race, Class, and Nation*. Stanford, CA: Stanford University Press.

Sharma, Aradhana. 2013. "State Transparency after the Neoliberal Turn: The Politics, Limits, and Paradoxes of India's Right to Information Law." *Political and Legal Anthropology Review* 36: 308–25.

Sharpe, Christina. 2016. *In the Wake: On Blackness and Being*. Durham, NC: Duke University Press.

Shore, Cris, and Susan Wright. 2000. "Coercive Accountability: The Rise of Audit Culture in Higher Education." In *Audit Cultures: Anthropological Studies in Accountability, Ethics, and the Academy*, edited by Marilyn Strathern, 57–89. London: Routledge.

Simon, Rita J., and Rhonda M. Roorda. 2000. *In Their Own Voices: Transracial Adoptees Tell Their Stories*. New York: Columbia University Press.

Solinger, Rickie. 2001. *Beggars and Choosers: How the Politics of Choice Shapes Adoption, Abortion, and Welfare in the United States*. New York: Hill and Wang.

Speier, Amy. 2016. *Fertility Holidays: IVF Tourism and the Reproduction of Whiteness*. New York: New York University Press.

Spillers, Hortense. 1987. "Mama's Baby, Papa's Maybe: An American Grammar Book." *Diacritics* 17: 64–81.

Spiro, Peter J. 2008. *Beyond Citizenship: American Identity after Globalization*. New York: Oxford University Press.

Spiro, Emma S., Ryan M. Acton, and Carter T. Butts. 2013. "Extended Structures of Mediation: Re-Examining Brokerage in Dynamic Networks." *Social Networks* 35: 130–43.

Stabile, Carole. 1998. "Shooting the Mother: Fetal Photography and the Politics of Disappearance." In *The Visible Woman: Imaging Technologies, Gender, and*

Science, edited by Paula A. Triechler, Lisa Cartwright, and Constance Penley, 171–97. New York: New York University Press.

Stack, Carol. 1974. *All Our Kin.* New York: Perseus.

Stewart, Kathleen. 2012. "Precarity's Forms." *Cultural Anthropology* 27(3): 518–25.

Strathern, Marilyn. 1992. *Reproducing the Future: Essays on Anthropology, Kinship and the New Reproductive Technologies.* New York: Routledge.

———. 2000. "New Accountabilities: Anthropological Studies in Audit, Ethics, and the Academy." In *Audit Cultures: Anthropological Studies in Accountability, Ethics, and the Academy*, edited by Marilyn Strathern, 1–18. London: Routledge.

Teurlings, Jan, and Marcus Stauff. 2014. "Introduction: The Transparency Issue." *Cultural Studies, Critical Methodologies* 14: 3–10.

Thomas, James M., and Jennifer G. Correa. 2016. *Affective Labour: (Dis)Assembling Distance and Difference.* London: Rowman & Littlefield.

Thompson, Charis. 2005. *Making Parents: The Ontological Choreography of Reproductive Technologies.* Cambridge, MA: MIT Press.

Ticktin, Miriam. 2017. "A World without Innocence." *American Ethnologist* 44(4): 577–90.

Timmermans, Stefan, and Mara Buchbinder. 2010. "Patients-in-Waiting: Living between Sickness and Health in the Genomics Era." *Journal of Health and Social Behavior* 51: 408–23.

Tsing, Anna Löwenhaupt. 2005. *Friction: An Ethnography of Global Connection.* Princeton, NJ: Princeton University Press.

Twohey, Megan. 2013. "The Child Exchange: Inside America's Underground Market for Adopted Children." *Reuters Investigates,* September 9. www.reuters.com /investigates/adoption/#article/part1. Accessed October 12, 2013.

United Nations. 2009. *Child Adoption: Trends and Policies.* www.un.org/esa /population/publications/adoption2010/child_adoption.pdf. Accessed May 29, 2018.

Urcuioli, Bonnie. 1998. "Acceptable Difference: The Cultural Evolution of the Model Ethnic American Citizen." In *Democracy and Ethnography: Constructing Identities in Multicultural Liberal States*, edited by Carol J. Greenhouse, 178–95. Albany: State University of New York Press.

U.S. Census Bureau. n.d. "American Fact Finder." http://factfinder.census.gov /faces/tableservices/jsf/pages/productview.xhtml?src = bkmk. Accessed March 6, 2015.

Villareal, Mireya. 2017. "Adoption Agency's Sudden Closure Leaves Prospective Parents Hanging." *CBS News*, February 9. www.cbsnews.com/news/adoption-agencys-sudden-closure-leaves-prospective-parents-hanging/. Accessed May 29, 2018.

Wacquant, Loïc. 2008. *Urban Outcasts: A Comparative Sociology of Advanced Marginality.* Malden, MA: Polity Press.

Wanzo, Rebecca. 2008. "The Era of Lost (White) Girls: On Body and Event." *Differences* 19(2): 99–126.

Weir, Kyle N. 2003. *Coming Out of the Adoptive Closet*. Lanham, MD: University Press of America.

Weismantel, Mary. 1995. "Marking Kin: Kinship Theory and Zumbagua Adoptions." *American Ethnologist* 22(4): 685–709.

Wendland, Claire L. 2007. "The Vanishing Mother: Cesarean Section and 'Evidence-Based Obstetrics.'" *Medical Anthropology Quarterly* 21(2): 218–33.

West, Harry G., and Todd Sanders, eds. 2003. *Transparency and Conspiracy: Ethnographies of Suspicion in the New World Order*. Durham, NC: Duke University Press.

Weston, Kath. 1997. *Families We Choose: Lesbians, Gays, Kinship*. New York: Columbia University Press.

WHWGF (White House Working Group on the Family). 1986. *The Family: Preserving America's Future: A Report to the President from the White House Working Group on the Family*. http://files.eric.ed.gov/fulltext/ED316515.pdf. Accessed March 6, 2015.

Yancy, George. 2008. *Black Bodies, White Gazes: The Continuing Significance of Race*. Lanham, MD: Rowman & Littlefield.

Yngvesson, Barbara. 2010. *Belonging in an Adopted World: Race, Identity, and Transnational Adoption*. Chicago: University of Chicago Press.

——— and Susan Bibler Coutin. 2006. "Backed by Papers: Undoing Persons, Histories, and Return." *American Ethnologist* 33(2): 177–90.

Zaloom, Caitlin. 2006. *Out of the Pits: Traders and Technology from Chicago to London*. Chicago: University of Chicago Press.

Zelizer, Viviana. 1985. *Pricing the Priceless Child: The Changing Social Value of Children*. Princeton, NJ: Princeton University Press.

———. 2005. *The Purchase of Intimacy*. Princeton, NJ: Princeton University Press.

———. 2010. "Caring Everywhere." In *Intimate Labors: Cultures, Technologies, and the Politics of Care*, edited by Eileen Boris and Rhacel Salazar Parrenas, 268–80. Stanford, CA: Stanford University Press.

———. 2011. *Economic Lives: How Culture Shapes the Economy*. Princeton, NJ: Princeton University Press.

Zimmerman, Shirley L. 1989. "Myths about Public Welfare: Poverty, Family Instability, and Teen Illegitimacy." *Policy Studies Review* 8(3): 674–88.

Zimring, Carl. 2016. *Clean and White: A History of Environmental Racism in the United States*. New York: New York University Press.

INDEX

adoption process: overview, 6–7; "Adoption at a Glance" diagram used to explain process, 21, 22–25, *22*, 102–3, *102*; adoption time (gestational clock), 23, 210–11n41; and divergence of interests of expectant parents and prospective adoptive parents, 14–15, 23–24, 211n44, 228n1; division of labor of social workers, 23, 144, 211nn42–43; expectant mothers as usual focus of, vs. birth fathers, 14–15, 54–55; and "going with the flow," 26–27, 193, 195, 212n51; as "high-risk pregnancy," 36, 97–98; informal, 31, 208–9n27; and invisibility of expectant mothers, 42–43; as "processing process," 195; and the stranger, figure of, 36–37, 213n4; as "stranger pregnancy," 36; three types of (*see* foster care adoption; private agency adoption; private non-agency-assisted adoption). *See also* adoption triad; biological fathers; exchange; expectant mothers; fall-through of adoptions; First Steps; home study process; prospective adoptive parents; social workers; surrenders of parental rights; uncertainty in the adoption process; uncertainty in the adoption process––waiting
Adoptions by Heart (CO), 169
Adoption Tax Credit, 155–56
adoption trainings. *See* adoption conferences
adoption triad: alternative constructions to, 211n46; definition of, 25; social worker role in, 25, 26. *See also* brokerage, adoption social workers as
adoptive parents: defined as post-adoption, 29. *See also* prospective adoptive parents
advanced marginality, 128, 224n1
affect and affective investment: anger/angry adoptees, 223n26; expectant mothers' affective heterogeneity, 223–24n27; and First Steps' closure, 186–93, 228nn13–17; speculative, 146. *See also* affective labor; anticipation; anxiety; emotional closure, lack of; futures/the future; happiness; hope; suspicion; uncertainty in the adoption process

affective labor: brokerage function of social workers as, 26, 130; and commodification of intimate labor, 211–12n49; definition of, 26, 129–30; detective work of social workers to stop "scams," 141–47; immaterial labor distinguished from use of term, 130, 224n2; neoliberalism and, 130, 174, 211–12n49. *See also* moral maintenance
Africa, international adoption programs in, 180, 181
African Americans: Chicago gun violence victims, 15–16; controlling images of black womanhood, 39–40; food deserts as disproportionately affecting, 128; police shootings of unarmed, 17–19, 209–10nn35–37,39; and subprime mortgage crisis, 176–77. *See also* black body; blackness; black people; expectant mothers; pregnant body—black; racial inequality; slave trade/slavery; transracial adoption
Aguilera, Christina, 185
Ahmed, Sara, 2, 36, 125, 204n5, 221n6, 224n28
ambiguous loss, 188, 228n15
Anagnost, Ann, 78, 205n3
Anderson, Ben, 103
anger/angry adoptees, 223n26
Anthroman (John Jackson), 204n4
anthropology: adoption, traditional approach to, 206n10; futures-oriented anthropology, 205n3; international adoption, traditional approach to, 206n10; as noninnocent, 199; and transparency, 219–20n19. *See also* methodology
anticipation: definition of, 222n13; as mode of intimate speculation, 7, 200; uncertainty and, 102–3, 116, 125–26, 222n13
anxieties, about biological parent returning for child, 60
anxiety: about absence of expectant mothers, 113; anticipation and, 222n13; about biological fathers, 56–57, 58; of childlessness, vs. anxiety of being with child, 125, 221n2; and closure of First Steps, 13, 191; about effect of researcher on adop-

tion process, 36–37, 74, 203n1, 220nn21,31; about fall-through risk, 7, 101, 118, 135; about fall-throughs, and turn to international adoption, 56–57, 123–24, 223n22; as future-oriented affect, 7, 94, 101–5, 107–8, 117–19, 126, 205n3; and home study process, 68, 74, 77, 84, 92, 94; kinship/certainty as mitigating, in popular culture, 95, 126, 224n29; about the pregnant body, 42; and "proof-of-pregnancy," 49; about roots/the past, 6; uncertainty and, 102–3, 104, 118–19, 125, 126, 224n28; and waiting, 110, 115, 221n8, 222n13

Appadurai, Arjun, 136–37, 205n3

Arman, Rebecka, 186–87, 228n14

audits. *See* home study process—as audit and inspection

Ayto, John, 34, 119

"Baby Scoop Era," 28, 131, 212n54

"Baby Tamia" case, 227n2

Baker, Josephine, 228n2

Baker Victory Services (Buffalo, NY), 169

Barnum, Sgt. Bret, 18, *18*, 209–10n37

Bartholet, Elizabeth, 220–21n34

Bear, Laura, 151, 200, 205n6, 219–20n19, 224n2, 225n13, 226n22

Becker, Gay, 119

Beck, John, 214–15n17, 219–20n19

Beck, Ulrich, 119

Behar, Ruth, 203–4n1,3, 208n24, 216n23

belonging, 6, 99, 198, 206n10

Berlant, Lauren, 46, 78, 80, 205n3, 222n15

Bernstein, Robin, 65, 196, 217n7, 220n28

biological fathers: absence from adoption process, 54–55, 56, 58; assertion of parental rights by, 55–56; Bill of Rights for birth and adoptive parents, 167; "birth father" as term used for, 55, 216n24; "expectant father" as term used for, 55; fears about, and prospective adoptive parents, 56–57, 58; final surrenders from, 55, 57–58, 100; identification of by expectant mother, 55; Illinois Putative Father Registry and protection of rights of, 55–56, 57; as "legal risk," 54, 55, 57–58, 59, 60, 101; and mother's

signing of surrenders, 58; paternity, establishment of, 56; as spectral, 56, 57, 58; and stereotypes of absent black fathers and "deadbeat dads," 24, 58

biological mothers. *See* expectant mothers

biological reproduction: amniocentesis and reality of tentative pregnancy, 120; home study perceived as "unfair" in light of, 72–73; surrogacy, 210n40; uncertainty and precarity as present in "traditional," 21, 210n40. *See also* infertility; reproductive technologies

Birchall, Clare, 219–20n19

Birla, Ritu, 205n6

birth fathers. *See* biological fathers

birth mothers: as "belonging" to the prospective adoptive parents, 131; closure of First Steps and concern about future contact of adoptees and, 190–91, 228nn16–17; defined and discussed as term, 27–29, 212nn53,55. *See also* birth mother as figure; expectant mothers

birth mother as figure: as spectral, 35, 41, 54; as suspect specter, 41; as threat, 60; as unknowable and contradictory, 38, 54

black body: as capital, 177–78; constructed as Other, 41; pregnant, 38, 41–43

Black Lives Matter, 17, 20

blackness: as being-in-collection, 176–77; surveillance of, 41; the womb as factory producing, as abjection, 177

black people: black womanhood, controlling images of, 39–40; vulnerability of, international adoption and, 180, 184–85, 227–28nn11–12. *See also* expectant mothers; international adoption; transracial adoption

Blagojevich, Rod, 167

Blind Side, The (film), 210n38

Boris, Eileen, 211–12n49

"born babies"/"sky babies": connections at area hospitals to find, 33; definition of, 52; in relation to fall-through, 121–22, 157

Boss, Pauline, 188, 228n15

Brace, Charles Loring, "orphan trains," 64–65, 218nn10–11

Bradley, Mindy S., 228n2

Briggs, Laura, 38, 176, 177, 200, 226n22, 229n7

Brighenti, Andrea Mubi, 42, 67, 214n9

Brinkley, Leslie, 169

Brinson, Jamal R., 209n32

Brodwin, Paul, 156

brokerage, adoption social workers as: as affective labor, 26, 130; definition of, 26, 211n48; and fee-for-service economic conditions, 66; and financial loss at fall-through, 146, 148; forces contributing to breakdown of, 27, 180, 211n48, 222n12; futures traders compared to, 150–51; inequality as produced by, 26, 212n50; and relinquishment, dependence on, 33

Browne, Katherine, 226n21

Browne, Simone, 41, 45, 50

Brown, Michael, 17, 18, 19, 209–10n37

Buchbinder, Mara, 221–22n9

Buckley, Betsy, 225n14

Buddhism, "beginner's mind," 95–96

Butts, Carter T., 26

Cacho, Lisa Marie, 214n11, 217n7

California, 153, 169, 226n16

Campbell, Lee, 212n53

capitalism: the black body as capital, 177–78; as cruise ship, 178. *See also* exchange; neoliberalism

Caribbean, international adoption programs in, 180, 181

Carp, E. Wayne, 64, 65–66

Carr, E. Summerson, 212–13n3, 217n3

Casper, Monica, 38, 42, 50, 216n20

Cassiman, Shawn A., 24, 58

Castañeda, Claudia, 205n3

categorical suspicion, 41

Certeau, Michel de, 51

Chakravartty, Paula, 153

Cherished Child, A (UT), 227

Chicago: academic achievement gap and, 16; African American population of, 8, 206n14; gun violence statistics, 15–16; low-income students, percentage of, 8, 207n17; poorest neighborhoods of, 8, 128, 207n19, 224n1; segregation of residences and schools in, 8

child abuse: and the privacy of the family as superseded, 80; and sacralization of the child, 65

child labor, 64, 65

childlessness: anxiety about, vs. anxiety of being with child, 125, 221n2; and heteronormative conception of family, 124–25, 223nn23–25

child protection: corporal punishment bans, 89–90; and educational disparities, 16; as First Steps' mission, 90; and gun violence campaigns, 15–16; Devonte Hart case, 17–21, *18*, 209–10nn35–39; innocence of children, 65, 218n13; and nineteenth-century "placing out" ("orphan trains"), 64, 218n11; and police shootings of unarmed African Americans, 17–19, 209–10nn35–37,39; product safety recalls on items for baby, 110–11; protected childhood, advent of, 65–66, 218n12; and relinquishment vs. abandonment of infants (Safe Haven laws), 16–17, 209n32; sacralization of the child, 64–65. *See also* Illinois Department of Children and Family Services (DCFS)

Child Protective Services: disproportionate removal of black children from homes, 220n20; removal of children at risk of future abuse or neglect, 90. *See also* Illinois Department of Children and Family Services (DCFS)

children: as essential in heteronormative definition of family, 124–25, 223nn23–25; illegitimate, as stigma, 6, 39, 40–41, 131, 132, 133, 213–14n8; as possession/dispossession, 178; as priceless, 158; trafficking of, distinguished from adoption, 137. *See also* adoptees; child abuse; child labor; child protection; Child Protective Services; education; infants; single motherhood

China, 23, 56–57, 123–24, 181–82, 221n8

class inequality: academic achievement gap and, 16; adoption rendered possible via, 19, 130, 131–33, 143, 146–47, 176–77, 196, 197–200; as contingency, 201; intersectionality of, 8, 38, 42, 65, 132, 137, 201,

domestic adoption: and age of prospective adoptive parents, limits on, 113, 222n11; decline of, and closure of First Steps, 168–69, 172–75, 178–81; divergence of interests of expectant parents and prospective adoptive parents, 14–15, 23–24, 211n44, 228n1; international adoption as eclipsing, 180–81; statistics, 208n23. *See also* transracial adoption

Dorow, Sara, 23, 25, 130, 134, 137, 204–5n2, 206n10, 221n7, 225nn4–5

Douglas, Mary, 217n7

Ducre, K. Animashaun, 132, 228n1

Duden, Barbara, 26n20, 48

Durham, Deborah, 222n13

duty of candor. *See* prospective adoptive parents—and transparency (duty of candor)

Ebola, 12, 185

economics. *See* class inequality; exchange; fees; financial losses due to fall-throughs; intimacy and economy; "legally allowable birth parent expenses"; moral maintenance (disavowal of market forces of adoption); neoliberalism; poverty and the poor; Recession (2008)

Edelman, Lee, 125, 205n3, 223n25

Edin, Kathryn J., 148

Education Commission of the States, 209n30

Ehrenreich, John H., 217n4

embryo adoption, 175–76, 227n5

emotional closure, lack of: ambiguity of loss and, 188, 228n15; closure of First Steps and, 188; fall-throughs and, 120, 148

emotional investment. *See* affect and affective investment

end, definitions of, 4, 44, 63, 119, 134, 147, 149, 162, 201, 211n45

Ertman, Martha, 225n11

Ethiopia, 88, 181–82, 196, 197

exchange: choosing to keep child (closure) as opposite of, 178; kinship and, 135–39, 225n4; literatures on, 205n10; and signing surrenders, 115, 147; and transi-

tion of First Steps to nonprofit, 168; vulnerability of First Steps to, 13. *See also* class inequality; fees; financial losses due to fall-throughs; intimacy and economy; "legally allowable birth parent expenses," paid by prospective parents; moral maintenance (disavowal of market forces of adoption); neoliberalism

expectant fathers. *See* biological fathers

expectant mothers: antisurveillance politics of, 49–50, 63; Bill of Rights for birth and adoptive parents, 167; choice as constrained for, 51, 198; class inequality and, adoption rendered possible via, 19, 130, 131–33, 143, 146–47, 176–77, 196, 197–200; definition of, 27–28; divergence of interests of, from prospective adoptive parents, 14–15, 23–24, 211n44, 228n1; as "familial stranger," 35–36; home visits with, 43–44; innocence as denied to, 65; interaction with prospective adoptive parents, 99–100; lies of omission by, 34; locations/living conditions of, 8, 128, 132, 207n19, 224n1; marketing/outreach to, 31–33, 51, 52–54, 173–74; Native ancestry, disavowing, 213n6; out-of-state, 27, 207n19; power differential between social workers and, 158–59; power of, custody of the child as, 51, 54, 67, 158–59; protocols, difficulty of getting compliance with, 45–46, 51; the right to choose to parent her child, 33, 123, 141, 158–59, 178–79; and scripts, 36, 212–13n3; suspicion of, 34–36, 63; and waiting, 114. *See also* fall-through of adoptions; invisibility of expectant mothers; "legally allowable birth parent expenses," paid by prospective parents; pregnancy, proof of; "scamming"; single motherhood; surrenders of parental rights; surveillance; unfit parent, expectant mothers cast as

—ABSENCE OF: overview, 31, 174–75; contraception and, 175, 178–79, 222n12; and death, connections to, 44; and decline in number of unplanned pregnancies, 175, 178–79; decline of domestic adoption and, 172–76, 178–80; difficulties in keeping track of expectant mothers, 35–36, 43–44; ethnography and, 37–38; as invisibility, 37–38, 42–43, 59; marketing/outreach to find, 31–33, 51, 52–54, 173–74; and positionality of researcher, 54; and simultaneous hypervisibility of poor black mothering, 38, 213n5; and single parenting, cultural acceptance of, 174, 179–80, 222n12

—PARTICIPANTS: Angeline, 142, 143, 157; Celeste, 157; Dawn, 1–4, 45, 144–45, 147–48, 199; Denise, 47–52, 59; Fiona, 45, 111–12; Jamie, 141–42; Jenna, 114–15; Lara, 54; Mallory, 134, 137; Marie, 223n19; Selene, 5, 9, 214–15n17; Sheena, 43–44, 45, 46–47, 50; Valerie, 128–29, 142, 143, 156–57

Fagan, Jeffrey, 220n23

Faist, Thomas, 212n50

FakeABaby.com, 49, 215–16n19

fall-through of adoptions: overview, 30–31; adoption disruption insurance (ADI), 154–55; anxiety of prospective adoptive parents about risk of, 7, 101, 118, 135; anxiety about, and turn to international adoption, 56–57, 123–24, 223n22; biological father asserting parental rights as cause of, 55; and "birth mother" vs. "expectant mother" as terms, 28; change of heart as basis of, 131, 140–41, 148, 153; and closure, lack of, 120, 148; and death, comparisons to, 44, 123, 159; definition of, 5; as disruptive, 119–20; emotional risks of, 5–6, 33, 120, 121–22, 129, 156, 159; for expectant mothers, 223n19; and "familiar stranger," 35–36; ghosting by expectant mother, 44, 214n12; and "keeping" vs. "parenting" as terms, 178, 179; loss of contact with expectant mothers as early sign of, 35, 135, 157; and miscarriage, comparisons to, 44, 120, 121; multiple, 6, 129, 153–54, 156–57; narratives of, 4, 5, 44, 105–7, 121–22, 128–29; the right of biological mother to parent her child, 33, 123, 141, 158–59, 178–79; and "slippery little eels" meta-

phor for expectant mothers, 30, 33, 34–36, 145, 212n2; and starting over, 101, 130, 159; statistics on number of, 96–97, 129; uptick in, following 2008 Recession, 5–6, 33, 129, 154. *See also* disruption of adoption; financial losses due to fall-throughs; "scamming"; uncertainty in the adoption process

fall-through of institution, closure of First Steps as, 13, 164

family: "forever family," 126; "happy," 124–25, 126; heteronormative conception of children as defining, 124–25, 223nn23–25; privacy of, 78, 80

Family, The: Preserving America's Future (WHWGF), 213–14n8

Fanon, Frantz, 41, 216n22

fathers. *See* biological fathers; prospective adoptive parents

fees for adoption: all-inclusive, as older model, 151–52; closure of First Steps and reimbursement of, 162, 163; fee-for-services structure of, 66, 130, 154, 167, 171; for First Steps adoptions, 9–10, 13, 24, 132, 171; gift industry to provide, 225–26n15; private non-agency-assisted adoption, 208–9n27; racial disparities in, 9–10, 207n21; and risk of small size of First Steps, 169–70. *See also* financial losses due to fall-throughs; "legally allowable birth parent expenses," paid by prospective parents

Feigenholtz, Sarah, 167

Ferguson, MO, 17, 18–19, *18*

Ferreira da Silva, Denise, 153

Fessler, Ann, 39, 212n54, 213n7

fetal alcohol spectrum disorders (FASD), 118–19, 222–23n17

fetus, as term, 29. *See also* imagined child; ultrasound

financial investment. *See* fees for adoption; financial losses due to fall-throughs; "legally allowable birth parent expenses," paid by prospective parents

financial losses due to fall-throughs: overview, 6, 129, 130; adoption disruption insurance (ADI), 154–55; and class dynamics of adoption, 130; First Steps'

financial losses *(continued)*
"birth mother fund"/insurance for, 154; and gift of funds as prevention of commodification, 130, 138, 152, 153, 156–57, 226n19; and gift of funds vs. adopted child as commodity, 130; and pressure for social worker vigilance, 144; and reciprocity, demand of expectant mother for, 146–47; reluctance of adoptive parents to discuss, 159; "scams" and, 47–48, 142–43, 144; surrenders demanded in order to prevent, 147; tax credit to offset, 155–56; withholding of money to temper, 146–47

first mother, as term, 28

First Steps (private adoption agency): "Adoption at a Glance" diagram used to explain process, 21, 22–25, *22*, 102–3, *102*; adoption time (gestational clock), 23, 210–11n41; as "agency of last resort," 12; as boundary place, 9; fee reimbursement in closure of, 162, 163; fee structure of, 9–10, 13, 24, 132, 171; foster care licensing guidelines used by, 79–80; and Hague Convention accreditation, 70, 219n18; international adoption programs of, 10, 12, 71, 180–86, 189; location of, 8–9, 35; mandated conversion from for-profit enterprise to nonprofit status, 12–13, 165, 166–69, 170, 172, 173, 186; marketing and outreach by, 31–33, 51, 52–54, 173–74, 184–86, 227n11; mission of, 9–10, 195–96, 200; numbers of placements, 33; offices and staffing of, 11–12, 21–22, 30, 165; open adoption as normative and preferred by, 98–99; personal level of attention offered by, 13, 169–70; and slavery, payment of money for children and implications of, 176–78, 225n11; small size of, 13, 167, 168, 169–70; and vulnerability to forces of economic exchange, 13; wait times, 12, 110; white expectant mothers, 226n20. *See also* adoption process; brokerage, adoption social workers as; closure of First Steps; expectant mothers; fall-through of adoptions; home study process; prospective adoptive parents;

social workers; transracial adoption; uncertainty of the adoption process

Firth, Mary Durnin, 225n14

Fleetwood, Nicole, 213n5

flipping the script, 36, 217n3

Floersch, Jerry, 135

flow, 26–27, 193, 195, 212n51

Fogg-Davis, H., 9, 206n10, 228n3

food deserts, 128

foster care: adoption from, 12, 181, 208–9n27, 227n3; corporal punishment banned by guidelines for, 88–90; First Steps' use of guidelines and licensing process for, 79–80; "illegitimate" black children removed from families, 39; interim care homes, 121

Foucault, Michel, 48, 63, 77, 82, 217n5

Franklin, Sarah, 206n10

Frekko, Susan, 217n3

future child. *See* imagined child

futures/the future: adoption as future-craft, 206n10; adoption as trafficking in imagined futures, 6; adult adoptees as possible embodiment of, 53; anthropology, futures-oriented, 205n3; anxiety as future-oriented affect, 7, 94, 101–5, 107–8, 117–19, 126, 205n3; assumption that adoption always produces better futures, 20–21; childless people as threat to, 124, 223n23; closure of First Steps and concern about future contact between birth parents and adoptees, 190–91, 228nn16–17; contingency/uncertainty and, 7, 205nn6–7; custody of the child as determining, 51; and figural Child, 223n25; happiness as future-oriented affect, 125; hope as future-oriented affect, 125; legally allowable birth mother expenses as investment in imagined, 130, 131–32, 133. *See also* child protection; uncertainty in the adoption process

futures trading, adoption as, 149, 150–51, 159, 225nn12–13

Gailey, Christine Ward, 214n11

Gallagher, Mari, 128

Gal, Susan, 77, 220n24

Garner, Eric, 17

Gates, Theaster, 204n

gaze: expectant mothers as object of, 41–42; prospective adoptive parents as object of, 63, 68, 77, 94; prospective adoptive parents' subversion of, 84–86; of social worker and the state, as intertwined, 80; women and minority groups as object of, 214n9

Gelman, Andrew, 220n23

gender inequality: as contingency, 201; controlling images of black womanhood, 39–40; intersectionality of, 38, 42, 132, 198, 201, 206n10; and moral maintenance, 137; noninnocence and, 199; norms of, and home study, 75; ultrasounds and, 50. *See also* birth mother as figure; class inequality; expectant mothers; invisibility of expectant mothers; poverty and the poor; racial inequality; single motherhood; surveillance; welfare queen, figure of

Georges, Eugenia, 48

Gift of Adoption Fund, 225–26n14–15

Gift of Life Adoptions, 225n14

gifts: adoptees as, 152–53, 198, 225n14; of fees, by industry of giving, 225–26n15; intimate speculation and, 153; "legally allowable birth parent expenses" constructed as, 130, 138, 152, 153, 156–57, 226n19

Gilens, Martin, 40

Gill, Brian, 66

Gilliom, John, 41, 50, 51, 80, 86

Ginsburg, Faye D., 203–4n3

Goodwin, Michele Bratcher, 137, 206n10

Gordon, Avery, 44, 203–4n3, 208n24

Gossage, J. Phillip, 222–23n17

Grand, Michael Phillip, 211n46

Gray, Freddie, 209n36

Guatemala, 124, 181

guilt, and framing of expectant mothers as potential "scammers," 34. *See also* noninnocence

gun violence: CeaseFire Illinois campaign against, 15; police shootings of unarmed African Americans, 17–19, 209–10nn35–37,39

Gupta, Akhil, 211–12n49

Guttmacher Institute, 175, 178

Guyer, Jane, 103

Habermas, Jürgen, 78

Hackin, Ian, 98

Hague Convention on the Protection of Children and Co-operation in Respect of Intercountry Adoption, 70, 181, 182, 219n18

Haiti, 71, 182–83, 184–86

Halbrook, Bernadette, 203–4n3

Hancock, Ange-Marie, 39

happiness, 124–25, 224n28

"happy family," 124–25, 126

Haraway, Donna, 46, 48, 199, 228–29n4

Hardt, Michael, 130

Hargitay, Mariska, 19

Harney, Robert F., 228n12

Harney, Stefano, 153, 170, 178, 186, 228n12

Harper, Douglas, 119, 216n27

Hart, Devonte, 17–21, *18*, 209–10nn35–39

Hart, Jennifer and Sarah, 19–21

Hartman, Saidiya, 193

Harvard University, Achievement Gap Initiative, 209n30

Harvey, David, 178

Hayden, Corinne P., 206n10

Heath, Deborah, 118

Herman, Ellen, 64, 98, 99, 116, 198, 218n10

Herold, Steph, 220n20

heteronormativity, the "happy family" and, 124–25, 223nn23–25

HIPAA (Health Insurance Portability and Accountability Act), 62, 216n1

HIV/AIDS+ adoptees, 12, 168

Hocevar, Andreja, 228n2

Hochschild, Arlie Russell, 222n16

Ho, Karen, 226n22

Holt, Marilyn I., 64, 218n10

Homer, Aaron, 19

home study process: overview, 61–63, 66–67; appointments for, as scheduled and announced, 82–84; checklist of compliance, 68; as disempowering, 74–77; interviews, 68–70; legal standards for compliance, 67; license as contingent on performance of, 216–

home study process *(continued)*
17n2; as mode of intimate speculation,
81, 93–94; as monitoring, 63, 83, 217n6;
narratives of, 73–77; pet animals
present in home, 69–70, 219nn16–17;
and power of social workers to grant
parental status, 67, 74; and predictive
knowledge production about future
parenting ability, 63, 69–70, 78, 90, 92,
93–94; as producing suitable parents,
62–63, 217n3; as protection for "our
kids," 68–69, 72–73; as public performance, 78; and risk management, 63, 69,
218n8; self-help preparation material,
67–68; strategic adaptations of behavior
in, 84–86, 220n31; as "unfair" compared
to biological reproduction, 72–73
—AS AUDIT AND INSPECTION: as aspirational, 94; and assurance, production
of, 94; as coercive accountability, 80;
and comfort, production of, 82, 84,
220n26; definition of terms, 216–17n2;
the glance and, 77; and intimate speculation, 81, 93–94; multiple scales of,
219n18; and performance of parental
fitness, 62, 66, 81–83, 94, 217n3,
220nn27–28; as political technology of
the self, 82, 220n27; as public performance, 78; and risk management, 63, 94,
218n8; roles of social workers created by,
218n14; and state social norms, reproduction of, 80, 220n25; and strategic
behavior adaptations, 82, 85; surveillance distinguished from, 217n6; and
trustworthiness, 70–71; and verification, 217n7
—FAILURE OF: overview, 86, 87; fear of
failing, 74–75, 75–76, 87; lack of candor
and, 91, 92; narrative of, 88–92; as
permanent bar against adoption, 87,
92–93, 220–21n34
—AND PUBLIC/PRIVATE DISTINCTION: as
co-constitutive cultural categories,
220n24; duty of candor and, 86; fractal
nature of, 77; invasion of privacy/
humiliation, 61–62, 67–68, 74–75, 94,
216n1; LGBTQ+ adoptive parents and,
217n4; narratives about, 61–62, 74–75,

76–77; and the state's role in private
agency adoption, 77–81, 220nn24–25;
vs. surveillance faced by poor women of
color, 68, 73, 220n20
hope: as future-oriented affect, 125; uncertainty in the adoption process and,
102–3, 116, 125, 126, 222nn13–14; will of
adoptive hope as creating certainty, 103,
105–7, 108, 126, 162, 185, 221nn5–7
Hope for Haiti Now (telethon), 185
Howell, Signe, 97, 110, 204–5n2, 206n10
"How to Adopt a Child without Losing
Yourself" (workshop), 95–96, *96*, 99, 101
Hyde Amendment (1976), 220n20
hyperghettos, 224n1
hypervisibility: definition of, 213n5; of poor
black mothering, 38, 213n5

identity: American, of equality, 198; "birth
mother" as term and assignment of, 41;
concern for, and opposition to transracial adoption, 9, 207n20; open adoption
and, 59, 221n3; traditional focus on, 6,
206n10. *See also* methodology—positionality of researcher
illegitimate children, as stigma, 6, 39,
40–41, 131, 132, 133, 213–14n8. *See also*
single motherhood
Illinois: Adoption Option Index figures
for, 175; Adoption Reform Act (2005),
12–13, 165, 167, 168, 227n2; foster care
license required for adoptions, 79–80;
legally allowable birth parent expenses,
137–39, 141, 152, 226n16; Safe Haven
program, 16–17, 209n32; state role in
private agency adoption, 77–81,
220nn24–25; voluntary surrender of
parental rights as irrevocable, 56
Illinois Department of Children and
Family Services (DCFS): corporal
punishment banned by, 89–90; file
relocation with, and closure of First
Steps, 165, 190; foster care adoption
and, 181; parental fitness guidelines
of, 80; Putative Father Registry,
55–56, 57; rules for closure of adoption
agencies, 163
Illinois Putative Father Registry, 55–56, 57

imagined child: and amniocentesis, 223n20; anticipatory logics of family formation and, 126–27; as the client, 14–15, 228n1; defined and discussed as term, 29; and futures trading, adoption as similar to, 150–51, 159, 225nn12–13; as happy object, 125, 223n26; as highly contingent, precarious figure, 97, 195; and intimate speculation, 199, 201

incarcerated women, forcible sterilization of, 220n20

Inception (film, dir. Christopher Nolan), 95, 126, 224n29

income, low-income, defined, 207n17

Independent Adoption Center (CA), 169

independent adoption. *See* private non-agency-assisted adoption

Indian Child Welfare Act (1978), 213n6

infants: custody of, as power of expectant mother, 51, 54, 67, 158–59; in interim care, 121; relinquishment via Safe Haven program, 16–17, 209n32. *See also* "born babies"/"sky babies"; children; substance exposure, trauma, or genetic issues

infertility: home study and exposure of private information, 74–75; and turn to international adoption, 124; and waiting periods of adoption, 113, 222n10. *See also* reproductive technologies

infrapolitics, 50

innocence: black children and, 65; the child constructed as (white), 65; as creating a savior subject, 218n13; denied to black expectant mothers, 65; mapped onto whiteness, 63, 217n7, 220n22; noninnocence, 199, 228–29n4; of prospective adoptive parents, 65, 72, 77, 86, 93, 94; racial innocence, 65

Interethnic Placement Act (1996), 9

international adoption: abuse of children in, 90–91, 191; age limits on prospective adoptive parents, 222n11; of American children to other countries, 156, 226n18; as anthropological subject, 206n10; closure of First Steps and clients in programs for, 189; decline of, and closure of First Steps, 173, 180–84; domestic adoption as eclipsed by, 180–81; and

failure of home study, 88–92; fear of fall-through or disruption and turn to, 56–57, 123–24, 223n22; First Steps' programs for, 10, 12, 71, 180–86, 189; Hague Convention regulations, 70, 181, 182, 219n18; humanitarian aid/disaster as fundraising focus, 184–85; infertility and turn to, 124; marketing/outreach/fundraising efforts for, 184–86, 227–28nn11–12; as "opening up," 99; precarity of, 12; and racialized black vulnerability, 180, 184–86, 227–28nn11–12; "re-homing" practices, 91, 181; statistics on, 208n23

internet: role in adoption, 27, 99, 222n12; as supplanting the brokerage function of adoption agency, 27, 222n12

intersectionality, of transracial adoption, 8, 38, 42, 65, 132, 137, 201, 206n10. *See also* class inequality; gender inequality; invisibility of expectant mothers; neoliberalism; poverty and the poor; racial inequality

intimacy, risk and, 205–6n7

intimacy and economy: overview, 130; as co-constituted, 135–36, 158, 226n21; and "natural continuum" between person and thing, 149–50, 225n11; and "scamming," 139; "separate spheres/hostile worlds" and "nothing-but" models of, 135

intimate labor, commodification of, 211–12n49. *See also* affective labor

intimate public sphere, 78

intimate speculation: and adoption as the neoliberalization of child welfare, 226n22; chattel slavery as original form of, 177–78; closure of First Steps and, 161, 193; definition of, 7, 59, 204n, 216n27; and failure of the adoption process to create new forms of kinship, 159; and family-building scale, 200; gifts and, 153; home study process and, 81, 93–94; the imagined child and, 199, 201; and kinship formation, 159, 195; and multiple forms of loss, 159; and noninnocence, 199, 228–29n4; observation/visualization and, 7, 200; risk and,

intimate speculation *(continued)*
7, 97, 126–27, 130; theoretical and practical applicability of, 200–201, 229n7; ultrasound as tool of, 50. *See also* contingent kinship; expectant mothers; futures/the future; imagined child; "legally allowable birth mother expenses"; risk; speculation; uncertainty in the adoption process

investments. *See* affect and affective investment; exchange; financial losses due to fall-throughs

invisibility of expectant mothers: and absence, 37–38, 42–43, 59; the gaze as forbidden to minority members and, 214n9; in history of adoption, 38; and risk, 59; "scamming" and, 50; ultrasound as producing, 46, 50, 60, 216n20

Jackson, John L., 3, 204n4
Jackson, Julia, *Children Are Forever—All Sales Final,* 112–13, 124, 126
Jackson, Michael, 98
Jacobson, Heather, 206n10
Jalongo, Mary Renck, 64
Jobs, Steve, 17
Johnson, Chloe, 19–20
Jones, Jo, 173, 175
Jones, Jonathan, 209–10n37
Jones, Monica, *Homestudy Boot Camp,* 67–68, 73–74
Jonsson, Lars-Eric, 19, 68
Jorjorian, Anoosh, 209–10n37
journey metaphor: and adoption process, 107, 126; and closure of First Steps, 160, 163, 186

Kaufman, Sharon R., 114, 115–16
Kennedy, Randall, 18, 196–97, 198
Kim, Eleana J., 206n10
Kim, Hosu, 54, 214n11
Kim, Jodi, 214n11
Kingsbury, Kathleen, 173
kinship: failure of adoption process to create new forms of, 159; "Make Kin, Not Babies," 199; and market exchanges, 135–39, 225n4; nonnormative, 21,

206n10; and sinking ship analogy, 178. *See also* contingent kinship
Kiss, Alex, 220n23
Knight, Kelly Ray, 2–3, 50–51, 148, 203n2, 210–11n41, 214n14
Koch, Wendy, 173
Kohler-Hausmann, Julilly, 139, 225n7
Kopytoff, Igor, 136, 150, 225n11
Koster, Martijn, 26
Kreider, Rose M., 208n23

Lakoff, Andrew, 154
Larson, Stevie, 84, 198–99, 220n33
Latinx, Chicago gun violence victims, 15
laws: HIPAA (Health Insurance Portability and Accountability Act), 62, 216n1; Hyde Amendment (1976), 220n20; Women's Ultrasound Right to Know Act (proposed), 214–15n17. *See also* laws on adoption
laws on adoption: foster care license required (IL), 79–80; Hague Convention, 70, 181, 182, 219n18; Illinois Adoption Reform Act (2005), 12–13, 165, 167, 168, 227n2; Illinois Putative Father Registry, 55–56, 57; Illinois Safe Haven laws, 16–17, 209n32; Indian Child Welfare Act (1978), 213n6; Interethnic Placement Act (1996), 9; "legally allowable birth parent expenses," 137–39; Massachusetts Adoption Act (1851), 38; Multiethnic Placement Act (1994), 9
lawyers, independent adoptions mediated by, 208–9n27
Layne, Linda L., 152
"legally allowable birth parent expenses," paid by prospective parents: agency handling of, 139; all-inclusive fees (in the past) compared to uncertainty of, 151–52, 155; and appearance of commodification of infants, 133; caps on, 153, 154, 226n16; and class inequity as forming the social base of adoption, 131–33, 143, 146–47; definition of, 138; expenses allowed, 138–39; expenses disallowed, 138; First Steps' central "birth mother fund" as insurance arrangement for, 154; as futures trading, 149, 150–51, 159,

225nn12–13; gift status of, as legally negated to avoid commodification, 130, 138, 152, 153, 156–57, 226n19; as investment in an imagined future, 130, 131–32, 133; laws on, 137–39, 141, 152, 226n16; losses of (*see* financial losses due to fall-throughs); narratives of delivery of, 1–4, 128–29, 137; and nutritional well-being of the fetus, 131–32, 133; paid by social workers, 45; prospective adoptive parents' ability to match need for, 132, 137, 142, 156; and reciprocity, demands for, 146–47; and reciprocity/reimbursement as legally prohibited, 153; as spectacular accumulation, 225n10; temporal limits on, 138. *See also* fees; financial losses due to fall-throughs; moral maintenance; "scamming"

Leinaweaver, Jessaca, 217n3

LGBTQ+ people: and heteronormative conception of "happy family," 124–25; nonnormative kinship and, 206n10, 223n24

LGBTQ+ prospective adoptive parents: adoption history and expansion of, 66; and radical inclusivity of First Steps, 12, 196; "rainbow families" of, 228n2; surveillance of the home study and, 217n4

Liberia, 12, 182, 184, 185–86, 189

licensing: foster care license required, 79–80; and inspection, definition of, 216–17n2; monitoring visits required to maintain, 83, 86; private adoption agency function in, 79; state final approval of, 79; state standards for, 78–79

Lipsky, Michael, 116, 219–20n19

Little Mermaid, The (film), 212n2

Lofquist, Daphne A., 208n23

Love Actually (film), 212n2

Low, Setha, 220n22

Lubiano, Wahneema, 139–40

Luhmann, Niklas, 98

L Word, The (TV), 113

McDonald, Carmen, 227n2

McDonald, Maria, 227n2

McKinzie, Ashleigh E., 228n2

Malaby, Thomas M., 23n21, 98, 205n6

Malkki, Liisa, 205n3

Manetti, Michelle, 117

Mankekar, Purnima, 211–12n49

Maquet, Jacques, 136

Maril, Robin S., 39

Mariner, Kathryn A., 217n3

market forces. *See* class inequality; exchange; fees; financial losses due to fall-throughs; "legally allowable birth parent expenses"; moral maintenance (disavowal of market forces of adoption); neoliberalism; poverty and the poor; Recession (2008)

Marre, Diana, 217n3

Martin, Trayvon, 17, 18

Marx, Gary T., 41, 42

Massachusetts Adoption Act (1851), 38

maternity homes ("Baby Scoop Era"), 28, 131, 212n54

Mattingly, Cheryl, 35–36

Mauss, Marcel, 153

May, Philip A., 222–23n17

media: adoptive interracial intimacy as visual canon in, 19, 210n38; and Chicago gun violence, 15–16; Devonte Hart case, 17–21, *18*, 209–10nn35–39; the white savior narrative in, 20

Medicaid, 220n20

medical special needs, children with, 12, 39, 214n16

Melosh, Barbara, 64, 99, 213nn4,7

methodology: overview, 10–12, 208n26; and absence of expectant mothers, 31, 37–38; access to adoption agencies, challenge of, 13–14; and closure of First Steps, 160; international adoption and, 180–81; limitations on data gathering, 14; and pre-adoption trainings, 221n1; pseudonyms, 14, 207n18, 209n28. *See also* anthropology

—POSITIONALITY OF RESEARCHER: overview, 10–11; and the absent subject (expectant mothers), awareness of, 37–38; affective intensity of, 216n23; anthropologist as vulture, 2–3, 203n2; anxiety about effect on adoption

methodology *(continued)*
process, 36–37, 74, 203n1, 220nn21,31;
dual hailing, 53, 216n22; ethnographic
countertransference, 3, 203–4n3; ethnographobia, 3, 204n4; as haunted, 10,
208n24; as haunting, 203–4n3; methodological approach to discomfort of,
203n1; mobilized to recruit expectant
mothers, and rejection of, 52–54; and
moral maintenance, 133; and native
anthropology, 2–4, 11, 208n25; and
noninnocence, 199; as "sky baby," 52;
and suffering, turning away vs. turning
toward, 3; trauma experienced vicariously, 3, 204n5
Mindfulness-Based Stress Reduction,
104–5
Mitchell, Harvey, 198
Miyazaki, Hirokazu, 159
Modell, Judith, 99, 206n10, 213n4
Moore, Lisa Jean, 38, 42
moral ambiguity: and completed adoption
vs. fall-through, 149; diversion of commodities and, 136–37
moral maintenance (disavowal of market
forces of adoption): and child trafficking distinguished from adoption, 137;
and conflict of intimate and economic
activity, 135–36, 158, 226n21; and cost of
adoption, questions about, 158; definition of, 134, 136; as enclaving, 136, 138,
149; and First Steps' "birth mother
fund" insurance program, 154; and
futures trading, 159; international
adoption and, 137; narratives of
instances of, 133, 134, 137; as protective
labor/affective labor of social workers,
129–30, 134–35; "scam" detection and
possible financial remediation, 135,
139; and slavery, 135, 137, 150, 225n11;
state restrictions on "legally allowable
birth parent expenses" as, 137–39;
suspicion of "scamming" and, 144;
and temporal lag between the circulation of money and delivery of an
infant, 158
Morfitt, Karen, 169
Moten, Fred, 153, 170, 177, 178, 186, 228n12

mothers. *See* expectant mothers; prospec-
tive adoptive parents
Moynihan Report (*The Negro Family: The
Case for National Action*), 39, 140, 176
Multiethnic Placement Act (1994), 9
Murray, Charles, 213–14n8

NABSW. *See* National Association of
Black Social Workers
Narayan, Kirin, 10–11, 208n25
National Association of Black Social Workers (NABSW), 9, 207n20
National Center for State Courts, 227n3
National Council for Adoption, 173, 175
Native Americans, and adoption, 213n6,
227n3
Negri, Antonio, 130
Nelms, Taylor C., 176
Nelson, Barbara, 65, 218nn11–12
neoliberalism: adoption as investment in
future and appeal to consumption of,
17, 209n34; adoption as neoliberalization of child welfare, 226n22; audit as
surveillance tool of, 220n25; and family-
building scale, 200; for-profit logics
retained in switch of First Steps to
nonprofit status, 166, 167, 168; and
intimate, affective, and reproductive
labor, 130, 174, 211–12n49; and state
involvement in private agency adoption,
81. *See also* exchange; poverty and the
poor; Recession (2008)
Newman, Jonah, 128
New York, 169
New Zealand, 19
Nguyen, Johnny, 18
noninnocence, 199, 228–29n4
nonprofit, mandated conversion of adoption agencies from for-profit enterprise
to, 12–13, 165, 166–69, 170, 172, 173, 186

observation/visualization, as mode of
intimate speculation, 7, 200
Oher, Michael, 210n38
open adoption: and desire for knowledge of
where the birth mother is, 59–60; and
normalization of adoption as identity
trait, 221n3; as normative and preferred

private non-agency-assisted adoption (independent adoption): and decline of agency adoptions, 179, 180; defined as type of adoption, 12, 208–9n27; and national quantitative data, 227n3; as supplanting brokerage function of adoption agencies, 222n12

Progressive Era, 38, 65

proof of pregnancy. *See* pregnancy, proof of

prospective adoptive parents: age limits on, 113, 222n11; Bill of Rights for birth and adoptive parents, 167; and biological father, fears about, 56–57, 58; and birth mother, fears of return for child, 60; defined and discussed as term, 29; divergence of interests of, from expectant parents, 14–15, 23–24, 211n44, 228n1; documentation required from, 68; encouraged to form relation with expectant mother, 99–100; historically narrow parameters for, 12; innocence of, 65, 72, 77, 86, 93, 94; loss/lack of control by, 101, 104, 107–8, 111, 120, 146–47; monitoring visits, 15, 89; norms of kinship and gender and, 75–76, 220n22; radical inclusiveness of First Steps for, 12, 196; risks for, social workers informing of, 98–99, 101, 120–22; subjectification of, 62–63, 217n5; three meetings with social workers, 66–67, 74–76, 98; training requirement of, 97; unpreparedness, perpetual sense of, 109–11. *See also* home study process; licensing AND TRANSPARENCY (DUTY OF CANDOR): overview, 70; "Duty of Candor" form required, 70–71; as ethnographic idea, 219–20n19; failure of home study for lack of, 91, 92; and failure of home study, reporting of, 87; as moral, 72–73; as producing transparency, 72; as racial, 73; social worker explanations of, 71–72; and strategic adaptations of behavior, reporting of, 85, 220n31; undisclosed transgressions and, 72; as visual, 72, 219–20n19

public/private distinction: fractal nature of, 77; and normative family life, 78, 80; and protection of children, need for, 80. *See also* home study process—public/private distinction

public sphere, intimate, 78

Puri, Stine Simonsen, 205n6

Quirk, Mary Beth, 169, 207n21

Quiroz, Pamela Anne, 206n10

Rabinow, Paul, 221n5

racial inequality: adoption rendered possible via, 19; as contingency, 201; and educational disparity, 15–16; and gun violence, 15–16; intersectionality of, 8, 38, 42, 65, 132, 137, 201, 206n10; noninnocence and, 199; and privacy of the family, 80; reversal of dynamics, in adoption, 51. *See also* class inequality; gender inequality; neoliberalism; slave trade/slavery

Ragone, Helena, 152, 206n10

"rainbow families," 197, 228n2

Rainbow Family of Living Light, 228n2

Rainbow Tribe, 228n2

Raleigh, Elizabeth, 26, 134, 137, 168, 180, 204–5n2, 206n10, 211nn44,48

Rapp, Rayna, 118, 152

Reagan, Ronald, 39, 148, 213–14n8

reasonable living expenses. *See* "legally allowable birth parent expenses," paid by prospective parents

Recession (2008): and blackness as being-in-collection, 176–77; closure of First Steps and, 160–61, 165, 172; uptick in fall-throughs and, 5–6, 33, 129, 154; uptick of poverty as primary precursor to relinquishment and, 39

Reeves, Madeleine, 212n1

Reich, Jennifer, 78, 80

relative leverage, 54

religion: and corporal punishment, 89, 92; and "orphan trains," 218n10; popular religiosity of "fate" in adoption, 221n7

relinquishment. *See* surrenders of parental rights

relinquishment vs. abandonment of infants (Safe Haven laws), 16–17, 209n32

reproductive freedom: forcible sterilization of prison inmates, 220n20; public/

Simon, Rita J., 206n10

single motherhood: acceptance of, and declining adoption rates, 39, 40, 174, 174–75, 179–80, 213n7, 222n12; and black "illegitimate" children removed to foster care, 39; blamed for pathological roots of poverty (Moynihan Report), 39, 140, 176; and child poverty (Reagan report), 213–14n8; middle-class vs. poor mothers and social acceptance of, 40–41; and poverty as major factor in adoption, 131, 132–33; and subprime mortgage crisis, 176–77. *See also* welfare queen, figure of

single-parent adoptions: and First Steps' radical inclusiveness, 12; history of adoption and expansion of, 39, 66, 133; and waiting, 109, 113

"sky babies." *See* "born babies"/"sky babies"

slave trade/slavery: and decline of adoption, 177–78; resistance in, feigned pregnancy as, 50; transracial adoption and implications of, 135, 137, 150, 176–78, 185–86, 225n11, 227–28nn11–12

social death, 44, 214n11

social inequality: as forming the basis of transracial adoption, 19, 130, 131–33, 143, 146–47, 176–77, 197–200; as power differential between expectant mothers and social workers, 158–59. *See also* class inequality; gender inequality; poverty and the poor; racial inequality

social workers: in "adoption triad," 25, 26; "best" families ideal of, 66; everyday practices of erasure and marginalization by, 33–35; expanded norms for adoptive families, 66; family case records, 65–66; history of, as "friendly visitors" to the poor, 217n4; moral judgments and power in broad context of, 135, 158; mother-like relationship converting to "the person who took away the baby," 158; power differential between expectant mothers and, 158–59; power of, to grant parental status, 67, 74, 108; professionalization of, 65–66, 217n4, 218n14; and waiting, 114. *See also* affective labor; brokerage, adoption social

workers as; expectant mothers; home study process; pregnancy, proof of; prospective adoptive parents; surveillance; uncertainty in the adoption process

Solinger, Rickie, 39, 40, 51, 133, 139, 213–14n8

South Korea, 214n11

Spain, 217n3

"special needs" adoption, 12, 39, 214n16

spectacular accumulation, 225n10

speculation: etymology of, 59, 216n27; tripartite definition of, 7, 200. *See also* intimate speculation

Speier, Amy, 211n48, 222n14, 227n5

Spillers, Hortense, 41, 177

Spiro, Emma S., 26

Spiro, Peter J., 198

square footage per child, legal requirement, 67, 68

Stabile, Carole, 42, 50, 216n20

Stack, Carol, 31

Stauff, Marcus, 219–20n19

Stewart, Kathleen, 211n47

stop-and-frisk, 220n23

stork euphemism, 197, 228n3

"stranger danger," 36

Strathern, Marilyn, 79, 82, 94, 206n10, 220n25

structural inequities. *See* class inequality; gender inequality; neoliberalism; racial inequality

subprime mortgage crisis, 167–68, 176–77

substance exposure, trauma, or genetic issues: and fall-through risk, 100–101; fetal alcohol spectrum disorders (FASD), 118–19, 222–23n17; lack of knowledge about, as risk, 59, 118–19; "you don't know what you're gonna get," 59

surrenders of parental rights: from biological father, difficulty of obtaining, 55, 57–58, 100; biological father signing allowable prior to birth, 55; biological mother signing, 58; demanded by social worker to prevent financial losses, 147; and exchange, feeling of, 115; lack of, utilized to control expectations ("the child isn't yours yet"), 67; narrative of, 114–15; out-of-area adoptive families urged not to travel until signing of, 122–23; 72 hour wait prior to mother's signing of, 113, 114, 123; 60-day period following birth for paternity claims, 56; voluntary surrender of, as irrevocable in Illinois, 56

surrogacy, 210n40

surveillance: antisurveillance politics of expectant mothers, 49–50, 63; of blackness, 41; of the black pregnant body, 41–43; categorical suspicion, 41; of lower-income parents, 80; of poor women of color, by state, 41–42, 73, 220n20; of the pregnant body, 42, 44–45; stop-and-frisk, 220n23; ultrasounds as, 45, 46, 48–50, 51, 59, 60, 214–15nn16–17,20; welfare and, 41–42. *See also* home study process; pregnancy, proof of

suspicion: of black pregnant body, 41–43; categorical, 41; of expectant mothers, 34–36, 63; as mode of governing uncertainty, 34, 212n1; of "scamming," 48–49, 135, 141–47, 148–49; of "scamming," as insufficient to end adoption plan, 142; speculative affect and, 146

Taussig, Karen-Sue, 118

taxes, Adoption Tax Credit, 155–56

temporality of adoption: and "birth mother" as term, vs. "expectant mother," 27–29, 212n55; in existing literature on adoption, 206n10; and "prospective adoptive parents" as term, 29; uncertainty of (when will they adopt), 104. *See also* futures/the future; surrenders of parental rights; uncertainty in the adoption process; uncertainty in the adoption process—waiting

Teurlings, Jan, 219–20n19

Thomas, James M., 130

Thompson, Charis, 206n10

Ticktin, Miriam, 65, 218n13

Timmermans, Stefan, 221–22n9

Todd, Leonard, 204n

transnational adoption. *See* international adoption

transparency. *See* prospective adoptive parents—and transparency (duty of candor)

transracial adoption: adoption history and expansion of, 66; adult adoptees presented as possible future to expectant mothers, 53; as "afterlife" of capital, intimacy, and inequality, 193; and animal-children comparison, 69, 219n16; the black body as capital in, 177–78; class inequality as forming the social base of, 19, 130, 131–33, 143, 146–47, 176–77, 197–200; condemnation of by National Association of Black Social Workers, 9, 207n20; fees for, racial disparities in, 9–10, 207n21; guilt/innocence mapped onto blackness/whiteness, 63, 217n7, 220n22; heartbreak as inextricable from, 197–98, 228n3; intersectionality of, 8, 38, 65, 132, 137, 206n10; as mission accomplished, 195–96, 200; and noninnocence, 199, 228–29n4; race-matching vs., 9, 207n20; "rainbow families" as created by, 197, 228n2; rosy pictures painted of, 196–97; and slave trade/slavery, implications of, 135, 137, 150, 176–78, 185–86, 225n11, 227–28nn11–12; social transformation narratives of, 19–21, 210n39; as symbol of American equality, 198; visual canon of interracial intimacy of, 19, 210n38. *See also* African Americans; futures/the future; imagined child; international adoption; *headings beginning with* black *and* blackness

Trump, Donald, 117

trust, and risk of intimacy, 205–6n7

Tsing, Anna, 225n10, 226n22

Tuohy, Leigh Anne, 210n38

Twohey, Megan, 91

Uganda, 181–82

ultrasounds/sonograms, as proof of pregnancy, 45, 46, 48–50, 51, 59, 60, 214–15nn16–17,20; feigned as, 46–50, 51, 59 unborn child. *See* imagined child

uncertainty in the adoption process: overview, 95–97, 125–26; anticipation and, 102–3, 116, 125–26, 222n13; anxiety and, 102–3, 104, 118–19, 125, 126, 224n28; auditing as risk management, 63, 94, 218n8; caution against buying items for the baby, 110–11, 122; and cruel optimism, 222n15; disappointment and, 125; and fate/adoption as "meant to be," 221n7; happiness and, 124–25, 224n28; hope and, 102–3, 116, 125, 126, 222n14; and infants as "patients-in-waiting" for genetic testing results, 221–22n9; interim care homes as strategy to cope with, 121; journey metaphor as strategy to cope with, 107, 126; "keep calm," 117–18; knowledge about pregnancy as mitigating, 59; knowledge of whereabouts of biological parents as mitigating, 59–60; and liminal temporal frames, 102–3, 115–16, 121; mindfulness strategies to cope with, 103–5; and perceived lack of control by prospective adoptive parents, 101, 104, 107–8, 111, 120, 146–47; and prediction of outcomes, social workers' inability for, 98; and "scamming," identification of, 48–49, 135, 140–41, 148–49; suspicion as mode of governing, 34, 212n1; temporal uncertainty (when they will adopt), 104; transformation of, to calculable risk, 96–97, 123; and unpreparedness, perpetual sense of, 109–11; the will of adoptive hope as creating certainty, 103, 105–7, 108, 126, 162, 185, 221nn5–7. *See also* contingency; intimate speculation; risk

—WAITING: anticipation and, 222n13; expectant mothers and, 114; First Steps' wait times, generally, 12, 110; social workers and, 114; and supply and demand, 115–16; "The Wait" for prospective adoptive parents, 12, 108–14, 115–16, 164; various periods of, 113–14

unfit parent, expectant mothers cast as: "birth mother" as label and, 28, 41; in

marketing/outreach materials, 32; stereotypes of, 41

United Nations, 227n3

United Negro College Fund (UNCF), 15–16

unpayable debt, 140, 153, 177–78, 201

Urcuioli, Bonnie, 198

U.S. Children's Bureau, 65

Ussery, Kimberly, 148

Utah, 227n2

Villareal, Mireya, 169

visualization: canon of interracial intimacy, 19, 210n38; of racialized vulnerability, 180, 184–85. *See also* gaze; hypervisibility; invisibility of expectant mothers; pregnancy, proof of; surveillance

Wacquant, Loïc, 128, 224n1

waiting. *See* uncertainty in the adoption process—waiting

Wanzo, Rebecca, 217n7

Weir, Kyle N., 99

Weismantel, Mary, 206n10

welfare: adoption viewed as lowering costs of, 213–14n8; surveillance of poor women and, 41–42

welfare queen, figure of: as "controlling image," 40; definition of, 39; as highly raced and gendered figure, 39; lies of omission as linking expectant mother to, 34; perceived hyper-fertility and laziness of, 39–40; and the prostitute, figure of, 139; Reagan's description of, 148; and reproduction as an economic tactic, 40; and "slippery little eels" metaphor for expectant mothers, 30, 33, 34–36, 145, 212n2; as unpayable debt, 140

Wendland, Claire L., 216n20

West, Harry G., 219–20n19

Weston, Kath, 206n10, 223n24

White House Working Group on the Family (WHWGF), 213–14n8

whiteness: "behaving badly," 92, 220n33; "candor" as etymologically derived from, 73; innocence mapped onto, 63,

217n7, 220n22; "nice" and "clean" as culturally linked to, 220n22; reproductive technologies as perpetuating, 227n5; as strategy, 84–85
white savior narrative, 20, 184, 218n13
will, 103, 105–7, 108, 126, 162, 185, 221nn5–7
Wilson, Darren, 18, 19, 209–10n37
Women's Ultrasound Right to Know Act (proposed), 214–15n17
World War I, 50
World War II, 64, 117, 118

Wright, Susan, 80, 82, 217nn7,14, 220nn25,27

Yanagisako, Sylvia, 226n22
Yancy, George, 41
Yngvesson, Barbara, 206n10

Zaloom, Caitlin, 150, 205n3, 225n12
Zelizer, Viviana, 64–65, 135–36, 158, 205n7
Zimmerman, Shirley L., 39
Zimring, Carl, 220n22
Zinn, Jon Kabat, 104